Philadelphia Quakers and
the Antislavery Movement

D1599371

ALSO BY BRIAN TEMPLE

The Union Prison at Fort Delaware: A Perfect Hell on Earth (McFarland, 2003; paperback 2012)

Philadelphia Quakers and the Antislavery Movement

BRIAN TEMPLE

McFarland & Company, Inc., Publishers
Jefferson, North Carolina

LIBRARY OF CONGRESS CATALOGUING-IN-PUBLICATION DATA

Temple, Brian, 1955–
    Philadelphia quakers and the antislavery
movement / Brian Temple.
        p.   cm.
    Includes bibliographical references and index.

    ISBN 978-0-7864-9407-1 (softcover : acid free paper) ∞
    ISBN 978-1-4766-1577-6 (ebook)

    1. Antislavery movements—Pennsylvania—Philadelphia—
History.   2. Quaker abolitionists—Pennsylvania—Philadelphia—
History.   3. Abolitionists—Pennsylvania—Philadelphia—
History.   4. Philadelphia (Pa.)—History—18th century.
5. Philadelphia (Pa.)—History—19th century.   I. Title.

F158.44.T59 2014
974.8'1102—dc23   2014015522

BRITISH LIBRARY CATALOGUING DATA ARE AVAILABLE

On the cover: *Slaves Learning* by H.C. Phillips & Bro., ca. 1863
(Friends Historical Library of Swarthmore College, Pennsylvania)

Printed in the United States of America

McFarland & Company, Inc., Publishers
    Box 611, Jefferson, North Carolina 28640
        www.mcfarlandpub.com

To Sarah and Lauren.
No father could be prouder.

Table of Contents

Preface

When I was about eight years old, my grandparents and I drove through the city of Salem, New Jersey. As we went past an old house on the main street, my grandmother pointed at it and said that it was part of the Underground Railroad. I didn't really know what the Underground Railroad was and I was a little confused about what she meant. I thought it was a strange place to put a railroad.

Many years later, a friend of my wife mentioned to her that the Quakers were very influential in the early history of our area and maybe I could write something about them. I thought I would be polite and look into them. I soon learned that the Quakers were fair in their treatment of the Native American tribes they came into contact with, had a far more liberal approach in their dealings with women than the rest of the country during the 18th and 19th centuries, and were early opponents of slavery. They were also so involved with the development of the Delaware Valley (Pennsylvania, New Jersey, and Delaware) that I thought that they were rather active for a group of pacifists.

To narrow the field that I was going to research, I needed a focal point. I decided to focus on the Quakers' attitude toward slavery. Many Quakers started out owning slaves and eventually the group became a strong opponent of slavery. Such a contrast interested me. It sounded like the Bible verse that said to remove the plank from your own eye before you remove the speck from another's eye. That brought everything into focus.

The more I delved into the Quakers and slavery, the more contrasts appeared. Not every member of the Underground Railroad was a Quaker and not every Quaker was involved in the railroad or even in the antislavery movement. There was another contrast that is not always discussed and that is while the Quakers grew to believe that slavery was wrong, it did not always translate into true equality. There were some Quakers who invited African Americans into their homes and others who demanded that they sit on segregated benches at the Quaker meetings.

I was also surprised that more books did not mention the many ways the Quakers fought slavery beyond the Underground Railroad. They routinely petitioned state and federal governments to protest the slave trade and slavery and used existing laws to help slaves gain their freedom. Some of those stories are as exciting as those of the Underground Railroad.

I have many people and organizations to thank for the information in this book. The Gloucester County (New Jersey), Rowan University, and particularly the Swarthmore College libraries were very helpful. Also, the Burlington, Gloucester and Salem County (New Jersey) and Greenwich and Haddonfield (New Jersey) historical societies and their personnel were very giving of their time and knowledge. I'd like to thank Sandy Ridgeway and Jim Merel for pointing me in the right direction and my wife Martha for keeping me there. Finally, I'd like to thank my grandmother Josephine Phillips for pointing out that old house so long ago.

Prologue

Tide Mill sat on a hill overlooking Mannington Creek near Salem, New Jersey. George Abbott, a member of the Society of Friends, also known as Quakers, built the house in 1845 for his bride. Occasionally, late at night, there would be boats traveling the waters near Tide Mill. The contents of these boats were not visible, but those who waited on the New Jersey shore for their arrival already knew who was coming. A blue light over a yellow light on a boat signaled that the boat was carrying escaped slaves.

In "Reflections of Ruth Abbott Rogers," she mentions an incident that occurred at Tide Mill. Her father once stumbled onto an escapee hiding in a hay mow. He ran to tell his father and when he did, George Abbott told his son to "just forget about it."

That was not necessarily bad advice. Laws against helping runaway slaves had been in effect since 1793 and anyone trying to help someone escape could risk prosecution from the authorities. Since he was a Quaker, Abbott also risked getting into trouble from the Society of Friends. Slavery had been banned from the Quakers for almost one hundred years, but they also did not openly defy the laws of the land.

George Abbott was a member of the Underground Railroad, a loose confederation of people, Quaker and non–Quaker alike, who hid and helped those who tried to escape from slavery. Why would anyone, especially those belonging to a religious organization known to avoid conflict, risk their wealth and standing in the community to help strangers who were persecuted and forced to conform to the standards of others? To understand why Abbott and other Quakers, known for their pacifist beliefs, were so active in fighting slavery, it is necessary to go back to their beginnings.[1]

PART I
REMOVING THE PLANK

1. Quaker Beginnings

Frustration is a powerful tool to enact social change. It's one thing to not like the world around you. It's quite another to actually work towards changing it. One such person was George Fox. At first glance, he might not seem someone who would rebel against the status quo. During his formative years, he was much more serious than his peers. His mother had the reputation of an upright woman and his father was called a "Righteous Christer" by their neighbors. In spite of George's strongly religious background, he had questions concerning the worship of God. What really troubled him were the divisions existing in organized religion in England during the first half of the 17th century.[1] The Protestants and Catholics were not happy with each other and the Protestants separated into different denominations that did not agree on their beliefs.[2] Not only was religion in England in turmoil, but the country as a whole was equally in a state of flux. The first English Civil War began in 1642, when King Charles I entered Parliament with armed guards to attempt to arrest four leaders of his opposition, and continued until 1646, when the king surrendered to the Scots.[3] In 1643, at the age of 19, Fox left his home in Leicestershire and began to wander in the hope of finding a religious path that he felt was the right one. He visited many members of the clergy and laypeople of different denominations, talking with them and asking questions. However, he never received an answer that satisfied him.

It was during his travels that Fox came to certain conclusions about religion. One day, while going to Coventry, Fox considered the idea that "it was said that all Christians are believers, both Protestants and Papists; and the Lord opened to me that, if all were believers, then they were all born of God and passed from death to life," no matter what their station in life. On another occasion, he was walking in a field when "the Lord opened unto me that being bred at Oxford or Cambridge was not enough to fit and qualify men to be ministers of Christ." This belief puzzled him because it was not the accepted viewpoint of people at that time.[4] It was felt that it was necessary to have some-one educated in universities such as Oxford or Cambridge to lead people to the Lord. This belief that only certain people were worthy to preach the Gospel kept power firmly in the hands of the existing churches. However, with the invention of the printing press, this type of control was threatened. Bibles became easy to obtain and this allowed people to read them whenever they pleased. This access to a book that previously only men of the cloth were able to read gave people the ability to study it, ask questions and make their own decisions about religion. This questioning forced organized religions to scram-ble to keep their flocks in line so that new denominations would not siphon off members. The established churches then pressured the British government to persecute those whose beliefs did not match their own. This would cause a great deal of hardship to George Fox and those like him.

As a child, Fox saw adults act in what he considered to be an unseemly manner and promised himself that when "I come to be a man, surely I should not do so nor be so wanton." This understanding not only guided his life, but it also was a basis for his religious beliefs. Fox later stated in his journal that the "Lord taught me to be faithful in all things, and to act faithfully two ways, viz, inwardly to God and outwardly to man, and to keep to 'yea' and 'nay' in all things. For the Lord showed me that though the people of the world have mouths full of deceit and changeable words, yet I was to keep to 'yea' and 'nay' in all things; and that my words should be few and savoury, seasoned with grace."

Soon he began to find others who felt as he did. In Nottingham, he found a group that had separated from the Baptists. They liked what he had to say and they joined together to become the "Children of the Light." The name came from a message Fox once gave that the light of Christ was the guiding light to eternal life. By the end of the 1640s, Fox felt compelled to go out and deliver his message to the world. The tenets of this religion were different than those of the other organized religions of the time. He had the need to "turn people to that inward light, Spirit and grace, by which all might know their salvation and their way to God—even that Divine Spirit which would lead them into all truth, and which I infallibly knew would never deceive any."[5]

He also believed that when "the Lord sent me forth into the world, He forbade me to put off my hat to any, high or low, and I was required to Thee and Thou all men and women, without any respect to rich or poor, great or small. And as I traveled up and down, I was not to bid people "Good morrow," or "Good evening," neither might I bow or scrape with my leg to any one, and this made the sects and professions to rage."[6]

Fox was also not afraid to lecture people on their sins. He spoke out against overindulgence in alcohol, implored merchants to be honest in their dealings with people and warned teachers to impress upon their students the need to be fearful of the Lord and to be examples of sobriety and virtue. He also lectured justices about how legal wages for farm laborers were set lower than was equitable. Justices were required to set a fair wage for laborers every Easter according to the Statute of Apprentices passed in 1563. However, this was not always done and Fox took them to task.[7]

His new group had different names as it grew in numbers. Fox liked to use the term "Children of Light." He also called them "People of God," "Royal Seed of God," and "Friends of the Truth." The official name became the "Religious Society of Friends." However, that name did not stick as well as a name used to describe them negatively. In 1650, Fox appeared before Justice Gervase Bennett of Derby on the charges of blasphemy and claiming to have infallible guidance. Fox told Bennett that he should fear the Lord. Bennett answered Fox by saying: "And quake, thou quaker, before the majesty of the law." Fox spent almost a year in jail in Derby. It was not the first time that Fox was thrown into prison for his beliefs, nor was it the only time that his fellow Quakers spent time in prison or otherwise faced the wrath of the powers that be.[8]

Thomas Holme was a man who did not mind letting the world know how he felt about other religions. He proved this by walking through the streets of Cheshire in 1655 naked, and was arrested for it. Elizabeth Fletcher did the same thing in Oxford to protest the Presbyterians and Independents. Quakers felt that those groups were hypocrites and walking naked through the streets was a symbol of a Quaker belief that the Lord would soon strip them of their profession. Fletcher and Elizabeth Leavens went to colleges and churches preaching their doctrine and were whipped by the authorities.

John Stubbs and William Caton went to Maidstone to preach and the law against vagrants was applied to them. They were seized by the authorities, who seized possessions. They were stripped naked, placed in the stocks, whipped, put in irons, and thrown into jail. A few days later, under the Vagrancy Act, they were escorted home. The relay of constables performing this task soon grew tired of this and left the Quakers to their own devices.

One of Fox's converts, Richard Sale, dramatically showed his displeasure toward other organized religions the same year by walking through Derby dressed in sackcloth, barefoot and barelegged. To complete the outfit, he wore ashes on his head and carried flowers in his right hand and weeds that did not smell like the flowers in his left. People who saw him either stared in astonishment or set their dogs on him. In 1657, he walked down Eastgate Street in Chester during the middle of the day carrying a lighted candle to mock the idea of candlelight services. His protests caused him to end up in Newgate Prison several times. The last time this happened, the guards placed him into a hole in a rock called Little Ease for hours at a time. It was four and a half feet high, seventeen inches across, and nine inches deep. Sale, unfortunately, was not a thin man and could not be placed into this cell unless he was shoved into it by four men. They pushed him in so violently that blood came from his nose and mouth. This type of treatment ruined his health and he died in August 1658.[9]

Not everything was bad for the Quakers. After Fox was released from Derby, he continued traveling and preaching in Yorkshire and Lancashire. This became a pivotal moment in the Quaker movement. When he was in Lancashire, Fox felt compelled to climb Pendle Hill. He looked out and felt the spirit of the Lord show him that there were many people there who were willing to hear his message.

A visit to Ulverston in Lancashire led Fox to Swarthmoor Hall in May of 1652. The owner, Thomas Fell, was a judge who invited Fox to stay at his home. This was another pivotal moment in the Quaker movement. Judge Fell and his wife Margaret went to hear Fox speak at the Ulverston church that Sunday. Mrs. Fell heard Fox and was converted to the Quaker faith. Due to her conversion, Swarthmoor Hall became a base of operations for the Quakers. Even though he never became a Friend, Judge Fell brought them support with both political connections and financial help[10] until his death in 1658.[11] The Fells supported the Quaker missionaries and opened their doors to any of them who came to their area. Sarah Fell, the judge's daughter, told a story about the time her father had returned from a business trip and found that his stable was filled with horses that he did not recognize. There was only one space left for his horse. He said to his wife that if this continued that he would be eaten out of house and home. She answered that she thought that they had enough to spare.

George Fox may have wanted to send Quaker missionaries throughout England to spread the word on the Friends faith, but that enterprise needed money to function. Margaret Fell had experience in managing finances due to her husband's holdings. She created the Kendal Fund to help those missionaries who needed financial help in carrying out their mission. It would also help Friends who were in prison and support their families. This kind of financial support was the beginning of the Yearly Meeting Fund, which is the cornerstone of the modern-day Society of Friends.[12]

Quaker beliefs and practices differed sharply from those of other organized religions of the time. Even though Quaker men held the same attitudes toward women as the rest of society, the one great difference was their belief that women were equal to men when it came to spiritual matters and were just as capable as men to preach. They also did not have designated people to stand before a congregation and lead them in services. The topics discussed were not predetermined. The Friends would gather together in their meeting houses and wait for the Holy Spirit to touch someone and lead that person to preach. They also did not do Holy Communion or baptism.

The Friends' belief that all were spiritually equal led them to reject all titles of rank. They either referred to people by their names or used the terms "thee" or "thou," according to Fox's teachings. People commonly referred to close friends in this manner, not judges, soldiers, or royalty. This shocking idea was not the only habit that the Friends adopted. They also did not remove their hats for anyone.[13] In 1655, Richard Bennett was fined two pounds for coming into court with his hat on. He was sent to prison, but was eventually released.[14] In 1656, Fox, along with two others, spent eight months in jail for the same offense.[15] A public display of vanity was considered wrong, so the typical garb for the Friends was plain. They also did not believe in swearing or taking oaths. Since they believed that all Christians should tell the truth at all times, the use of oaths was pointless. This proved to be a problem when they were in court because not taking an oath could either cost them money in fines or time in jail. They got around the problem by proclaiming the truth of the statements that they made in court without taking an oath.

Arguably the most famous trait of the Friends is their belief in nonviolence. They believed that fighting was immoral and that no member should be involved in any form of violence.[16] George Fox practiced this while in prison in 1651. Some of the prisoners were going to become soldiers and they asked him to be their captain because of his integrity. He told them that he "lived in the virtue of that life and power that took away the occasion of all wars." They told him that they offered the captaincy to him with respect and kindness. He replied, "If that were their love and kindness I trampled it under my feet." That statement angered the men and they told the jailer to "cast him into the dungeon amongst the rogues and felons." Fox spent another six months in jail.[17]

Just because Friends practiced nonviolence did not mean that those they came into contact with did the same thing. Mary Fisher and Elizabeth Williams spoke to Cambridge students at a college gate in December 1653. They were seized, stripped to the waist and flogged. A year later, Margaret Killam visited the college and spoke as she walked through the streets. People started to follow her and chased her away. They threw dirt at her face and by the time she left the area, her clothes were almost covered with it.

Oxford University was the site of other acts of violence against the Friends. In 1658, Oxford scholars went to the home of Richard Bettris, a Friend and surgeon, where the Friends gathered, and burst in to

act their wickedness and abuses toward us, as pulling of Friends' hair off their heads, and beards by the roots, plaiting their hair into knots, pluck off Friends' hats and throw them at others and then beat them on the heads. They took one Friend by the neckcloth and held him up from the ground until they had near chocked [sic] him, and stopped another Friend's mouth ready to strangle him, ... [They] pull Friends up and down the meeting-room and some out of doors, ... bring in nettles and thrust them in Friends' faces, throw down forms with Friends on them, bind some with cords and draw them up and down the meeting-room abusing them, tear Friends' clothes, shoot bullets in Friends' faces ... with a pair of scissors cut one side of a Friend's beard off and left the other remaining, ... thrust pins in their flesh, ride on Friends' backs, ... They have brought hogs into our meeting and pulled them about the room to make a noise, and likewise madmen. One Mack of Trinity College brought into our meeting a pistol and cocked it and sware he would shoot Friends ... they have come into meetings, whooping and halloing, houghing, scoffing, swearing and cursing and ... calling for ... beer and tobacco, calling Friends rogues and whores, dogs, bitches and toads ... making a noise like cats and doge, throw squibs into our meeting, squeeze and abuse Friends going in and coming out, break the porch of the door and break the windows of the house.[18]

The violence against the Friends existed at other places of learning besides Oxford. Scholars at Sidney-Sussex College harassed the meetings of the nearby Friends. In 1658 and 1659, they threw stones at the windows of their meeting house and shot bullets inside. They also ran through the meeting place "like wild horses, throwing down all before them, halloing, stamping, and making a noise, as if several drums had been beating, to prevent [Friends'] being heard." During three successive Sundays in May of 1660, there was more harassment. The worst was on the third Sunday. James Blackley sent a letter describing the incident to Friends in London. He said that

in our meeting-house when we had been together two hours, the soldiers came and set upon us with swords and their staves, and brake in upon us and gat smiths' hammers and brake the windows and doors in pieces, and with shivered boards and window-bars fell upon us and beat and wounded many Friends, that few or done did escape without a wound, and haled [sic] every one out, and would not suffer one to stay within the house; only I stayed there to see what they would do. And when the house was emptied of Friends they brake down all the glass windows, the stairs, the forms, benches, chairs, etc., whatever could be broken in the house. The soldiers and scholars began and the rude people in the town made an end.

This continued on the first Monday in July. A mob gathered around the meeting-house, encouraged by wholesale consumption of alcohol. They attacked the Friends while they were in their meeting place. They struck

> at those they could reach, flinging at others, and making an hideous noise, with scoffing, laughing, railing, shouting, knocking, drumming upon the boards, and sometimes throwing wildfire and gunpowder into the meeting to drown the sound of that which was spoken to us in the name of the Lord, and continually exercising themselves in one act of mischief or other to make a disturbance and weary us out of the place: and when they saw they could not do it by all those means, they brake and battered down the doors and walls next the street with bolt-hammers and other engines, and ... called us rebels ... and used us as if our lives were all at their mercies ... so that very many of us were sorely hurt and bruised, twenty-two had their blood shed, one so lamed that he was left behind unable to walk abroad, and a woman almost killed by their cruel usage ... and [they] quite battered down the walls and bays on each side of the meeting-house.

In January 1661, the Friends decided that they needed to clarify their beliefs to the outside world. They drew up a declaration that explained their position on nonviolence and wars and sent it to the king. In it, they stated that their

> principle is, and our practices have always been, to seek peace and ensue it and to follow after righteousness and the knowledge of God, seeking the good and welfare and doing that which tends to the peace of all. We know that wars and fightings proceed from the lusts of men (as Jas. IV. 1–3), out of which lusts the Lord hath redeemed us, and so out of the occasion of war. The occasion of which war, and war itself (wherein envious men, who are lovers of themselves more than lovers of God, lust, kill, and desire to have men's lives or estates) ariseth from the lust. All bloody principles and practices, we, as to our own particulars, do utterly deny, with all outward wars and strife and fightings with outward weapons, for any end or under any pretence whatsoever." They also stated that "whereas men come against us with clubs, staves, drawn swords, pistols cocked, and do beat, cut, and abuse us, yet we never resisted them, but to them our hair, backs, and cheeks have been ready.

When the king heard this declaration, he proclaimed that all Friends held in prison for their stand on nonviolence should be set free without paying a fee.[19]

In the 1660s, the Friends became a more organized and structured religion. They toned down the more outrageous parts of their beliefs, such as walking through the streets naked. They still believed in waiting until they were moved to speak. However, they changed the church by creating monthly, quarterly, and yearly meetings. During the monthly and quarterly meetings, they had separate meetings for men and women. This was so that they could manage the affairs of their own gender.[20] The first monthly meeting had been arranged in 1653 when members went to George Fox and asked if they could hold a meeting to look after the poor and to insure that all members acted in a proper way. They also had general meetings for a district and occasional monthly meetings.[21]

They also felt a need to branch out. Part of this was a desire to go to places that might be more tolerant of their beliefs. Another reason was the desire to spread their faith. Their destination was the American colonies.

2. Quaker
Beginnings in America

Once a religious organization becomes established, it often feels the need to send missionaries out into the world. The Quakers were no different. However, they had another reason to investigate their chances out in the world. They had been victims of persecution and wanted to find other places that would be more hospitable to their beliefs. Invariably, the New World called to them. The first Quaker missionaries came to America in either 1655 or 1656. Elizabeth Harris landed in the Chesapeake area and by 1662, approximately sixty Friends had traveled to Maryland and Virginia and several meeting houses had been created. Maryland was tolerant of them, but Virginia was not. Friends were thrown into jail for not paying tithes to the established church or attending services.

In 1656, Friends also went to Massachusetts and found that the attitude there was even more intolerant than in Virginia. When Ann Austin and Mary Fisher landed at the Puritan colony there, the authorities immediately put them in jail, burned their books on Quakerism, and checked them to see if they bore marks of witchcraft. They were then placed on a ship headed for Barbados. For the next three years, whenever Friends came to Massachusetts, they were dealt with in a swift and harsh manner. They were all expelled and many were whipped, branded, and otherwise mutilated beforehand.[1] One of those who were whipped was Katherine Marbury Scott, the sister of religious dissenter Anne Hutchinson. Scott's crime was to complain about the right ear of her future son-in-law being cut off because he was a Quaker.[2] Any Quaker man or woman could count on being treated in much the same way, along with being banished and having their property taken from them. The authorities in Salem even went so far as to order that the two children of a Quaker couple be sold as indentured servants in the Caribbean. The sentence was not

13

carried out because they could not find a sea captain who was willing to take the children away.

In October 1658, Massachusetts passed a law stating that any Quaker who had been banished twice and still came back would be executed.[3] William Robinson and Marmaduke Stephenson, who had been banished the month before, decided to test the law. They had heard that other Friends had stayed away after their banishments and the two men felt that they had to defy the law. They traveled to Boston and the authorities arrested them as promised.[4] Another Quaker arrested for the same crime, Mary Dyer of Rhode Island, who was a former follower of Anne Hutchinson, was sentenced to die with them.[5] On October 27, 1659, the three went hand in hand to Boston Commons, where the gallows was located,[6] walking to the beat of drums which were used to stop them from speaking to the assembled crowd.[7] Robinson and Stephenson were executed, but Mary Dyer was spared at the last moment. She returned to Boston in May of 1660, and this time the execution was carried out. Another victim of the law, William Leddra of Barbados, was killed in March of 1661.[8]

When the news of this arrived in England, a Friend named Edward Burrough was determined to stop the violence. He went to Charles II and told him that "a vein of innocent blood opened in his dominions, which, if it were not stopped, would overrun all." The king agreed and had the order written to put a halt to the persecution, but did not have any ships heading to New England to carry the order at that time. Burrough was worried that time was of the essence, so he suggested that a Quaker, Samuel Shattuck, who had been banished from New England and came to England because of the law, be granted a deputation to carry the mandate to Boston. Permission was granted and a ship owned by Ralph Goldsmith, another Friend, was hired to set sail. The ship arrived in Boston six weeks later on a Sunday with many Friends on board.

When they arrived, the citizens of Boston went out to the ship that flew the British flag and asked for the captain. Goldsmith came out and they asked him if he had any letters to deliver. He said yes, but not on Sunday. They went away and quickly spread the word that they saw a ship full of Quakers and Samuel Shattuck was one of them. The next day, Shattuck and Goldsmith went to the governor's house and delivered the mandate. It said, in part, that

> if there be any of those people called Quakers amongst you, now already condemned to suffer death or other corporal punishment, or that are imprisoned, and obnoxious to the like condemnation, you are to forbear to proceed any further therein; but that you forthwith send the said persons (whether condemned or imprisoned) over into this our kingdom of England, together with the respective crimes or offences laid to their charge; to the end such course may be taken

with them here, as shall be agreeable to our laws and their demerits." This ruling was subscribed to "all and every other the governour or governours of our plantations of New England, and of all the colonies thereunto belonging, that now are, or hereafter shall be: and to all and every the ministers and officers of our plantations and colonies whatsoever within the continent of New England."

The governor, John Endicott, read the order and told the Friends that the king's order would be obeyed. Once this announcement was made, Goldsmith allowed his passengers to come ashore. The Friends on the ship met with the Friends in Boston to give thanks. They were also joined by a Friend who had been held in prison. The ruling had saved his life and he came to celebrate with his fellow believers.[9]

The Puritans despised the Quakers because they perceived them as a threat to their way of life. They felt that Friends were blasphemous, heretical in their actions, and disrespectful to authority. They believed Friends gave too much power to women, and thought the habit of Friends continuing to come to a place where they were treated so brutally was a sign of demonic possession. Except for Rhode Island, which was set up to be more tolerant of other religions, New England was not a hospitable place to be for a Friend. Therefore, they searched for another area to go to,[10] and it all began with a visit to Ireland in 1658.

Thomas Loe was a Friend who went to Ireland to spread the Quaker faith and preached to an English family living there. There was a boy in the family who listened and never forgot the man. Nine years later, the boy, now grown, was in Cork, Ireland, when he met a Quaker shopkeeper. He learned from the shopkeeper that Loe was in Ireland again and going to preach that night. He went to listen to Loe speak on "a faith that overcomes the world." The young man heard this and became a devout Quaker. This convincement, as the Quakers called converting to their faith, affected the future of the entire Quaker movement because that man was William Penn.[11]

William Penn was born into the aristocracy. His father was a wealthy man, educated at Oxford, and an admiral of the English Commonwealth. William was in Ireland in 1667 running the family estates when he became convinced into the Quaker religion. As time went on, Penn evolved into a fine speaker and tireless writer about the Quaker movement. His political connections gave the Friends access to a part of society they had never reached before. He was even able to reach King Charles II. That was how he was able to make his greatest contribution to Quakerism.[12]

Great Britain did not take much interest in colonization due to the English Civil War and the creation of the English Commonwealth under Cromwell. That changed when the monarchy was restored in 1660. England was nearly bankrupt due to the political upheavals and was desperate to generate income. Exploitation of the New World would solve that problem and allow the monarchy to reward those who helped them.[13]

George Fox was interested in having a Quaker colony in America. He had learned that except for a small amount of Swedes and Finns living between present-day northern New Jersey and northern Maryland, there were no European settlements in the area. He sent Josiah Coale there in 1660 to ascertain if the area would be a good place to colonize. William Penn had heard of the scheme when he was a student in Oxford, and the idea of a Quaker colony in America stuck with him.[14]

Penn was in favor in the court of Charles II because of himself as well as because of his father. The king owed not only a personal but also a financial debt to Admiral Penn since he had loaned the Crown sixteen thousand pounds.[15] When his father died, Penn had not only inherited his father's lands and properties, but also the debt the king owed his father. Penn saw this debt as an opportunity to give the Quakers a place where they could practice their beliefs and he asked for repayment of the debt in land. Charles did so by granting a charter stating that Penn would be the proprietor of land running from north of Maryland to south of New York. Penn wanted to make money from this venture, but he also used it as an opportunity to provide a safe haven for Quakers. He aimed his promotion for the land to rural Quaker families of little means so he originally charged one hundred pounds for 5,000 acres. So many families took advantage of the price of land and moved to America that some feared that some of the rural monthly meetings would run out of members in England.[16]

There was a strong reason for the Friends to take advantage of this opportunity. Persecution of Quakers on both sides of the Atlantic made the idea of a safe haven look like the place to go. In 1656, the Massachusetts Puritans passed the first anti–Quaker law in America. The Conventicles Act of 1664 allowed England to ship repeat dissenters against Puritanism to America to stay for seven years. The only places they could not be sent were Virginia and New England. Even though the law was to pertain only to dissenters, Quakers qualified in the eyes of the government, and large numbers were sent to New Jersey and Pennsylvania.

Fox's attempt to start a Friends colony was hampered by events out of his control. The second Anglo-Dutch war broke out in 1664 and disrupted communications and shipping between Europe and North America for the next three years. Also, King Charles II gave his brother James, the Duke of York, the title to land on both sides of the Delaware River where Fox was looking at land. James then gave the land on the east side of the Delaware River to Lord John Berkeley and Sir George Carteret.[17]

Berkeley wanted to sell his half of the New Jersey proprietorship and offered it to a friend of his, Edward Byllynge, for 1,000 pounds. Byllynge was a London brewer, a former officer in Cromwell's army, and had recently convinced to the Quaker faith. Even though it was a great opportunity for Byllynge, he did not have the money because he had gone bankrupt due to fines levied against him because of his membership in the Friends society. He needed to have someone buy the land for him because he was not legally permitted to have his name listed as the owner. Byllynge then turned to another Friend, John Fenwick, for help.[18] Fenwick, who was a farmer, a lawyer, and a major under Cromwell, had once been a tenant on the land of the future Mrs. William Penn.[19] He agreed to buy the land to hold in trust for Byllynge.[20]

On March 18, 1674, the sale of the land took place, but that was only the beginning of the legal problems. The third Anglo-Dutch War had ended on February 19, 1674. However, the Dutch had retaken the land briefly during the war, which made the proprietorship null and void. It had to be renewed by the Crown. When James heard about Berkeley selling his half of the land, he only renewed the proprietorship to Carteret. This meant that Fenwick and Byllynge needed to get the situation straightened out before they could govern the land they had purchased.

Here is where the peaceful Quakers had a dispute among themselves. Fenwick did not want to wait. He had the deeds to the land and refused to give them to Byllynge unless Byllynge agreed to give him two-thirds of the land. Byllynge refused.[21] Fenwick made plans for his colony and advertised that the land was for sale before everything was legally settled. The majority of the land he sold was purchased by fellow Quakers. Even after selling some of the land, he did not have enough money to finance his trip, so he mortgaged the land to fellow Friends John Eldridge and Edmond Warner.[22] He then set sail on the *Griffin* with 48 others, including his three daughters, two sons-in-law, five grandchildren, and ten servants. They sailed up along the eastern shore of New Jersey from modern-day Cape May for about fifty miles and anchored opposite the Old Swedes' Fort Elsborg near the mouth of the Assamhocking River on September 23, 1675. The next day, they went up the river, now called the Salem River, about three miles and landed on the south side. They named this place where they landed, after a two-and-a-half-month ocean crossing, Salem, meaning "the City of Peace."[23]

The first Caucasians who settled in New Jersey were the Dutch in 1624. They created an outpost on an island in the Delaware River near modern-day Trenton. They then established the West India Company and claimed the area between Long Island and the Delaware Bay. They built Fort Nassau in 1626 where the Delaware River and Big Timber Creek met. The Swedes and Finns founded New Sweden in 1638 by slipping past Fort Nassau and building new settlements. The Dutch took over the area again in 1655 and kept control until the Anglo-Dutch wars occurred.

Once he had arrived, Fenwick set out to buy the land from the Lenapi tribe, which already lived there. On November 17, 1675, Fenwick and Lenapi representatives met under an oak tree in Salem and Fenwick bought the rights to the land. They met again in 1675 and 1676, eventually buying what is now Salem and Cumberland counties in trade for guns, powder, rum, and cloth. During the time of the purchases of the land and afterward, Fenwick's people and the Lenapi coexisted peacefully. However, that was not the case between Fenwick and his fellow Friends.

When he mortgaged the land to Eldridge and Warner, Fenwick believed that he would be able to buy it back. Instead, the two men sold the mortgage to William Penn, Gawen Lawrie and Nicholas Lucas while Fenwick was in America.[24] The situation between the Friends was also disrupting Penn's plans for his own colony on the western side of the Delaware. As was the custom with the Friends, they decided to work it out among themselves. Fenwick and

John Fenwick built his settlement and was buried near this marker in modern-day Salem County, New Jersey (photograph by the author).

Byllynge agreed to submit their disagreement to arbitration by a group headed by Penn.[25] They wanted the problems concerning the land to be settled so that "things may go on easy without hurt or jar; which is the desire of all Friends." They worked out the troubles with the Crown and made a boundary between the Carteret family's holdings and the Fenwick-Byllynge purchase with the Quintipartite Deed in 1676. This deed drew a dividing line between Barnegat Bay on the Atlantic Ocean side and the mouth of the Pennsauken River on the Delaware River side. The Carteret holdings were named East Jersey and south of the line became West Jersey. The Friends also created a joint stock company for West Jersey, which divided it into one hundred proprietary shares. Fenwick received ten shares and the rest went to other Friends who wanted to be free from the persecution they had experienced in England.

More Friends sailed to the Delaware Valley in 1677, but these people did not want to settle at Salem Creek because Fenwick was in charge there. They went upriver on Raccoon Creek until they reached New Stockholm, where the Swedish community took them in during the winter of 1677–78. The Friends moved north in the spring and created the town of Burlington. Some of the Friends did not like the plots of land there, so they moved south and settled along the Cooper, Newton, and Timber Creeks.[26]

Henry Wood was an eighty-year-old Quaker from Bury, Lancaster, England, who had been beaten, imprisoned, and lost the use of one eye due to religious persecution. In 1681 he left England with his son John and his family to live on three hundred acres in New Jersey that he had bought from Byllynge. This became the city of Woodbury. They had a letter of introduction from their monthly meeting in Clithrice, England, that stated, "Henry Wood and John Wood, with their families, going to these parts is with the consent of Friends. And we further certify you that they have been faithful to their testimonies." They had no trouble with the Native Americans in the area. One time, the settlement had run short of food, so the men decided to go to Burlington for supplies. While they were gone, a storm arrived that kept them from returning as quickly as they would have. The women and children in the settlement ran out of food, but a woman from the nearby tribe found out about their troubles and supplied them with venison and other supplies until the men returned.[27]

Now that the situation in West Jersey was at an end, Penn was free to enact his own plans. In 1681, Penn received a royal grant for the land west of the Delaware River, which now makes up Pennsylvania and the three counties of Delaware. Since he was the sole proprietor, he could set the government up in the way he wanted. Therefore, he created the government of Pennsylvania based on Quaker principles.[28] The Frame of Government of Pennsylvania, created on April 25, 1682, allowed for the creation of a provincial Council and General Assembly. Penn, as governor, and the council would bring up laws to the assembly, elected by free men every year, who would discuss the bill before them for eight days. On the ninth day, the "General Assembly, after reading over the proposed bills by the clerk of the provisional Council, ... shall give their affirmative or negative." The governor, council, or the assembly was not able to change the charter without six-sevenths of the council assembly agreeing. The governor also did not have the right to do anything to restrict the laws set down in the charter.[29]

Penn also created a rule that stated that no one was able to own more than one thousand acres connected unless that owner was planning to plant a family on every thousand acres within three years. He also made sure that any trade with the Native Americans would occur in an open market to ensure fairness. Penn's reputation was so great on this issue that for many years, the greatest compliment a Native American could give a Caucasian was to compare him to Onas, the name they gave to Penn.[30]

Not only were the Friends organizing their government, they were also organizing their religion. The earliest monthly meeting was in Salem in 1676, and Burlington followed in 1678. The monthly meeting conducted all of the Friends' important business such as recording births and deaths, brought in members from other meetings, and disciplined members who were acting in a way the Friends did not approve of. The local meetings, which met at least once a week, brought their business to the monthly meetings. The local meeting was like a congregation in other religions. If the number of members in a monthly meeting became too big, a quarterly meeting was created. This meeting was made up of members from the monthly meetings from a specified area who met every three months to rule on disputes between monthly meetings or as a court of appeal to decisions from a monthly meeting. The first quarterly meeting in America was in Burlington in 1681. Salem had its first in 1683. The most important meeting was the yearly meeting. This meeting decided policy in an area covered by several colonies. All yearly meetings kept in contact with the London meeting. West Jersey did not have a yearly meeting for a long time because the Friends there felt that any major decisions could be handled by their quarterly meeting. The Jersey Friends eventually became a part of the Philadelphia yearly meeting, which became the most powerful meeting in the Middle Colonies.[31] The Friends had brought their organization over from England. They had found a place in America where they could worship without fear of persecution. They also brought their slaves.

3. Friends and Slavery

In 1619, the first indentured servants came to Jamestown, Virginia, to create a workforce of sufficient size to work on plantations. Indentured servants were those people who became servants to an employer, bound by either a written or verbal contractual agreement for a set amount of time. About 75 to 80 percent of the people who left England for the Chesapeake area during the 17th century were indentured servants. Because the male indentured servants outnumbered the women by 5 or 6 to 1, the workforce failed to reproduce itself in sufficient size to handle future labor demands. Also, they were reluctant to continue being servants at the end of their term, which was usually five years. Therefore, slavery was used to combat the shrinking workforce. The Dutch saw great profits in the slave trade and this did not go unnoticed by English merchants and shippers, who created the Royal African Company in 1672 to offer planters slave workers. English merchants were also willing to offer credit to plantation owners so that they could buy slaves.[1]

The first Africans imported as slaves in New Jersey arrived in 1639 in Pavonia, which was the first permanent settlement by the Dutch in New Jersey and a part of what became known as Jersey City. Slaves continued to come into the area under Carteret and Berkeley. They pushed the use of slaves by putting into the constitution of their colony in 1664 the proviso that immigrants would receive seventy-five acres for every slave they bought before January 1, 1665. The law continued with giving sixty acres for every slave bought in 1666, forty-five acres in 1667, and thirty acres in 1668.[2]

In November of 1684, the *Isabella* sailed up the Delaware River from Bristol, England, and landed in Philadelphia carrying 150 Africans. They were sold on the wharves to the highest bidder, some of those buyers being Friends. These slaves then cleared the land around Philadelphia. They wore chains and had bells attached to them to prevent escape attempts and to announce if an attempt was made.[3]

On the other side of the Delaware River, New Jersey created laws to restrict the actions of enslaved Africans. In 1682, a statute was passed to prohibit the buying of goods from slaves. The penalty was five pounds for the first offense and ten pounds for the second. If an African attempted to sell anything to a Caucasian, that man had the right to flog him and receive half a crown from his master. Also in 1682, no one could sell alcohol to slaves unless for medicinal purposes. A treaty signed by Native Americans the next year stated that they too were not permitted to trade with slaves. In 1685, another law about alcohol stated that anyone convicted of selling or giving alcohol to either Native Americans or Africans, except as a medicine, would receive a fine of five pounds. But there were others who wanted another kind of law passed.[4]

Francis Daniel Pastorius was a German who met Penn and had become convinced to Quakerism.[5] He led thirteen Quaker families from Krefeld in Germany to America to escape religious persecution, and they landed in Philadelphia on October 8, 1683. Leading Quaker families to a new home was just the beginning of his accomplishments. He held the first fair in Philadelphia on November 16, 1684, which later became a role model for American county fairs. Pastorius founded Germantown on October 25, 1685, which became a section of Philadelphia, and was its mayor. He was also a lawyer, teacher and poet. In spite of these accomplishments, Pastorius became known for something else.[6]

Germantown was an area settled by skilled artisans who had no need or liking for slavery. In 1688, the Friends gathered at the home of Tones Kunders to prepare a document outlining their feelings on slavery. Four men, Pastorius, Derick up de Greaff, Abraham up de Graef, and the clerk of the meeting, Garret Henderich, signed the document and were assigned to deliver and present the document to the monthly meeting at nearby Dublin.[7] Without preamble, they declared that they were "against the traffic of men-body," and stated,

> "There is a saying, that we should do to all men like as we will be done ourselves; making no difference of what generation, descent, or colour they are. And those who steal or rob men, and those who buy or purchase them, are they not all alike? Here is liberty of conscience, which is right and reasonable; here ought to be likewise liberty of the body, except of evil-doers, which is another case. But to bring men hither, or to rob and sell them against their will, we stand against."[8]

The Monthly Meeting decided that the issue was "so weighty that we think it not expedient for us to meddle with it here." Therefore, they referred the matter to the quarterly meeting in Philadelphia. That meeting assigned the men to present their document to the yearly meeting in Burlington, New Jersey, on September 5, 1688. That meeting considered the document, but no action was taken because the Friends could not arrive at a unanimous opinion.[9]

In 1693, the question of slavery was again approached. The Yearly Meeting in Philadelphia asked its members not to buy slaves unless it was for the purpose of freeing them. There was, however, no penalty for not following this suggestion. This conciliatory response toward slavery was not enough for others. George Keith, a prolific writer of pamphlets and tracts who was already in trouble with the more conservative Quakers because of his belief that the Inner Light was not enough to base their faith on, wrote a paper called "An Exhortation and Caution to Friends Concerning Buying or Keeping of Negroes."[10] In this paper, Keith asked the Friends to not buy slaves unless they planned to free them, and if they owned slaves, to free them after they had taught "them to read, and give[n] them a Christian education." His reasoning was that it was against their practices "to buy Prize or stolen Goods" and since the slaves were stolen from their own country, the Friends should not have anything to do with the practice.[11] Instead of not having anything to do with slavery, the Quakers wanted nothing to do with Keith or anyone who followed him. He angered many Friends because he had published his paper for the whole world to see, which went against the Quaker belief about keeping any disagreements between Friends. Keith, who had founded a branch of the Friends called Christian Quakers, went to England to plead his case. He lost, and on May 25, 1695, the London meeting threw him out. He then created a Christian Quaker group in England, but it soon disbanded. Keith gravitated towards the Anglican Church and eventually became a priest for that church.[12] Keith's abandonment of the Friends' faith shook them, but it would not be the last time that Friends would argue among themselves.[13]

Just because the yearly meeting did not come out quickly against slavery did not mean that the subject was closed. The members wrestled with the idea of giving their slaves religious instruction. At the yearly meeting of 1696, it was decided to advise the Quakers to bring their slaves to meetings or have meetings for them at the members' homes. It was to keep them from "loose and lewd-living, as much as in them lies, and from rambling abroad on First-days or other times."

That particular meeting also had several members once again question the idea of slavery. William Southeby spoke out against slavery at the meeting. Cadwalader Morgan, a minister from Merion, near Philadelphia, did as well and spoke of the conflict within him concerning slavery. He had needed help around his farm, but there were not enough men in his area to hire, so he ordered a slave. However, he became troubled by the decision. He asked other Friends, and some of them said to buy a slave and others said not to. Finally, he went to the Lord on the subject, and soon it was made known to him that he should not have anything to do with slavery. Once he had heard that others were troubled by slavery, he decided to share his feelings with his fellow Friends and encourage them to speak their minds concerning slavery. The meeting decided to not only instruct Friends who owned slaves to care for their morals, but also to stay away from the slave trade. It was not a direct ban of the slave trade; it was more of a suggestion. Either way, it was a first small step toward turning against slavery.

Voices continued to rise up in the Quaker community against slavery. In 1698, Robert Pyle wrote down his objections toward slavery. Pyle was an important member of the Concord Monthly Meeting, which was located a few miles southwest of Philadelphia.

He also expressed his concerns about, not just the immorality of owning slaves, but also his fears of a slave uprising and his belief that holding slaves went against the Golden Rule. He also made the suggestion that the various quarterly meetings should be responsible for talking with Quaker slaveholders and pinning them down for a definite time frame to free their slaves. Pyle also believed that the Quakers and their ex-slaves should meet and arrange for payment for the labor given while they were slaves.

The Philadelphia Meeting tried to limit the importation of slaves from Barbados, a major source of slaves for the Quakers, by continuous pushing against slavery. After a paper was read at the Philadelphia Monthly Meeting of 1698 concerning the selling of slaves on the auction block, the mood of the meeting was that Quakers should not be involved in these types of actions. They also wrote to Friends in Barbados asking them to help stop the slave trade to Pennsylvania because they believed that there were too many slaves in Pennsylvania.

On William Penn's second visit to Pennsylvania in 1699, he made several statements concerning slaves. He requested his fellow Friends to care for their slaves' souls and tried to get the assembly to legalize slave marriages. Neither one of these wishes were granted.[14] Penn left America because he heard a report that proprietary governments were possibly going to be abolished. When he returned to England in 1701, a new charter was granted to him.

Even though there were some in the Quaker community who wanted to keep slaves from coming into Pennsylvania, this idea was at odds with what the Crown wanted for the colonies. In 1702, the proprietors of East and West Jersey had tired of fighting each other, as well as not making money on the land, and surrendered their land to the Crown. The provinces were joined together and New Jersey became a royal colony.[15] When Queen Anne gave instructions to Edward Lord Cornbury on November 16, 1702, as he prepared to become her captain general and governor in chief in New Jersey, among the instructions were orders that affected slavery and the Quakers. She informed him that he was to

> give all due Encouragement and invitation to Merchants and others who shall bring Trade unto Our said Province, or any way contribute to the Advantage thereof, and in particular the Royal African Company of England.
>
> And whereas we are willing to recommend unto the said Company that the said Province may have a Constant and Sufficient Supply of Merchantable Negroes at moderate Rates in money or Commodities, so you are to take especial care that Payment be duly made, and within a competent time according to their agreements.
>
> And You are to take care that there be no Trading from Our said Province to any place in Africa within the charter of the Royal African Company, otherwise than prescribed by an Act of Parliament, Intituled An Act to Settle the Trade to Africa.
>
> And You are yearly to give unto Us and to Our Commissioners for Trade and Plantations an Account of what number of Negroes our said Province is yearly supplied with, and at what Rates.

The queen also told Cornbury that he should

> endeavour to get a Law pass for the restraining of any Inhuman Severity, which by ill Masters or Overseers may be used towards their Christian Servants and their Slaves; And that provision be made therein, that the Wilful killing of Indians and Negroes may be punished by Death, and that a fit Penality [*sic*] be Imposed for the maiming of them.
>
> And You are also with the Assistance of the Council and Assembly to find out the best means to facilitate and incourage the Conversion of Negroes and Indians to the Christian Religion.[16]

Queen Anne also informed Cornbury that he was "to permit a liberty of conscience to all persons, except papists, so they may be contented with a quiet and peaceable enjoyment of the same, not giving offense or scandal to the government." The queen was specific in her order to practice tolerance for most religious beliefs, but Cornbury did not follow it when it came to the Quakers. He hated the Friends because they refused to fight against France during the war. When Burlington County elected three Quakers into the Provincial Assembly, he refused to allow them in because he thought they would not swear allegiance to the Crown. Lewis Morris, one of the three men, wrote to Queen Anne's secretary of state in London complaining about Cornbury as well as his fears that the Friends would be persecuted. He also informed the secretary of state of Cornbury's habit of dressing in women's clothing in public. The New Jersey Assembly publicly censured Cornbury and the New York Assembly did the same thing in September 1708. The queen then removed him from office.[17]

Friends were also dealing with conflicts from within. In the early 18th century, there was a movement among the Quakers called Quietism. This meant that they were concerned with keeping to their belief of the Inner Light and making sure that all members stayed focused on that principle. Nothing was to be done in their lives from free will. Everything had to be from the will of God. If someone spoke at a meeting, it had better be from divine will. This was also a time when elders, the older, more experienced Friends, were in charge of keeping the other members in line. This move toward introspection also meant that the Friends were not as concerned with gaining converts and spreading their beliefs as they had been in the past. It also meant that anyone speaking out about a topic that might upset the other members was taking a huge risk. Members who were against slavery had an uphill battle, not only with the general public, but also with their fellow Friends.[18]

The Pennsylvania Assembly, controlled by Quakers, in 1711 prohibited the importation of slaves. This was a continuation of the road the Quakers wanted to walk of being against the slave trade, but not slavery so as to not offend those Quakers who owned slaves.[19] However, the proposal was vetoed because it went against the wishes of the Crown. The slave trade was very lucrative to England and the prohibition had to be removed. The next year, a head duty of 20 pounds that was proposed by the assembly was also vetoed.

In September of 1711, the Chester (Pennsylvania) Quarterly Meeting was concerned about Quakers buying slaves from the West Indies. They broached the subject to the yearly meeting and asked them to consider some action against slavery. The only thing the meeting mentioned was that they advised fellow Quakers to not buy slaves from other countries and that other Quakers in other areas were concerned about it.

Since the bill prohibiting the slave trade failed to go into law and their Yearly Meeting was not very clear on their intentions on the subject, the Quakers wrote in September 1712 to the London Yearly Meeting for advice on the subject. They told the meeting that they had tried to stop their members from dealing with the slave trade in Barbados, but with not much success. Therefore, they wanted advice on what to do in this situation. The English Friends wrote back, saying that the Philadelphia Friends should have asked the opinion of the other Friends in America and then formed a plan to deal with the situation. They agreed that the African slave trade was wrong, but they did not give a definite answer on how to end it.[20]

Not taking the vague answer as the final word on the subject, the Epistle of the 1714 Yearly Meeting to the London Yearly Meeting mentioned that they "kindly received your advise about negro slaves and we are one with you that the multiplying of them may be of a dangerous consequence." They continued by stating that they wished

> that a way might be found to stop the bringing in more here, or at least that Friends may be less concerned in buying and selling of any that may be brought in and hope for your assistance with the Government if any farther Law should be made discouraging the importation. We know not of any Friend amongst us that has any hand or concern in bringing any out of their country. And we are of the same mind with you that the practice is not commendable nor allowable amongst Friends and we take the freedom to acquaint you, that our request unto you that you would be pleased to consult or otherwise with Friends in other plantations where they are more numerous than with us because they hold a correspondence with you, but not with us and your meeting may better prevail with them.[21]

The Chester Friends continued to press the yearly meeting about the importation of slaves. At the 1715 Yearly Meeting, the Chester contingent mentioned that they were still concerned that "some Friends bring yet in the practice of importing buying and selling of Negro slaves." The Yearly Meeting answered their concern by stating that "the argument and minutes of the former Yearly Meetings may be observed and put into practice." They also observed that Friends should "avoid judging one another in this matter publicly or otherwise." It was also stated in their yearly epistle that if any Friends were involved "in the importation of Negroes, let them be dealt with and advised to avoid that practice according to the sense of former meetings in that behalf and that all Friends who have or keep Negroes do use and treat them with humanity and a Christian spirit and that all do forbear judging or reflecting on one another either in public or private."[22]

The next year, at the yearly meeting at Burlington, New Jersey, the Chester Friends expressed their concerns. They felt that "former minutes and Orders are not sufficient to discourage their importation and therefore request that no Friends may buy any Negro slaves that may be imported for the future." The Yearly Meeting disagreed and said they thought that what had already been written was sufficient. However, to appease the Chester Friends, they did state that "it is desired that Friends generally do as much as may be to avoid buying such Negroes as shall hereafter be brought in rather than offend any Friends who are against it. Yet this is only caution and not Censure."[23]

The Friends may have not wanted inner strife concerning slavery, but they received it anyway. William Southeby, who spoke out against slavery at the yearly meeting in 1696, continued the fight by appearing in front of the Pennsylvania Assembly in 1712. He gave them a petition asking for the prohibition of slavery. It was rejected because the assembly believed that it was not a good idea to set the slaves free. Southeby continued to argue about slavery with the Pennsylvania Friends. When they refused to listen, he published a paper denouncing slavery. This was considered an act of rebellion by the Pennsylvania Friends because Friends did not allow Friends to publish anything without the approval of senior Friends. In June of 1716, the Philadelphia Monthly Meeting disciplined him and forced him to apologize. Three months later, when the yearly meeting refused to come out completely against slavery, Southeby took back his apology and published another paper about the cruelty of slavery. He was warned that if he did not stop this, he would be disowned from the Friends. In December of 1718, the meeting declared its intention to disown Southeby. Apparently, it never became more than an intention because when he died on September 7, 1722, he was still listed as a Friend of good standing.

John Farmer, a British Friend, got into the same kind of trouble with the Philadelphia Yearly Meeting as Southeby. In 1716, he traveled to America and joined in the anti-slavery fight in New York and New England. He was disowned in New England and he went to Philadelphia to appeal the ruling. While he was appealing his disownment, he read his anti-slavery essay, "Epistle Concerning Negroes," both in and out of Friends meetings. The Philadelphia Yearly Meeting did not appreciate these readings and endorsed his disownment in 1718.This was enough to silence him, and within a year or two, Farmer dropped from sight.

After the attacks on Southeby and Farmer, there was no one to restart the anti-slavery movement among the Quakers. John Hepburn had tried to continue the fight with his pamphlet entitled "The American Defense of the Christian Golden Rule" in 1715, but it was mostly ignored. It was more important to the leading Friends to keep unity within their ranks and not criticize the actions of the slaveholding members than to correct a wrong. America would face that same problem throughout its early history until the explosion called the Civil War wiped the stain of slavery off the collective soul of the country.[24]

The Pennsylvania Assembly was concerned about the possibility of a slave revolt or having too many slaves in the area. Therefore, they raised the tariff on slaves in 1726 to ten pounds. Three years later, they decided to reduce it to forty shillings and the floodgates of slavery opened wide. It was the same year that another Quaker would stand up against the status quo. Ralph Sandiford, a shop owner in Philadelphia, whose place of business overlooked the marketplace where slaves were sold, was disgusted with slavery and wrote a book called "A Brief Examination of the Practice of the Times," which was published by Ben Franklin. In it, Sandiford attacked the rationalization of slavery that claimed that Africans were descended from Cain and therefore deserved to be slaves. He stated that since Cain's descendants died in the Great Flood, the rationale was without merit. Sandiford then jumped straight into the heart of the issue by stating,

> What greater injustice can be acted, than to rob a man of his liberty, which is more valuable than life, and especially after such a manner as this, to take a man from his native country, his parents and brethren, and other natural enjoyments, and that by stealth, or by way of purchase from them that have no right to sell them, whereby thou receiveth the theft, which is as bad.
>
> And take them amongst a people of a strange language, and unnatural climates, which is hard for them to bear whose constitutions are tendered by the heat of their native country; for God that made the world, and all men of one blood, that dwell upon the face of the Earth, has appointed them bounds of their habitations, shall we then undertake to remove them, wheresoever interest shall lead us, to sell them for slaves, separating husband from wife, and children from both, like beasts, with all their increase, to the vilest of men, and their offspring after to all Eternity.

His attack on slavery did not spare the Quakers. He also lectured the Quakers by saying that if they had stood against slavery, they would have been "a burning and shining light" to those who were in the slave trade and would have set "a precedent to the nations throughout the universe, which might have brought them to have seen the evil of it in themselves." Instead, the Friends were involved in a practice that converted "men's liberty to our wills." He wondered how the Friends could "minister to spirits in prison? Thou, that teachest a man should not steal, but work with his hands the thing which is good; and yet does thou become a receiver" when they traded in slaves. He said that it was "far wide of Friend's principles in the beginning, and is so to all them that are led by the same truth. And shall we be so implicit, as not to see so unjust a practice."

He cautioned his readers to consider the price a slave owner would pay to continue in the slave trade. He wondered how anyone who owned slaves could

> "die in peace, to leave these poor creatures in such unhappy circumstances; for though their Maker might grant them all enjoyment but liberty, how does he know what barbarous hands they may fall into when he is gone, which then would make their bondage and severity more grievous to them; which often happens; for those that are trained up in this sin, become more hard and dark than the rest of the human race; which I have often experienced in my travels amongst men concerned; and the more men have pretended to religion, the more dark have they been, striving to cover their sin." He warned anyone who had not become involved in slavery to "shun it as thou value thine own soul, which should be more to thee than the gain of the whole world, that if thy father should offer to give thee slaves, center thou to the Witness of Jesus in thy soul,

which cannot consent to sin, and in the openings of the universal love of God in Christ for all mankind, resist the temptation, whereby thou mayest be an example to thy parents for good, by thy denying an inheritance so near to thee."

He finished his book by stating that if "any are offended with me, for the foregoing Treatise, because it came not forth with the concurrence of the meeting, it is in my heart to desire your freedom with me therein, that all offences may be removed according to the ability the Lord gives me."[25]

The book started the debate against slavery among the Quakers again. The more conservative of the Friends considered him an enemy, but those against slavery used it as a jumping-off point to fight again. The Chester Friends again confronted the Philadelphia Yearly Meeting in 1729 about slave holding among the Friends. They stated that if "we are restricted by a rule of discipline from being concerned in fetching or importing Negro slaves from their own country," they wondered "whether it is not as reasonable we should be restricted from buying of them when imported." This time, the yearly meeting passed on their concerns to their Quarterly Meetings so that they could give them advice on the subject.

Sandiford went back to Franklin and published a second edition of the book. This time, events were on the side of the anti-slavery forces. The Friends in England had condemned the importation of slaves in their Yearly Meeting in 1727. Sandiford sent word to them for help in convincing the meetings in America to do the same. He worried constantly about this issue and this made him ill. Things did not change much, but he did make a difference. The Philadelphia Quarterly Meeting felt that since it had already been ruled upon, there was no need to talk about the subject. The Bucks Meeting left the matter up to the yearly meeting to deal with. In New Jersey, the Burlington Meeting thought that buying slaves was wrong because it encouraged the slave trade, but it was only offering advice. However, Sandiford's words struck home in the Gloucester, Salem, and Shrewsbury Meetings. They all agreed that Friends should not be allowed to own slaves and that slavery was wrong.[26]

The fight against slavery continued in the Pennsylvania Yearly Meeting of 1730. The Chester Friends had put forth a proposal to stop Friends from buying slaves and the anti-slavery forces had support. The Quarterly Meeting of Gloucester and Salem reported that after "having considered the said Proposition. It is the Sense of That Meeting that Friends ought to be restricted from purchasing of Negroes as well as from importing them." The Shrewsbury Quarterly Meeting said in their report that it was "the Sense of that meeting that the Practice of buying Negroes is wrong and therefore they Desire Friends may be restricted from purchasing of them." The final outcome was that the meeting put out a statement saying that it was under the opinion "that Friends ought to be very cautious of making any such Purchases for the Future. It being Disagreeable to the sense of this Meeting." They also said that "this Meeting recommends it to the Care of the Several Monthly Meetings to see that Such who may be, or are likely to be found in that Practice may be admonished."[27]

An incident in Burlington County, New Jersey, created concerns about slave insurrections. In 1734, a group of slaves were convinced that England had abolished slavery. Feeling that their owners had no right to hold them, they decided to free themselves. The leaders of the slaves ordered the others to rise up at midnight on a designated night and kill their owners and their sons. The women would be ravished the next day. Afterward, the slaves would then run away to the French and Indians. The plot fell apart when one of the conspirators got into an argument with a Caucasian and told him that he was as good as any slave owner and he would soon prove it. An investigation began and most of the county's slaves were believed to be a part of the intended uprising. Thirty of the suspected leaders were tried and convicted. Most of them were flogged, several had their ears cut off, and one was hanged. Another plot was discovered the same year in Somerville, New Jersey and was stopped before it was carried out.[28]

The tide was turning, slowly, against slavery in the Friends community. During the 1737 Pennsylvania Yearly Meeting, it was written that the meeting "repeats their advice and Caution against the encouraging of the Importation of Negroes by buying them after imports and again recommend it to the several Quarterly Meetings belonging to this Meeting." The Meeting also requested information from the quarterly meetings on how this was proceeding by the next Yearly Meeting.[29] The next year, the reports from the quarterly meetings stated that it "also appears by the said Reports (that from the quarterly meeting from Bucks—accepted) that the Care of Friends is continued to avoid the Encouragement of the Importation of Negroes by buying them after Importation."[30] Sandiford did not live to see these changes because he died in 1733 at the age of forty.

One of the Friends who visited Sandiford while he was ill was Benjamin Lay. Whereas Sandiford fought slavery but did not wish to offend his fellow Quakers, Lay had no such qualms. As John Greenleaf Whittier, the poet, described him in his introduction to "The Journal of John Woolman," Lay was a

figure only four and a half feet high, hunchbacked, with projecting chest, legs small and uneven, arms longer than his legs; a huge head, showing only beneath the enormous white hat, large, solemn eyes and a prominent nose; the rest of his face covered with a snowy semicircle of beard falling low on his breast, ... a figure to recall the old legends of troll, brownie, and kobold. Such was the irrepressible prophet who troubled the Israel of slaveholding Quakersism, clinging like a rough chestnut-burr to the skirts of its respectability, and settling like a pertinacious gad-fly on the sore places of its conscience.

Lay was born in Colchester, Essex, England, in 1681. His family was Quaker and he supported himself over the years as a farmer, glove maker, sailor, and bookseller. In 1730, the English Friends disowned him and he moved to Barbados, where he became a storekeeper. It was there that he and his wife Sarah had several run-ins with slavery. Lay used to save scraps of food for the slaves and give them out at his store on Sundays, which was the one free day they had. This did not turn out well because the slaves would rush in and take not only the scraps, but other items in the store. That would make him furious and he would beat them to stop the theft. He was conflicted and later sorry for his actions. In another incidence, Sarah Lay went to visit a fellow Friend and witnessed the beating of a runaway. These occurrences fueled Lay's hatred of slavery and he began to speak out against it and was soon convinced to leave Barbados.[31] Lay and his wife moved back to England and then went to Philadelphia in 1731. He was disappointed that slavery was tolerated among the Friends in America. The Lays soon left Philadelphia and set up a farm in Abington, six miles away.[32] He lived in a natural cave that he amended slightly for his use. He drank the nearby spring water and ate just vegetables. He also refused to wear any clothes or eat anything made by the labor of slaves.[33]

Sarah Lay died in 1735, and afterward Benjamin spent his time confronting the Friends on their acceptance of slavery. His technique to hammer home his opinion recalled the actions of the English Quakers at their most outrageous. One time, he stood at the gate of a meetinghouse with one bare foot in the snow. This was to show how slaves had to deal with no shoes in the winter.[34] At the Market Street Meeting in Philadelphia, he walked into the building and one of the Friends asked that someone remove him, perhaps fearing that Lay would make a scene. Another Friend, a blacksmith, volunteered and led him to the gate. The man then hurled Lay through the gate with such enthusiasm that he landed in the gutter of the street. Never letting an opportunity to make his point pass, Lay stayed where he landed until the meeting ended. He told the people passing him on the street that he did not feel that that he should pick himself up and that "those who cast me here raise me up. It is their business, not mine."[35] There is even a story that claimed that Lay kidnapped a boy for a day so that the parents would know what is was like to be separated from their child like the slave parents dealt with when they or their children were sold and separated.[36]

His most famous attempt to shake the Friends from their acceptance of slavery occurred at a Yearly Meeting in Burlington. John Greenleaf Whittier mentioned that during the meeting,

> in the midst of the solemn silence of the great assembly, the unwelcome figure of Benjamin Lay, wrapped in his long white overcoat, was seen passing up the aisle. Stopping midway, he exclaimed, "You slaveholders! Why don't you throw off your Quaker coats as I do mine, and show yourselves as you are?" Casting off as he spoke, his outer garment, he disclosed to the astonished assembly a military coat underneath and a sword dangling at his heels. Holding in one hand a large bible, he drew his sword with the other. "In the sight of God," he cried, "you are as guilty as if you stabbed your slaves to the heart, as I do this book!" suiting the action to the word, and piercing a small bladder filled with the juice of poke-weed (phytolacca decandra), which he had concealed between the covers, and sprinkling as with fresh blood those who sat near him.[37]

Lay's attack on slavery did not end there. In 1737, he wrote a book entitled "All Slave-Keepers That Keep the Innocent in Bondage" and, like Sandiford, took it to Benjamin Franklin to publish. In his book, Lay began by saying that the book is "so far from offending or grieving my very dear true and tender Friends, called Quakers, who love the truth more than all, that it is by their request and desire that they are made public." He then used an address by William Burling written in 1718 and delivered to Friends Elders that attacked slavery. Lay continued by writing his own attack, mentioning how years before, the English and Dutch who were captured by the Turks were forced into slavery. He wrote that it was the same thing that

> our brave Christians so-call'd do; and have done for many years in Philadelphia, and elsewhere in America, by the poor Negroes, which is ten times worse in us, all things consider'd; but what crying, wringing of hands, what mourning and lamentations there was then by their relations, wives for their husbands, parents for their children, relations for their friends, one neighbour for another! What exclaiming against the Turk for his tyranny and oppression, and cruel dealing and treatment, towards their friends.

He pointed an accusing finger at the Friends by saying that they "pretend not to love fighting with carnal weapons, nor to carry swords by our sides, but carry a worse thing in the heart, as will I believe appear by and by; what, I pray and beseech you, dear Friends, by the tender mercies of our God."

He also mentioned his friend Ralph Sandiford as a man who spoke out against slavery. Lay defended Sandiford from attacks that said he was bitter and did not end his life well. He wrote that Sandiford "was in great perplexity of mind, and having oppression, which makes a wise man mad, by which he was brought very low, with many bodily infirmities, long before he died." He also mentioned that Sandiford was "a very tender hearted man before he came amongst Friends, as well as after, as I have heard from

Benjamin Lay's take-no-prisoners attacks against slavery earned him the scorn of many
of his fellow Quakers (Swarthmore College, Friends Historical Library).

many honest Friends, that had much dealing, and intimate conversation with him."

Lay specifically attacked those Friends who owned slaves and asked them to

> examine your own Hearts, and see and feel too, if you have not the same answer from Truth now within; while you preach and exhort others to Equity, and to do Justice and love Mercy, and to walk humbly before the Lord and his People, and you yourselves live and act quite contrary, behave proudly, do unjustly and unmercifully, and live in and encourage the grossest iniquity in the whole world. For I say, you are got beyond gospel, Law, Abraham, Prophets, Patriarchs, to Cain the Murderer, and beyond him too, to the Devil himself, beyond Cain, for he murdered but one, that we know of, but you have many thousands, or caused 'em to be so.[38]

The Philadelphia Friends answered the claim that they supported Lay's book during their Yearly Meeting of 1738 by ordering one of their members to

> draw an Advertisement to be printed in the newspapers of Philadelphia In order to inform all whom it may concern that the Book lately published by Benjamin Lay Entitled ... was not published by the Approbation of Friends, that he is not in Unity with us. And that his Book contains false Charges as well against particular persons of our Society as against Friends in general.[39]

The Friends may not have liked their way of life challenged, but circumstances, both in and out of their society, were waiting to change their world.

4. Victory and Retreat

Benjamin Lay was the type of man who would force his fellow Friends to look at slavery with his in-your-face tactics, but he could not make them change their opinions on it. That took another reformer who had a much milder approach, yet was just as determined as the more politically incorrect Lay. John Woolman was born in Northampton, in Burlington County, New Jersey, in 1720. When he was 21, he apprenticed himself, with his father's permission, to work in a shop in Mount Holly, New Jersey, and keep the shopkeeper's books. One day, the shopkeeper came to Woolman and asked him to write a bill of sale for a woman that he owned. Woolman was troubled by doing this, but he felt that he had to do this because the man was a fellow Friend as well as his employer. He wrote it, but when he gave the bill of sale to the shopkeeper, Woolman told him that he felt slavery was not a practice that a Christian should partake in. A short time later, another Friend came to him and asked Woolman to write paperwork for a slave he had just received. Woolman told him politely that he was uncomfortable with writing a bill of sale for another human being. The young man replied that he was not happy with the idea of owning a slave, but he accepted the slave because she was a gift to his wife. Woolman did not bend on his opinion and the young man had to go to another scribe.[1]

Woolman continued to work at the shop, learned the tailor business from his employer and eventually bought the business from him. He had also developed a reputation as a scribe and wrote legal papers for others. He eventually sold the shop and supported his wife, Sarah Ellis, whom he married in 1749, and their daughter as a tailor, scribe, and farmer.

Even though Woolman was uncomfortable with slavery, he was not a stranger to it. The wealthier Friends in the area owned slaves. Henry Burr, his grandfather, owned a slave woman and so did Woolman's employer. These slaves were treated well, so he did not immediately see the dark side of slavery.

However, it was when his employer wanted to sell his slave that Woolman was awakened to its evils.[2]

The evolution of Woolman's feelings toward slavery continued in 1746 when he felt the call to visit other Friends meetings in Pennsylvania, Maryland, Virginia, and North Carolina. During this trip, he sometimes stayed with Friends who owned slaves. He was troubled by it, but he had different feelings about it with different slave owners. If the owners lived simply and did not treat their slaves badly, he was able to deal with it better. However, if the family who owned slaves lived expensively and treated their slaves badly, he would privately talk to the slave owners about his misgivings. He also felt that slave trading brought to the land "so many vices and corruptions, increased by this trade and this way of life, that it appeared to me as a dark gloominess hanging over the land; and though now many willingly run into it, yet in future the consequence will be grievous to posterity."[3]

While John Woolman was dealing with his feelings on slavery, other members of the Society of Friends were dealing with another problem that affected both Quakers and non–Quakers alike. There had been disagreements for many years about whether or not Pennsylvania should have a militia. In 1671, Pennsylvania passed a militia law which stated that every man between the ages of 16 and 60 be given enough powder and bullets to use for defense. The law was soon abandoned, but in 1703, John Evans became the lieutenant-governor. Evans was a strong supporter of the idea of a militia and was determined to create one for Pennsylvania. David Lloyd, the speaker of the assembly and a Quaker, delayed the issue as much as he could to avoid voting on it. Evans went around the stalling by using executive orders to create a militia. He also made sure that anyone who was in the militia was exempt from watch duty in Philadelphia. The Quakers countered that by ordering constables to arrest anyone who did not report for watch duty. This made many men not want to volunteer for the militia, and enlistments were low. Delaying tactics and opposition continued until November 1705, when the assembly approved a bill creating a volunteer militia.[4]

Indication of the way the Quakers in the New Jersey and Pennsylvania assemblies reacted toward any talk of militias came in 1744 when England was at war with France. Governor Morris of New Jersey summoned the legislature into session in June to read them the declaration of war. He complained that the militia act was not being enforced properly. He also complained that offenses in the militia were not being punished and basic duties such as drilling were being ignored. The legislature answered that a revision of the act was not necessary because it was up to the officers of the militia to enact discipline. Morris tried again to effect a stronger act, but the legislature refused. He then dissolved the legislature. His reasoning for his actions was that he felt the legislature came together determined to do nothing for the defense of the state. Two months later, he met with the new assembly and received the same rejection.

Governor Shirley of Massachusetts came up with a plan to attack a major French fort, and he contacted Governor Morris in January of 1745 to ask for troops and ships. Morris told him that he seriously doubted that he or Pennsylvania could help him because of the Quakers. Shirley tried again in May, stating that the king liked the idea of the expedition. The fort was taken by New England troops, but Shirley then asked for help in keeping the position by sending money. The New Jersey legislature did send him 2,000 pounds. The money was taken from funds earmarked for the support of government.[5]

On the other side of the Delaware River, war clouds were growing. Bad feelings between the white settlers and the Lenapi tribe had been building for some time. It began when William Penn's son, Thomas, inherited the Pennsylvania Proprietorship after his father's death. Unfortunately for the Lenapi, he turned his back on Quakerism and the idea of treating them in a fair manner. The elder Penn had bought land from them in 1686 in what was called "The Walking Purchase." This agreement consisted of land in Bucks County that could be covered by a man walking for a day and a half. Thomas Penn wanted to sell land to Caucasians who had already occupied it illegally. To make the sale legal, Penn arranged a walk to change the boundaries. He did this by hiring trained athletes to run across land that had already been cleared to make travel easier for his walkers. The men covered sixty miles in the allotted time that a normal man would have covered only thirty and the surveyors who measured out the boundaries added several more miles. This kind of business dealing that the elder Penn would have never done so enraged the Lenapi that they sided with the French against the English and the colonists when the war broke out.[6]

Benjamin Franklin, in his autobiography, mentioned how he watched the Quakers in the assembly struggle with their conscience when it came to voting on anything concerning war or fighting. He felt that their beliefs caused them embarrassment whenever a vote came up

> to grant aids for military purposes. They were unwilling to offend government, on the one hand, by a direct refusal; and their friends, the body of the Quakers, on the other, by a compliance contrary to their principles; hence a variety of evasions to avoid complying, and modes of disguising the compliance when it became unavoidable. The common mode at last was, to grant money under the phrase of its being "for the king's use," and never to inquire how it was applied.[7]

If this phrase did not accomplish its goal, other strategies were put to work. In 1745, the Pennsylvania Assembly refused to give Governor George Thomas money for buying gunpowder[8]

> because that was an ingredient of war; but they voted an aid to New England of three thousand pounds, to be put into the hands of the governor, and appropriated it for the purchasing of bread, flour, wheat, or other grain. Some of the council, desirous of giving the House still further embarrassment, advis'd the governor not to accept provisions, as not being the thing he had demanded; but he reply'd, "I shall take the money, for I understand very well their meaning; other grain is gunpowder," which he accordingly bought, and they never objected to it.

Franklin used this flexibility for his own purposes. He had wanted to use money from a lottery to pay for a fire company and was concerned that the assembly would reject the proposal. He said to a friend in the assembly that if "we fail, let us move the purchase of a fire-engine with the money; the Quakers can have no objection to that; and then, if you nominate me and I you as a committee for that purpose, we will buy a great gun, which is certainly a fire-engine."[9]

In 1747, French and Spanish privateers sailed up the Delaware River and attacked two plantations and a ship. The governor wanted to create a militia, but the assembly did not. This prompted Franklin to urge the people of the colony to create their own militia. He also proposed a lottery that would generate income to pay for their equipment. Franklin commented on the continuing problem with the Quakers by saying: "Indeed I had some cause to believe that the defense of the country was not disagreeable to any of them provided they were not required to assist in it. And I found that a much greater number of them than I could have imagined, though against offensive war, were clearly for the defense."

The governor approved of Franklin's actions, but Thomas Penn did not, and he wrote that what had happened was "founded on a Contempt to Government, and cannot end in anything but Anarchy and Confusion." Eventually, he was proven right.[10]

While those who wanted to have a militia fought the Friends in the assembly, John Woolman was preparing his attack against slavery and the Friends' support of it. Woolman waited seven years to publish "Some Considerations on the Keeping of Negroes." Before he released the essay, he wished to discuss it with others to see how they felt about the topic. He showed it to his father, Samuel, who also had anti-slavery feelings.[11] He also discussed his opinion of slavery with other Friends, such as Anthony Benezet, who became his close friend and partner in attacking the slave trade, and the leaders of the Philadelphia Yearly Meeting, such as the Pemberton brothers, James, John, and Israel, who was known as the "King of the Quakers."[12] They all supported what he wrote, so finally, in 1754, Woolman sent the essay to the Overseers of the Press of Philadelphia Yearly Meeting for their approval. They thought so highly of it that the meeting paid for its publication[13] by Benjamin Franklin[14] and sent copies of it to every Yearly Meeting in America and to England. They also devoted their 1754 epistle to slavery. The epistle stated that

> if we continually bear in mind the royal Law of doing to others, as we would be done by, we shall never think of bereaving our Fellow Creatures of that valuable Blessing Liberty; nor endure to grow rich by their Bondage. To live in ease and plenty by the toil of those whom Violence and Cruelty have put in our power, is neither consistent with Christianity, nor common Justice; and we have good reason to believe, draws down the Displeasure of Heaven.[15]

The essay had such an impact that in 1755, the Philadelphia Yearly Meeting declared that Friends who were a part of the slave trade, either by buying slaves locally or importing them, would be spoken to about it. It also caused some Friends to rebel by ignoring the yearly meeting's stand against the slave trade.[16]

Woolman started by saying in his "Considerations" that people should remember that we all are "subject to the like afflictions and infirmities of body, the like disorders and frailties in mind" and this should create in people a sense of brotherhood. But, he wrote, when people forget those things about one another and are "filled with fond notions of superiority, there is danger of erring in our conduct toward them."

He then turned the argument for slavery around by asking the reader to picture himself in the position of a slave. If

> our ancestors and we had been exposed to constant servitude, in the more servile and inferior employments of life; that we had been destitute of the help of reading and good company; that amongst ourselves we had few wise and pious instructors; that the religious amongst our superiors seldom took notice of us; that while others, in ease, have plentifully heaped up the fruit of our labour, we had received barely enough to relieve nature; and being wholly at the command of others, had generally been treated as a contemptible, ignorant part of mankind: should we, in that case, be less abject than they now are?

Woolman was concerned not only for those held in slavery but also for those who owned slaves. This attitude made his attack on slavery far different from other more confrontational anti-slavery advocates, both before and after him. Woolman thought that anyone who considered "mankind otherwise than brethren, to think favors are peculiar to one nation, and exclude others, plainly supposes a darkness in the understanding: for as God's love is universal, so where the mind is sufficiently influenced by it, it begats a likeness of itself, and the heart is enlarged toward all men."

Woolman realized that it was difficult to change people's beliefs in the sin of slavery. In his journal, he stated, "Deep-rooted customs, though wrong, are not easily altered; but it is the duty of all to be firm in that which they certainly know is right for them." He also explained his refusal to write a will that would have children inherit their parents' slaves. He believed that someone who was "well acquainted with a negro, may, I believe, under some circumstances keep him in his family as a servant, on no other motives than the negro's good; but man, as man, knows not what shall be after him, nor hath he any assurance that his children will attain to that perfection in wisdom and goodness necessary rightly to exercise such power."[17]

The effort to convince the Friends that slavery was wrong was an uphill battle. Isaac Jackson reported to a Quarterly Meeting that he had visited the homes of people who owned in total eleven hundred slaves. They had a variety of reasons for not releasing their slaves. An older man did not want to release his slaves because he felt that he had raised his eleven slaves and now it was their turn to take care of him. Another man knew that slavery was wrong, but he could not free them. This caused his wife to be greatly upset about his decision. Jackson also reported that one man owned fifty slaves and knew it was wrong, but did not know how he could free them. This man's reluctance may have come from the idea that a great deal of his wealth was tied up in slavery. Another man wanted to release his slaves, but his wife and daughters wanted to keep them.[18]

While some Friends were pushing for changes in the way the Society of Friends looked at slavery, others wanted to change the Friends themselves. A movement within the Friends was pushing to rebel against the influences of the world. They felt that the prosperity that they enjoyed through hard work and a reputation for fair dealing in business, along with the end of Quaker persecution, was beginning to make many Friends lax in their beliefs due to living a life of ease. These Friends wanted reform to protect themselves from the outside world and its temptations. They saw Friends building great homes, wearing fine clothes, and buying slaves as a sign that Friends were becoming enamored of the world. They also disapproved of Friends who were not as wealthy as others doing things such as marrying outside of the Friends faith, trafficking in goods taken during war, and turning away from the plain talk and dress.

They decided to push for reforms that would crack down on anyone deviating from the Friends Discipline. They would try to convince Friends to stay true to the ideas of plain speech and clothing, to discourage Friends from attending worship with other denominations, and dissuade them from marrying "out of meeting." They were also against Friends taking part in the political process. It was another way they felt that the outside world corrupted the Quakers involved. To them, the idea of Friends in the assembly or other political offices smacked of heresy. Therefore, the push was on to convince office-holding Friends to give up their positions.[19]

In 1755, war had reached the frontier regions of Pennsylvania and this gave the reform-minded Friends ammunition for their movement. Native Americans were killing and capturing settlers. Committees were meeting in Philadelphia assigned by the yearly meeting to discuss whether or not to continue paying taxes, that were going to pay for the fighting. While they were meeting, a man who was killed in the fighting was brought into town in a wagon and driven through the streets to incite the citizens of Philadelphia to support the war.

There was a division among the Friends on how to stand on this issue. Some of them were afraid that not paying the taxes would be thought of as being disloyal to the Crown. There were others who did not mind paying the taxes and the rest did not want to because it supported war. The ones who had no problem paying the taxes eventually withdrew from the committee and allowed the ones who were against it to write an epistle against the payment of taxes to support war.

English Friends were also concerned with the battle in the assembly over the war. They feared that those in the assembly might be forced to go against their principles and agree to an escalation to the fighting. Therefore, they urged the Friends to resign their posts rather than put themselves in a position that they did not want. The situation finally reached its boiling point. In 1756, due to the constant pressure, those Friends who were involved in politics finally gave the warlike members of the assembly, the English Friends and the separatist members of the American Friends exactly what they wanted. They removed themselves from public life.

John Woolman continued his crusade in 1757 when he felt once again compelled to travel to Maryland and Virginia. He obtained a certificate from his Monthly Meeting and went with his brother, who had business of his own in North Carolina. It was the custom of Friends to take in travelers who were Friends and let them stay in their homes free of charge. He felt that staying in homes that had slaves meant that he would save money with people who profited from slavery and he was disturbed by this. He based this opinion on Exodus 23:8, which states: "Thou shalt not receive any gift; for a gift blindeth the wise, and perverteth the words of the righteous." He felt that "the disciples were sent forth without any provisions for their journey, and our Lord said the workman is worthy of his meat, their labor in the gospel was considered as a reward for their entertainment, and therefore not received as a gift; yet, in regard to my present journey, I could not see my way clear in that respect." He was finally able to get past the problem by either giving money privately to a member of the household to give to a worthy slave and explain why he was doing this or by simply giving the money to a slave.

As he was traveling to Virginia, Woolman met a man who was a colonel of militia. He went with Woolman for a time and Woolman discussed the issue of slavery with him. He started on the topic with the colonel by mentioning his belief that people who raise their children to work moderately and be careful with their money are usually happier than people who live off of the labor of slaves. The colonel agreed and mentioned that slaves were so lazy that one free laborer could do the work of two slaves. Woolman's answer was that free men worked to provide for and improve the lives of their families while slaves worked to support others who owned them and could only expect to be slaves for the rest of their lives, thus had no real incentive to be productive. The colonel then went on to add that "the lives of the negroes were so wretched in their own country that many of them lived better here than there."

Later in the trip Woolman met another man who used the excuse that Africans were better off being slaves in this country than being free in Africa. Woolman replied that if the real reason for slavery was compassion toward the Africans, then that would mean that the owners should treat their slaves kindly. He also felt that slavery was continued for the betterment of those who profited from it. When Africans were bought for slavery, Woolman felt that it incited those who sold them to continue the war that created the slaves, thereby creating more desolation in Africa. He also believed that if the slave owners did not change their ways, the "burden will grow heavier and heavier, until times change in a way disagreeable to us." Woolman's companion replied that he "had sometimes thought it might be just in the Almighty so to order it."

As he traveled, Woolman wrote down what he saw of the treatment of slaves. It was painful for him to do so, but he felt that it was necessary. He did not like that slave owners had no respect toward marriages between slaves and separated husbands from their wives by selling them. He did not approve of overseers beating the slaves or not giving them enough to eat, as well as the slaves barely having enough clothes to cover themselves. Some Friends and other people tried to teach slaves how to read, but the actions were looked upon with disfavor by the slave owners. Woolman felt that the slaves were "the souls for whom Christ died, and for our conduct towards them we must answer before Him who is no respecter of persons."[20]

The Friends' removal from public life did not make interacting with the world any easier. In October of 1757, the military officers of Burlington County, New Jersey, were under orders to draft a militia to help the English soldiers at Fort William Henry. When the first draft did not contain enough men, a second draft occurred. Some of the men targeted were young Friends. The Friends affected were of different minds about the draft. Some of them left town to avoid, it but the ones who stayed knew that it would not be easy for them. The English officers were under orders to collect a certain amount of troops and were warned that some men would claim that it was against their religion to go to war, whether or not it was true. When the captain came to town to collect the draftees, some of the Friends affected by the draft went to see him. They told him that they could not go to war because of their beliefs and that they did not have enough money to hire someone to take their place. The captain took pity on them and sent them home, but told them that they should prepare themselves for war in case the situation demanded more troops. There was no need for them because the French captured the fort and destroyed it. The men from the first draft came home and the men of the second draft did not have to leave.

Seven months later, orders came down for officers to find housing for about one hundred troops in Mount Holly, New Jersey. An officer and two of his men came to see Woolman and asked him if he would provide food and entertainment for two soldiers in his home. They would pay him six shillings a week per man. Woolman told them that if he was only to entertain the men, then he would do so. Only one man came for a week, and was a good guest. When the officer came to Woolman to pay him, he refused because he told him that he only allowed the man into his home because the officer had the authority to order the man to stay. He then explained to the officer his religious feelings on the subject.

The road to an anti-slavery belief was not an easy one. Some Friends bought slaves and then proposed to their Quarterly Meeting in Chester County, Pennsylvania, in the summer of 1758 that they reconsider the ruling on how to deal with Friends who owned slaves. The Quarterly Meeting decided to put the request before the Philadelphia Yearly Meeting. Woolman attended the meeting and spoke to those in attendance. He said that he felt that the matter be settled

> with a clear understanding of the mind of truth, and follow it; this would be of more advantage to the society than any medium not in the clearness of Divine wisdom. The case is difficult to some who have slaves, but if such set aside all self-interest, and come to be weaned from the desire of getting estates, or even from holding them together, when truth requires the contrary, I believe the way will be so open that they will know how to steer through such difficulties.

No one at the meeting supported slavery, but some were concerned that anti-slavery rulings by the Friends might upset those Friends who did. Those people believed that the Friends should wait patiently for a time when the Lord might help the slaves gain their freedom. Woolman replied that many

> slaves on this continent are oppressed, and their cries have reached the ears of the Most High. Such are the purity and certainty of his judgments, that he cannot be partial in our favor. In infinite love and goodness he hath opened our understanding from one time to another concerning our duty towards this people, and it is not a time for delay. Should we now be sensible of what he requires of us, and through a respect to the private interest of some persons, or through a regard to some friendships which do not stand on an immutable foundation, neglect to do our duty in firmness and constancy, still waiting for some extraordinary means to bring about their deliverance, God may by terrible things in righteousness answer us in this matter.

The Friends debated the issue for a time. During the meeting, there was a suggestion that slavery would never be completely removed from the Friends until it was known how many Friends actually owned slaves and what was the reasoning for keeping them. Once this information was known, justice could be given for all Friends. Then it was suggested that several Friends be assigned to visit those who owned slaves and talk to them about why they continued the practice. Many in attendance declared that it was the right of the slaves to be free. No one objected, and several Friends were selected to visit the slave-owning Friends.

Three months later, Woolman returned to the area to visit their Quarterly Meeting. After the meeting, he went with two other Friends, Daniel Stanton and John Scarborough, to visit other members who owned slaves. A few weeks later, he went again with Stanton and John Sykes to visit other Friends slave owners. Some Friends were receptive of their visit, but others were not. When he spoke to those who did not want to change, Woolman felt that he had to stay focused on "that root from whence our concern proceeded, and have cause, in reverent thankfulness, humbly to bow before the Lord, who was near to me, and preserved my mind in calmness under some sharp conflicts, and begat a spirit of sympathy and tenderness in me towards some who were grievously entangled by the spirit of this world."[21]

The 1758 Yearly Meeting on September 29 finally ended the debate on slavery among the Friends in America. It was written in their epistle that if there were members who persisted in supporting slavery or were involved in "importing, selling or purchasing slaves the respective Monthly Meetings to us they belong should manifest their Disunion which such persons be refusing to permit them to sit in Meetings for Discipline or to be employed in the Affairs of Truth or to receive from them any Contributions towards the Relief of the Poor or other Services of the Meeting."[22]

When Benjamin Lay heard of the decision to disown members who bought or owned slaves, he declared: "Thanksgiving and praise be rendered unto the Lord God. I can now die in peace." Lay passed away the following year.[23] The Friends had decided to make a stand against slavery. However, the changes to their society were not yet finished and they, like the thirteen colonies, were soon to discover that change may be good, but sometimes, it is not easy.

PART II
REMOVING THE SPLINTER

5. The Revolution

Even though the 1758 Yearly Meeting banned the Friends from any dealings in slavery, the end of their involvement did not happen immediately. Nathan Browne, a blacksmith in Philadelphia, admitted to his meeting on January 25, 1760, that he had bought a slave to replace the white apprentice who had worked for him until he enlisted in the army. Browne stated that he intended to give the slave some education, teach him a trade, and set him free when he turned thirty-two. Browne's meeting allowed him to keep the slave without punishment because he had not only set a time to free the slave but also promised to help the Friends to discourage the holding of slaves by others.

Just because the Friends removed themselves from holding political office did not mean that they divorced themselves from the world. A Friends petition against the slave trade arrived at the Pennsylvania Legislature in 1761. The result was that the Legislature passed a law placing a ten-pound import duty on slaves.[1] The merchants of Philadelphia were not happy about this latest attempt of the Quakers to limit the slave trade. In March of 1761, they sent a petition they had circulated among themselves to the lieutenant governor of Pennsylvania, James Hamilton, to complain about the duty on importing slaves. They stated that they were concerned that the people of Pennsylvania suffered because of the lack of laborers due to enlistments into "His Majesty's Service, and near a total stop to the importation of German and other white Servants, have for some time encouraged the importation of Negroes." They argued that bringing slaves into the area would "be a means of reducing the exorbitant price of Labour, and in all probability, bring our staple Commoditys to their usual prices." They finished their petition by begging the lieutenant governor to "take into consideration the hardships we shall Labour under by such a Law taking immediate effect, when we have it not in our power to countermand our Orders or advise our friends; therefore humbly pray that such time may be allowed (before the Law takes place) as your honour shall think most Conducive to extricate your petitioners from the impending danger."

Hamilton did not give them what they wanted, so the merchants got around this problem by simply going across the Delaware River to Cooper's Ferry in New Jersey.[2] In 1744, New Jersey had removed all import duties on slave traders.[3] The Cooper family were Quakers who owned ferries that ran between Philadelphia and Cooper's Ferry, which later became known as Camden.[4] In May of 1761, Stocker and Fuller and Willing, Morris and Co., several of the signers of the petition, were selling slaves at the ferry landing. In August of the same year, Thomas Riche, David Franks, and Daniel Rundle, three more signers of the petition, were selling slaves direct from Guinea on the schooner *Hannah* which was lying in the Delaware River near Cooper's Ferry. In October, another ship, the sloop *Company*, from Africa, was selling slaves which could "be seen on board said Sloop, lying off Cooper's Ferry. For Terms, apply to Samuel and Archibald M'Call, and James Wallace and Company." These men were also signers of the petition.

They were not the only people who were selling slaves in the area. Even though the Friends in Philadelphia were trying to remove slavery from their daily lives, it did not stop the Coopers from being involved in slave trading.[5] In May of 1762, slaves were being sold at Benjamin Cooper's Ferry in New Jersey. It was announced that they would be sold "from the hours of nine to twelve o'clock in the Morning, and from three to six in the Afternoon, by W. Coxe, S. Oldman, and Company." W. Coxe was another merchant who signed his name to the petition.[6]

In the same year, Woolman wrote Part 2 of "Considerations on the Keeping of Negroes." The Friends offered to pay for the printing of the essay, but Woolman decided against it. He wanted it to reach the greatest amount of people. His opinion was that if he paid for the printing himself and charged a fee, rather than the Friends printing it and giving it out to their members for free, it would be treated as a book that should be taken seriously. The Philadelphia Friends promoted it among their monthly meetings, letting their members know where it could be bought and that its price only covered the cost of printing and binding the book. Woolman sent copies to Virginia, New York, and Newport, and kept copies for himself so that he could hand them out if he saw an opportunity to do some good.

Woolman continued his attack against slavery by writing that when men place on other men the

> title SLAVE, dressing them in uncomely garments, keeping them to servile labour, in which they are often dirty, tends gradually to fix a notion in the mind, that they are a sort of people below us in nature, and leads us to consider them as

such in all our conclusions about them. And, moreover, a person which in our esteem is mean and contemptible, if their language or behaviour toward us is unseemly or disrespectful, it excites wrath more powerfully than the like conduct in one we accounted our equal or superior; and where this happens to be the case, it disqualifies for candid judgement; for it is unfit for a person to sit as judge in a case where his own personal resentments are stirred up; and, as members of society in a well framed government, we are mutually dependent.[7]

The Haddonfield (New Jersey) Friends began to slowly free their slaves. Samuel Clement left to his wife Ruth, at the time of his death in 1765, his slave Acteon. When she died, Acteon was to be freed. He also left his son Samuel Jr. two male slaves whom he eventually freed. Aaron Aaronson, who owned a plantation on Grove St. on the other side of Cooper's Creek, placed in his will the following: "I give and bequeath in manner following, that is to say my Negro man Anthony to my daughter Mary, my Negro man James to my daughter Keziah, and my Negro girl Margaret to my daughter Rebecca to serve them until my said Negroes shall severally arrive to the age of thirty-five years, at which age them and each of them shall be set at their own liberties as free persons."[8]

In 1765, the Stamp Act was passed. The intent of this legislation was to make the colonies more self-supporting. It created a tax on paper-made products used in the colonies. The payment was anywhere between a halfpenny on newspapers to two pounds for diplomas. Instead of making the colonies more self-supporting, this extra tax enraged many of the colonists and created greater tensions between Great Britain and the colonies. However, the Friends supported the act because of their belief in obeying the laws of the land. This attitude did not endear them to those who wanted to break away from Great Britain and would cause them a great deal of trouble in the years to come.[9]

Regardless of what was going on between the colonies and Great Britain, the Friends continued to remove slavery from their own lives. Abner Woolman, a brother of John Woolman, had married Mary Aaronson and placed in his will in 1771 the following: "My executors are to pay to the three negroes who were under the government of my father-in-law as follows: to negro Anthony 15 pounds, to negro James 5 pounds, to negro Margaret 2 pounds, which sums are to be paid them as they need it, and my executors are to advise with the monthly meetings of Haddonfield in the case. My negro Isable is to have 15 pounds and her sister Mariah who lived with my brother Asher."

The Record of Manumissions of Negroes showed that within the Haddonfield Monthly Meeting between 1771 and 1794 there were seventy-three manumissions. Some of the members who freed their slaves were Griffin Morgan, Mary Roberts, Isaac Ellis, John Gill, and Hugh Creighton. Hepsibah

Evans, who lived on a farm near Mount Laurel, New Jersey, freed five slaves gradually, with the last one freed in 1780. Edward Gibbs also freed his slaves the same year and the two ex-slave-owners were married in 1781.[10]

Sometimes, freeing a slave became more complicated than just granting a man or woman their freedom. A law in New Jersey in 1769 only allowed a master to free his slave if he put up a 200-pound bond so that a town would not be liable to support a former slave if he was unable to support himself. In 1773, the town of Chesterfield in Burlington County, New Jersey, asked the legislature to prohibit the importation of slaves and for a change on the manumission laws. It was suggested several times, but the legislature always put it off until the next session. This continued until the Revolution.[11]

The Quakers were not concerned with the actions of the colonial government and continued to push for the abolishment of slavery within their society. In March 1770, the Philadelphia Yearly Meeting wanted to know how well Friends had been following their advice. They sent out members to visit "those who are possessed of slaves." It was also recommended to "the Several Monthly Meetings to send account in their reports, how far they have proceeded." By September 21, "a Committee had been appointed to Visit such who are possessed of slaves to good Satification, there appearing a considerable openness in the owners to give them their liberty, tho' some are for putting the Time off to too great a distance:; the reports from Evesham express much the same; Haddonfield Reports say they have it under consideration, but Way hath not yet opened a process." On March 26, 1775, the quarterly report from Salem noted that members had spoken to "such of their members who hold Slaves as far as appears convenient."[12]

The freedom of slaves was not the only concern of the Friends. At the Philadelphia Monthly Meeting in January 1770, a motion was proposed to provide education for children of African descent. A committee was appointed to study the matter and it suggested

> that a committee of seven Friends be nominated by the monthly meeting, who shall be authorized to employ a schoolmistress of prudent and exemplary conduct, to teach not more at one time than thirty children in the first rudiments of school learning, and in sewing and knitting. That the admission of scholars into said school be entrusted to the said committee, giving to the children of free Negroes and Mulattoes the preference, and the opportunity of being taught clear of expense to their parents.

The school would be funded by a subscription of 100 pounds. The recommendation passed and the school was opened on June 28, 1770. Between 1770 and 1775, two hundred and fifty children and adults were taught.[13] The driving force behind this school was Anthony Benezet.

Anthony Benezet was born in France in 1713 and his family eventually moved to Philadelphia when he was eighteen. It was also that year that he became a Friend. In 1742, he became a teacher at the Friends' English School of Philadelphia, and stayed there for twelve years. He was a gifted and dedicated teacher, using innovative instructional techniques to instruct children with special needs as well as creative means to temper inappropriate behavior without resorting to corporal punishment. In 1750, he began to teach students of African descent in his home during the evening; he did this until 1770. Benezet resigned his position in the school in 1754 due to wanting a less taxing schedule. He had a change of heart, and a month later he started teaching at a Quaker girls' school. He resigned a year later, but returned in 1757. Benezet again resigned due to health reasons in 1766 and moved across the Delaware River to Burlington, New Jersey. The need to teach was still strong, so he returned to Philadelphia and teaching nine months later. He was still teaching young women when the school for people of African descent was created.[14]

Benezet's fight against the inequality of the races continued with the publication of anti-slavery books. He started in 1759 with "Observations on the Enslaving, Importing, and Purchasing of Negroes." In 1762, he published "A Short Account of That Part of Africa Inhabited by the Negroes ... and the Manner by Which the Slave Trade Is Carried On." In it, he knocked down the argument that slavery was an economic necessity by saying that "no other Necessity appears but that arising from the Desire of amassing Riches; a Necessity laid on worldly Men by their hard Task-master the Devil." He also published anti-slavery tracts in 1766 and 1771.

Benezet had another concern when it came to the anti-slavery movement. He felt that some people were against slavery but still harbored racial prejudices. His thought was that when anti-slavery supporters agreed with the idea that Africans were inferior to Caucasians due to reasons such as race or religion, they gave the proslavery forces a weapon they could use to defend their position.

That Benezet actually lived his beliefs was proven by Benjamin Rush in a letter from May 1774. In it, Rush stated that Benezet "appears in every thing to be free from prejudices of all kinds, and talks and acts as if he believed all mankind however diversified by color—nation—or religion to be members of one grand family."[15]

The fight against slavery continued that year in New Jersey when Quakers created a public petition against slavery in the state and it was signed by 3,000 people. Benezet's former pupil, William Dillwyn of Burlington, was a well-known member of the New Jersey Quakers who took the petition to the state capital of Trenton to give to the assembly. They then stiffened the law of 1769 so much that the Governor's Council rejected it because they believed that it was intended to prohibit the importation of slaves. The year before, Dillwyn and two other Quakers had Isaac Collins, a Quaker printer from Burlington, print an anonymous pamphlet which championed an immediate ban on importing slaves and encouraging the voluntary manumission of slaves in New Jersey.

As the talk grew around them of freedom from British rule, the Friends were solidifying their stand for freedom of another kind. The Philadelphia and Buckingham Quarterly Meeting in 1774 wanted a stronger statement against slavery than the previous ruling of 1758.[16] Anthony Benezet and the Pemberton brothers, John, Israel, and James, led the push for this reform. The Pembertons owned a merchant firm that was very successful in trading in the West Indies. They had also been very active in the slave trade. However, the brothers had a change of heart, renounced slavery and became determined enemies of it.[17] It was much easier for the antislavery proponents to push through their agenda because the groundwork had already been laid. In 1758, any Friend who owned a slave was banned from any leadership position. The new ruling declared that any Friend who was involved in buying or selling slaves, unless it was for the purpose of freeing them, would be disowned. All quarterly and monthly meetings were to study any type of slaveholding within their jurisdiction to make sure these parameters were being upheld. They were also warned to not hire slaves for wages or be the executor or administrator to a will that dealt with slaves.[18]

The years preceding the Revolutionary War were stressful ones for the Friends. Not only did they have to deal with the upheaval concerning slavery within their ranks, but they also had to contend with the spirit of revolution around them. Since many of them were businessmen directly affected by British taxation, the Friends agreed with those who petitioned the Crown to right the wrongs of the system. On the other hand, the Friends in the colonies had close ties with the Friends in England. The English Quakers warned their American cousins to stay away from anything that looked like treason. Not every Friend took that advice.[19]

On September 5, 1774, delegates from the colonies met in Philadelphia at the First Continental Congress to discuss their treatment at the hands of Great Britain. The Congress was not held in the Pennsylvania statehouse, which was later called Independence Hall, but at the nearby Carpenters' Hall. The leaders from New England, Virginia, and Pennsylvania all agreed to meet in a union hall to stay away from a place that might have Loyalist supporters who would report on the proceedings to the Crown. The atmosphere in Philadelphia was tense due to the news that Boston had been attacked by the

British. Pennsylvania militiamen drilled and marched through the streets while the last British regiment in the middle colonies marched to the waterfront to be loaded onto ships headed to Boston. It was in this air of fear and confusion that the delegates met.[20]

Benezet and the Quakers saw the Continental Congress as an opportunity to push for a ban on the slave trade. They lobbied hard for the delegates to include some sort of ban, and there was some hope that something might happen.[21] The reason for this hope was that the delegates felt that the policies adopted by the British ministry in 1763 such as the inability of the colonists to be tried in America were created to enslave the colonies. To fight against these policies, they created the Articles of Association on October 20, 1774, that listed various nonviolent acts that would be done until the British policies were changed. The delegates felt that "a non-importation, non-consumption, and non-exportation agreement, faithfully adhered to, will prove the most speedy, effectual, and peaceable measure" to correct the problems. The second item in the articles was a vow that the colonies "will neither import nor purchase, any slave imported after the first day of December next; after which time, we will wholly discontinue the slave trade, and will neither be concerned in it ourselves, nor will we hire our vessels, nor sell our commodities or manufactures to those who are concerned in it." It appeared that the delegates' desire to end the slave trade in America was less of a human rights issue than an economic one, since the articles were a list of items the colonists would not be importing or exporting to Great Britain, Ireland, and the West Indies.[22] One of the people affected by this embargo was Thomas Jefferson. Congress had requested that every county and town publish the names of anyone who broke the embargo. Jefferson did support the measure, but was embarrassed when his name appeared on the list due to an order of sash windows for Monticello that had been cancelled which accidentally continued on its journey to Virginia.[23]

In the early part of 1775, feelings toward the Crown divided Philadelphia. The convention of provincial delegates that took place there pushed for open rebellion. Anyone who lived in the city who did not share these feelings would be either silenced or driven out of town. That was done by harassment such as handbills, warnings, and, if that didn't work, tar and feathering. While this was going on, the meeting for Suffering of Pennsylvania and New Jersey Quakers released a testimony against rebelling against authority.[24] They were alarmed by the growing rebellion and could "foresee the most fatal consequences both to themselves and the parent country" and "thought it necessary to address their brethren in the adjacent provinces." So they released an epistle which declared their "disapprobation of the measures prosecuting for obtaining redress, and earnestly requesting all of their communion to avoid joining in such measures as are totally inconsistent with their religious principles."

The epistle was directed toward their members, but at the same time, it explained the reasons for their reluctance to join in the rebellion. The Friends declared that their religion was based on "the doctrines and precepts of our Lord Jesus Christ, who expressly declared, "If my kingdom were of this world, then would my servants fight, that I should not be delivered to the Jews; but now is my kingdom not from hence." Which ever since we were a people, we have publicly professed should be religiously observed by us as the rule of our conduct."

They also expressed their concern that some of their members "have been lately nominated to attend on and engage in some public affairs, which they cannot undertake without deviating from these our religious principles." They requested those Quakers and non–Quakers "to pursue those measures which make for peace, and tend to the reconciliation of contending parties, on principles dictated by the spirit of Christ, who 'came not to destroy lives, but to save them.'"

They wished that the colonists would "guard against and reject all such measures and councils, as may increase and perpetuate the discord, animosities, and unhappy contentions which now sorrowfully abound." The epistle also reminded the readers that when the early Quakers were "persecuted and subjected to severe sufferings, as a people unworthy of the benefits of religious or civil society; the hearts of the king and rulers, under whom they suffered, were inclined to grant them these fruitful countries, and entrust them with charters of very extensive powers and privileges" and that they were allowed to live in peace.[25]

The Quakers wanted to live quietly and they also wanted to free their slaves. Warner Mifflin, born in 1745 in Virginia, was a Quaker whose family owned more than one hundred slaves. His attitude toward slavery changed at the age of fourteen when he had a conversation with one of his father's slaves. Mifflin was then convinced by the slave that slavery was evil and that he should never be a slaveholder. However, he did become a slaveholder due to inheritance and marriage and brought at least thirty-seven slaves with him when he moved his family to Kent County, Delaware, in 1767. That was not the end of Mifflin's anti-slavery feelings. His friend Govey Emerson, also a Quaker, freed his slaves in 1773. The next year and in 1775, Mifflin acted on his beliefs and freed his slaves. He convinced his father to do the same thing in 1775. They also followed George Fox's advice that when a slave was freed, they should not be sent into the world with nothing. Emerson made sure that his slaves, men and women alike, knew how to read and possessed a good set of clothes to work in. Mifflin gave his freed slaves livestock and land in return for half of their crops. Other Friends also made sure that the slaves they intended to free were able to read the Bible by the time they were old enough to be freed.[26]

Some slaves did not wait for help to escape from slavery. In 1775, Lord Dunmore, the royal governor of Virginia, promised freedom to any slave who enlisted in the British army. Many seized the opportunity and hundreds of former slaves came to Philadelphia during the British occupation as members of the Black Guides and Pioneers, a regiment made up of escaped slaves who fought under Scottish officers.[27]

Another man who was able to win his freedom during the Revolutionary War was Cyrus Bustill. He was born in Burlington, New Jersey, in 1732, to Samuel Bustill, a lawyer and Quaker, and his slave Parthenia. When the elder Bustill died in 1742, Cyrus was given to his father's widow, Grace, who later sold Cyrus to another Quaker who was a local baker. Mrs. Bustill sold him with the understanding that Cyrus would be allowed to be taken on as an apprentice so that he could earn enough money to buy his freedom. He was able to do so in 1774, and soon afterward set up a bakery in Burlington. He later received an official commendation for his baking services during the war, in particular for baking bread for General Washington's troops during the winter of 1777–1778 at Valley Forge, Pennsylvania. After the war was over, Bustill moved his family to Philadelphia, where he became a prominent leader in the African American community. He was a founding member of the Free African Society in 1787 and later set up a school for African American children in his home. He was also the great-great-grandfather of Paul Robeson, an actor, singer, and activist in the twentieth century.[28]

The Battle of Lexington in April of 1775 changed the attitude of many Loyalists, Quakers and non–Quakers alike. Many of the Loyalists turned their backs on their former opinions and joined the army. Some of the younger Quakers went against the advice of other Friends and created a company of light infantry called the "Quakers Blues" that was led by Sheriff Joseph Cowperthwait. This was not the only change that the revolution inflicted on the Quakers.

The Pennsylvania Assembly created a Committee of Safety on June 30, 1775, to deal with suspected Loyalists in a far stronger way than had been done in the past. The committee demanded that known Loyalists confess their allegiance to the Crown and then renounce it. Around this time, the Quakers, Mennonites, and German Baptists opposed the order for enlistment in the militia. The Committee of Safety then went to the Pennsylvania State House, insisting that this opposition was not supportive of America and would damage the government and society. The committee also felt that the past allowances for these groups were a grave mistake. In November, the assembly made defense service mandatory and taxed "all non-associators (2 pounds, 10 shillings) above the regular assessment."[29]

In July of 1775, the Second Continental Congress recommended that all conscientious objectors make amends for not supporting the rebellion by helping those who were suffering because of the hostilities. The Quakers set up Meetings for Suffering to direct fund-raising for these charities and to coordinate efforts to help those in need. The Philadelphia Friends were suspicious about helping people in Boston, because of the Bostonians' support of the rebellion. The Friends feared that any help they would give them might be interpreted as support for the radicals. However, by November of 1775, the Philadelphia Friends sent two thousand pounds to the New England Meeting to distribute to those who needed help.[30]

Another Quaker who wanted to help others was Joshua Fisher. The successful merchant from Philadelphia had bought and sold slaves for many years, but by 1776 had had a change of heart. The sixty-nine-year-old Fisher decided to not only free all of his slaves, but he also decided to track down all of the slaves he had sold and purchase their freedom as well as their children's. Some of the slaves had died and he was unable to find everyone he had formerly owned. However, until his death in 1784, Fisher continued to locate, buy, and then manumit his ex-slaves and their children.[31]

The Continental Congress wrangled over whether or not to split from Great Britain in early 1776. Thomas Jefferson, with some help from John Adams and Benjamin Franklin, wrote the Declaration of Independence and presented it before the Congress on July 3. Approximately one-fourth of the Declaration was removed, part of it being a criticism of slavery and attaching blame of the slave trade in America on King George III. The delegates from South Carolina and Georgia objected to the accusation in the declaration that King George III was to blame for the slave trade in America, and several of the northern colonies were not happy with the wording either. They were against the charge being included because no one could logically blame the entire slave trade on George III.

There were questions, even at the beginning of the United States, about why slavery existed where so many were so vocal in their wish for liberty. In the end, the passage was removed even though men like John Adams were strongly opposed to slavery. Those who were against slavery let the removal happen to satisfy South Carolina and Georgia, as well as those delegates from other colonies who had been involved in the slave trade. The question of why a democracy allowed slavery did not end with the Declaration of Independence. It would be continually brought up for the next eighty-five years.[32]

The New Jersey State Loyalty Oath was created on September 19, 1776, for all civil and military officials in the state. The oath was worded so that the Quakers could take it without going against their religion. It asked them to not be bound to allegiance to the king and to "profess and swear (or if one of the People called Quakers, affirm) that I do and will bear true Faith and Allegiance to the Government established in this State, under the Authority of the People."[33]

When the New Jersey Constitution was written in 1776, certain parts of it were very liberal for its time. It permitted "all Inhabitants of this colony of Full Age" who were worth fifty pounds the right to vote. Whether or not this loophole was intentional, it allowed widowed or single women as well as free Africans with property to vote. Some of them did avail themselves of this right in the 1790s. It was overruled in 1807 when the legislature passed a law that allowed only "white adult males" to vote. Later, this became a part of the constitution of 1844.[34]

The Quakers continued to have trouble due to trying to stay out of trouble. Later in 1776, several Quaker meetinghouses around Philadelphia were appropriated to house soldiers. Continental soldiers coming from Maryland to New York broke into the Market Street Meetinghouse in Philadelphia and occupied it for their own purposes. The Friends talked with the soldiers for permission to continue to use it for worship. The soldiers agreed, but they would continue to keep control of the building.[35] This pattern continued throughout the war. The larger meetinghouses with open areas inside were used for hospitals and headquarters, as when General Henry Clinton used the Evesham Friends Meetinghouse in 1778 as the British marched from Philadelphia to New York. Also, the Woodbury, New Jersey, Meetinghouse was used as a hospital for colonial troops after the Battle of Red Bank and by General Cornwallis to quarter British officers.[36]

On March 5, 1777, Thomas Wharton, Jr., was elected president of the Supreme Executive Council. The council was created in the 1776 Pennsylvania constitution. It was made up of one representative from Philadelphia and one from each county in Pennsylvania. It was to take over from the Council of Safety. The Supreme Executive Council would soon turn its attentions to the Quakers.

On March 12, the Continental Congress asked all of the states to supply blankets to the Continental Army.[37] On May 2, a resolution was released stating that Pennsylvania would be collecting 4,000 blankets for the army. It was felt that "the want of Blankets for the Troops may occasion sickness and the death of many valuable men, and reduce the strength of our army" and that "an immediate supply is necessary." Also, it was announced that twelve men would be assigned to Philadelphia and twelve for the surrounding counties, "to aid and assist" in collecting the blankets. These were to be collected "immediately from every family their proportion of Blankets."[38] Elizabeth Drinker, a Quaker, received a visit from an officer with two constables on June 5 for blankets, but she refused to comply. Others had also tried three or four times with the same amount of success.[39]

Although attempts to abolish the slave trade all but dried up during the Revolutionary War, the Friends still continued to reduce the amount of slaveholders among themselves. Thomas Goodwin from Salem, New Jersey, manumitted his slave Will on April 26, 1777; he was to be freed when he reached age twenty-one in May of 1782. Goodwin's brother, William, from Elsonborough, New Jersey, manumitted Frank, Harry, and Robin on April 14, 1777, to be freed on their twenty-first birthdays and Phyllis on her eighteenth birthday.[40] The example the Goodwin brothers set for their family would continue into the next generation. William's daughters, Abigail and Elizabeth, would play an important part in the anti-slavery movement in New Jersey.[41]

Because the Friends did not hide their opposition to the rebellion, they paid for their lack of support. The Friends did not acknowledge any of the days set aside to celebrate July 4 or any American military victories, which made some people very angry. On July 4, 1777, a mob in Philadelphia celebrated by breaking the windows of Friends' houses because they did not illuminate their windows to celebrate.[42] However, that was only the beginning of the persecution of the Quakers for their anti-rebellion stance.

On August 25, 1777, the British landed at the head of the Chesapeake Bay and headed for Philadelphia. That same day, Congress passed two resolutions. The first one requested that Pennsylvania and Maryland detain anyone considered against the colonial cause until they could be released without doing harm to the rebels. The other ruling declared that every house in Philadelphia be searched for weapons such as pistols, rifles, swords, and bayonets. If any weapons were found, the owners would be offered a fair price for them. The weapons would then be given to any state militia that needed them. Three days later, Congress, thinking that the Quakers of Philadelphia might help the British, strongly suggested to the Supreme Executive Council of Pennsylvania that Joshua Fisher and his two sons, Thomas and Samuel, Henry Drinker, Abel and John James, Israel and James Pemberton, Samuel Pleasants, and Thomas Wharton, Sr., be detained. The council, which controlled Pennsylvania after the assembly was disbanded, ordered the commanding officer of each regiment of the city militia to create search parties and have David Rittenhouse, the treasurer of state, and three military officers to make up a list of those people considered dangerous to Pennsylvania. Once this list was completed, the men listed would be arrested and any papers they possessed that were considered political would be taken from them. This order included the records of the meetings of Suffering of the Society of Friends. The list was written on August 31, 1777 and had the names of thirty-one other men than the ones listed by Congress. Most of the men were Quakers.[43]

On September 3, 1777, Henry Drinker had been ill and stayed home from meeting. At noon, he sat in the front parlor of his home to copy the minutes from his monthly meeting. Three men entered the home and handed Drinker a parole to sign. Drinker refused and the men seized the book with the minutes in it and other papers. They left, but not before telling Drinker that they would be back at 9:00 a.m. the next day and he should be there waiting for them. He had not planned on leaving because of his illness, but, as promised, they returned and took Drinker to the Masonic Lodge to be held as a prisoner along with the other men on the list.

The prisoners sent letters to the Continental Congress and the Supreme Executive Council to protest their imprisonment. Congress demanded that the council give the prisoners a hearing, but the council replied that because events were happening so quickly, they were unable to do so. Congress backed away from the problem and claimed that it was the jurisdiction of the Supreme Council and they would not interfere in state business.

On the same day that the men broke into Drinker's house, Congress received a letter from George Bryan, the vice-president of the Supreme Council, requesting approval to send anyone arrested, especially Quakers who refused to take an oath of allegiance, to Staunton, Virginia. Congress approved the action and the council, whose leader had a cousin on the list of those affected, carried out their plan. The destination was later changed to Winchester, Virginia. On September 11, 1777, wagons lined up outside of the Masonic Lodge and the prisoners were loaded on, while their families said goodbye, and taken away. The prisoners were not the only ones who were leaving Philadelphia. Eight days later, the Continental Congress left town for Lancaster, Pennsylvania, because they expected the city to fall to the British. On September 26, 3,000 troops under the command of Lord Charles Cornwallis took command of Philadelphia. Most of the occupying army stayed in Germantown, five miles from Philadelphia, under the command of General Howe.[44]

On October 7, 1777, the Quakers sent a delegation to both General Howe and General Washington, expressing their opinions on the war. The Quakers also sent a delegation to Washington asserting of their innocence of the claims that they were traitors. They also asked Washington to help them win the release of their friends in Winchester. Washington told them to go to Lancaster, Pennsylvania, and express their wishes to the Supreme Council and Congress in person. The delegation thought that Washington would send them away once he gave them an answer, but instead he invited them to have dinner with him.[45]

While Elizabeth Drinker and the other wives of the prisoners waited for their husbands' release, other Quakers had their lives altered by the war. On October 21, 1777, 2,000 Hessian troops under the command of Count Carl Emil Ulrich Von Donop marched into Haddonfield, New Jersey, and spent the night there before moving south to Fort Mercer at Red Bank. The mostly Quaker population was not happy about their presence because of their obnoxious behavior. Colonel Christopher Greene, the commander of Fort Mercer, was aware that the Hessians had crossed the Delaware River into New Jersey, but did not know that they were coming toward him.[46] Jonas Cattell, a 16-year-old apprentice blacksmith in Haddonfield, New Jersey, was at his forge when the Hessians came into town. Cattell left before the Hessians did, and, using his knowledge of the countryside,[47] ran the 9.6 miles from Haddonfield to Red Bank and arrived before the Hessians to warn Colonel Greene of the

Site of the Battle of Red Bank. Quaker Ann Whitall cared for the wounded in her house after the battle (photograph by the author).

approach of Von Donop's troops. Greene had been using the home of Quakers James and Ann Whitall as a headquarters. The troops under Greene's command included free Africans and mulattoes from his 1st Rhode Island Regiment and the 2nd Rhode Island. Cattell's warning gave Greene time to prepare for battle.

When the Hessians arrived, the colonials were ready and defeated them.[48] The rest of the Whitall family wanted to escape the fighting, but Ann Whitall refused. She told her family that "God's arm is strong and will protect me. I may do good by staying." As the battle raged around her, she continued working at her spinning wheel in an upper room of the house. She did not even bother to look out of the window to watch the battle. A twelve-pound shot from a British ship went through the brick wall of her house's north gable and lodged into a wall near where she was sitting in her high-back chair. She then picked up her spinning wheel and went to the cellar to continue her work. She did not stop until she was asked to help nurse the wounded.[49]

The battle enacted its toll. Samuel Mickle, who was a Friend from nearby Woodbury, described the human and physical wreckage that surrounded the area. He mentioned that

> their fine apple orchard cut down and ground dug up in great trenches and works thrown up in erecting a Fort there, their dwelling house walls battered in holes while the family were endeavering [sic] to live quietly therein, fruits of a battle between ye Americans & Hessian solders in 1777 when I saw men lying naked on ye ground except in part covered with a little straw and some of them with their limbs off having died of their wounds.[50]

The house became filled with wounded men, even the attic. When some of the wounded complained about the noise from so many sick men, Mrs. Whitall reminded them that they "must not complain, who had brought it on themselves."[51]

On January 29, 1778, the Continental Congress ordered the release of Henry Drinker and the rest of the prisoners in Lancaster if they would take an oath to Pennsylvania declaring that they would be faithful subjects. Since the Quakers did not take oaths due to their beliefs, Elizabeth Drinker did not believe that it was a legitimate offer of freedom for her husband. On March 31, the relatives of the prisoners, as well as Anthony Benezet, banded together to sign a petition to give to Congress to have the prisoners released. After it was signed, it was decided that a delegation, including Elizabeth Drinker, would deliver it. They left on April 3 and arrived at Valley Forge three days later. They requested a meeting with General Washington and were sent to stay "with his Wife, (a sociable pretty kind of Woman) until he came in." Shortly afterward, the general came and discoursed with us freely, but not so long as we could have wished, as dinner was served, to which he had invited us, there was 15 of the Officers besides the General and his Wife, Gen. Green, and G. Lee we had an elegant dinner, which was soon over; when we went out with the General Wife up to her Chamber, and saw no more of him,—he told us, he could do nothing in our business further than granting us a pass to Lancaster, which he did.

They traveled to Lancaster and on April 25, Mrs. Drinker could not remember what happened to her that morning because "about one o'clock my Henry arrived at J. Webbs, just in time to dine with us; all the rest of our Friends came this day to Lancaster." Henry Drinker surprised his wife by being "much hardier than I expected, he looked fat and well."[52]

Before Elizabeth Drinker and her friends were able to obtain their loved ones' release, there was another incident that showed that no matter how hard the Quakers tried to stay neutral, their stance would not protect them from the war. On March 21, 1778, British troops under the command of Major John Simcoe attacked the house of William Hancock, a Quaker, at Hancock's Bridge in New Jersey because the British had reports that the South Jersey Militia was staying at the property. Simcoe's men rushed the front and back doors of the house while those inside were asleep. The militia had left the evening before and had left twenty to thirty men behind. Everyone in the house was killed by bayonet, including Hancock and his brother. Later, Major Simcoe excused his actions in the death of the elderly Hancock by stating that he had asked about Hancock's whereabouts and "was informed that he did not live at home, since the rebels had occupied the bridge." He also stated that Hancock had "unfortunately returned home at night; events like these are the real miseries of war."[53]

It was a dangerous time to live in this area of New Jersey. The Reverend Nicholas Collin of the Lutheran Church in Raccoon, which later became Swedesboro, wrote about how conditions were in 1778. He wrote that everywhere

distrust, fear, hatred and abominable selfishness were met with. Parents and children, brothers and sisters, wife and husband, were enemies to one another. The militia and some regular troops on one side and refugees with the Englishmen on the other were constantly roving about in smaller or greater numbers plundering and destroying everything in a barbarous manner, cattle, furniture, clothing and food. They smashed mirrors, tables, chinas, etc. and plundered women and children of their most necessary clothing, cut up bolsters and scattered the feathers to the winds, burned houses, whipped and imprisoned each other and surprised people when they were deep asleep.[54]

There were also dangers on the other side of the Delaware River. When the British finally left Philadelphia, the city's political leaders formed a Patriotic Society. The Society's purpose was to find and punish Loyalists. The Supreme

The Hancock House was the site of a British massacre in 1777. It proved that being a pacifist was no protection from the violence of war (photograph by the author).

Executive Council, encouraged by the society, published a list of 139 suspected Loyalists. The list eventually shrunk to forty-five suspects, who were given over to a grand jury. Of these, twenty went to trial and four were convicted of treason. The only defendants sentenced to death were Abraham Carlyle and John Roberts, both Quakers. In spite of the jurors and justices of the State Supreme Court asking for mercy, as well as petitions with thousands of signatures sent to the Supreme Executive Council also asking for clemency, the sentence on the two men was carried out on November 4, 1778.[55]

Quakers continued to work for the end of slavery throughout the Revolutionary War, both with the New Jersey legislature and Governor William Livingston. The Quakers were fortunate in that the governor was willing to listen. In 1778, he wrote to Samuel Allinson, a Friend who had written a compilation of New Jersey state laws, that he felt that slavery was "utterly inconsistent, both with the principles of Christianity and Humanity; and in Americans who have almost idolized liberty." Governor Livingston was against slavery, but he was unable to push the Friends' request through the legislature due to his limited constitutional powers and the task of keeping the state together during the war.[56]

The abolition of slavery among the Friends continued. At the Women's Meeting at Haddonfield, New Jersey, in August 1777, it was reported that "twenty-eight slaves in the compass of Haddonfield Meeting [were] freed." Those Friends who had not complied had their names recorded. Punishment for anyone who did not free their slaves later went farther than just putting their name on record or receiving a visit from another Friend. The Haddonfield Meeting "disowned" Marmaduke Cooper and Isaac Horner in September 1780 for not freeing their slaves. This strict position made it possible that by September 1788, the Haddonfield Meeting could state, "No negroes held in bondage among us."[57]

The Friends in Delaware dealt with a different issue at this time. They were concerned about restitution to former slaves for their work. In 1778, there were gatherings at five different Friends weekly meetings as Friends who were former slaveholders and a total of two hundred and seventy of their former slaves came together to discuss how the Quakers could pay restitution for their services. The devotion of the Friends against slavery so impressed Francis Asbury, the leading Methodist preacher in America, that while he was in Kent County, Delaware, he decided that the Methodists had to follow the lead of the Friends and support abolitionism. This was later followed by John Wesley, the English founder of Methodism, who strengthened his belief in the anti-slavery movement after reading a pamphlet by Anthony Benezet.[58]

In 1775, the fledgling organization, called the Society for the Relief of Free Negroes Unlawfully Held in Bondage, heard of the case of Dinah Nevill. She and her children had been sold by Nathaniel Lowry of New Jersey to Benjamin Bannerman of Virginia. Nevill, who was of Native American, African, and European ancestry, had insisted that she had been born free. The Society, led by Quakers Israel Pemberton and Thomas Harrison, brought the case to court on behalf of Nevill. The case dragged on for years, but in 1779, Harrison coordinated with Philadelphia brewer Samuel Moore to settle the problem. Moore purchased Nevill and her children and then transferred their ownership to Harrison. The Quaker then set the Nevill family free.[59]

The next year, Pennsylvania went farther to ensure freedom for everybody within its boundaries. On March 1, 1780, the

representatives of the freeman of the commonwealth of Pennsylvania, in general assembly met, and by the authority of the same, That all persons, as well Negroes and Mulattoes as others, who shall be born within this state from and after the passing of this act, shall not be deemed and considered as servants for life, or slaves; and that all servitude for life, or slavery of children, in consequence of the slavery of their mothers, in the case of all children born within this state, from and after the passing of this act as aforesaid, shall be, and hereby is utterly taken away, extinguished and for ever abolished.

Their reasoning was that it was not

for us to enquire why, in the creation of mankind, the inhabitants of the several parts of the earth were distinguished by a difference in feature or complexion. It is sufficient to know that all are the work of an almighty Hand.... We esteem it a peculiar blessing granted to us, ... by removing as much as possible the sorrows of those who have lived in undeserved bondage, and from which, by the assumed authority of the kings of Great Britain, no effectual, legal relief could be obtained.[60]

John Cooper of Gloucester County, New Jersey, had served at the Continental Congress in 1776 and was on the committee that wrote the New Jersey Constitution the same year. He was also a Quaker who was against slavery. He wrote in the *New-Jersey Gazette* on September 20, 1780, that while

we are spilling our blood and exhausting our treasure in defense of our own liberty, it would not perhaps be amiss to turn our eyes towards those of our fellowmen who are now groaning in bondage under us. We say "all men are equally entitled to liberty and the pursuit of happiness"; but are we willing to grant this liberty to all men? The sentiment no doubt is just as well generous; and must ever be read to our praise, provided our actions correspond therewith. But after we have made such a declaration to the world, we continue to hold our fellow creatures in slavery, our words must rise up in judgment against us, and by the breath of our own mouths we shall stand condemned.

He continued his attack on the hypocrisy of the colonies by wondering how anyone could ask God's help "to defend ourselves against tyranny and oppression, whilst we are acting the part of tyrants and oppressors?" Cooper also said that if

we are determined not to emancipate our slaves, but to hold them still in bondage, let us alter our language upon the subject of tyranny; let us no longer speak of it as a thing in its own nature detestable, because in so doing, as hath been observed, we shall condemn ourselves. But let us rather declare to the world, that tyranny is a thing we are not principled against, but that we are resolved not to be slaves, because we ourselves mean to be tyrants.

He feared that where slavery was allowed, "the tyranny becomes national, and the iniquity also; and in such case a national scourge may very well be looked for."[61]

Cooper signed his name to the essay in spite of the possibility that his beliefs might cause him harm. However, his anti-slavery stance apparently did not cause him a problem, because he won election to the Legislative Council a month later. On December 30, 1780, he asked permission to introduce a bill to abolish slavery in New Jersey. However, he lost the opportunity by a vote of 6 to 4.[62]

Even though the ability to restrict slavery was not in the grasp of the antislavery supporters, victory of another sort did occur. News of the surrender of General Cornwallis at Yorktown arrived in Philadelphia on October 22, 1781. The surrender marked the ending of most of the military actions in the colonies. Two days later, most of the citizens of Philadelphia celebrated in much the same way they celebrated July 4. Elizabeth Drinker wrote how

> a mob assembled about 7 o'clock or before, and continued their insults until near 10; to those whose Houses were not illuminated scarcely one Friends House escaped. We had near 70 panes of Glass broken the sash lights and two panels of the front parlor broke in pieces—the Door cracked and Violently burst open, when they threw Stones into the House for some time but did not enter—some far better and some worse—some Houses after breaking the door they entered, and destroyed the furniture &c—many women and Children were frightened into fits, and 'tis a mercy no lives were lost.[63]

The war between the colonies and England was over, but there was still a war to fight against slavery and those who supported it.

6. Creating a Free Nation, Not a Free People

In the summer of 1783, two free African Americans were accused of being runaway slaves. They were unable to prove their claims that they were free, so they committed suicide instead of wearing the yoke of slavery. Anthony Benezet, who had tried to help them, decided to call the Pennsylvania Abolition Society back into action after a nine-year layoff due to the war. What Benezet wanted was to give "assistance to the Black People, who we have set free, but have not yet been able to fix any effectual mode of giving them the necessary assistance, which many of their afflictive cases require."[1]

The inconsistency of a new country declaring itself a free nation while slavery was still permitted on its shores was not lost on everyone. David Cooper, a Quaker farmer from Woodbury, New Jersey, published a pamphlet in 1783 entitled "A Serious Address to the Rulers of America, on the Inconsistency of Their Conduct Respecting Slavery: Forming a Contrast Between the Encroachments of England on American Liberty, and American Injustice in Tolerating Slavery." In this pamphlet, Cooper highlighted how the American ideals of freedom lived side by side with slavery and the slave trade. Benezet was so impressed with it that he delivered thirty copies to the president of the Congress to distribute to each member. He also gave a copy to every member of the New Jersey Assembly.[2]

However, the Quakers did not stop there. The Revolutionary War had all but stopped the slave trade. With the end of the fighting, the Friends feared that the slave trade would begin again. Therefore, they sent a petition from the Philadelphia Yearly Meeting, dated October 4, 1783, to the newly formed Congress asking them to outlaw slavery. They felt that it was their "indispensable duty to revive the lamentable grievance of that oppressed people in your view as an interesting subject evidently claiming the serious attention of those who are entrusted with the powers of Government, as Guardians of the common rights of Mankind and advocates for liberty."

They feared that "some forgetfulness of the days of Distress are prompted from avaricious motives to renew the iniquitous trade for slaves to the African Coasts, contrary to every humane and righteous consideration, and in opposition to the solemn declarations often repeated in favour of universal liberty." They concluded with the request to "earnestly solicit your Christian interposition to discourage and prevent so obvious an Evil, in such manner as under the influence of divine Wisdom you shall see meet." It was signed by, among other people, Henry Drinker.[3]

The Quaker delegation, which included Benezet, James Pemberton, and Warner Mifflin, delivered the petition to Princeton, New Jersey, the site of the Continental Congress. The Congress had moved from Philadelphia because of a yellow fever outbreak and was unable to be very helpful to the Quakers. The president of the Congress, Elias Boudinot of New Jersey, met with Benezet and the petition was referred to a committee headed by David Howell. Both Boudinot and Howell were against slavery, but the lawmakers were restricted on what they could do by the Articles of Confederation. The Quakers' best chance at getting what they wanted would have to wait until a more stable form of government was put into place.[4]

Benezet had better luck improving the lives of African Americans in another manner. After the war was over, Benezet revived the Quaker School for Negro Children and held it in his home on Third and Chestnut in Philadelphia. He had been teaching for many years and in 1767, debunked the idea that intelligence could be determined by the color of someone's skin. He stated that based on his years of experience in teaching, he could "with truth and sincerity declare amongst them as a great a variety of talents, equally capable of improvement, as amongst a like number of whites."[5] Unfortunately, he was unable to go back to the New Jersey legislature to fight the slave trade because he passed away in 1784 at the age of seventy-one. His continuous attempts to better the plight of African Americans did not go unnoticed. The people who attended Benezet's funeral were "a collection of all ranks and professions among the inhabitants, thus manifesting the universal esteem in which he was held. Among others who paid that last tribute, of respect were many hundreds of black people, testifying by their attendance, and by their tears, the grateful sense they entertained of his pious efforts in their behalf."

Even after his death, he made provisions to continue helping African Americans. In his will, he gave to "James Starr and Thomas Harrison the sum of fifty pounds in trust for the use of a certain society who are forming themselves for the relief of such Black People and other who apprehend themselves illegally detained on slavery to enable them to employ lawyers" to fight for their freedom.[6]

He also continued to provide for the education of the children. He had made provisions in his will to "hire and employ a religious-minded person or persons to teach a number of Negro, Mulatto or Indian children, to read, write, arithmetric [*sic*], plain accounts, needle-work, etc." Other people also left money to help, and the school, which moved to Raspberry Street in 1844, taught a total of eight thousand people until 1866.[7]

The Delaware Quakers were no less committed to end slavery than their counterparts in other states, but their ability to act was restricted. The Quakers were influential but were less than 10 percent of the population of Delaware. However, they did not act alone. The Methodists, who had entered Delaware a few years before the Revolutionary War and by 1784 had more members than all other religions combined, worked together with the Friends toward freedom for slaves. Slavery stayed alive in Delaware because the majority of the wealthy landowners, who owned slaves, were either Anglican, Episcopalian, or did not go to church.

It was more difficult for the Delaware Friends to free their slaves than for the Friends in Pennsylvania because they owned far more slaves. However, by 1784, the Delaware Friends had freed 7 to 10 percent of the slave population of the state and almost all of their slaves. There were still a few Friends who owned slaves after this time because they co-owned slaves with non–Friends and did not have the legal right to free them.

They also went farther than just freeing their slaves. Some of the Friends gave restitution payments to former slaves for the work they had done while in bondage. This thinking came from a gathering of Friends in 1778 in Kent County, Delaware, who met to discuss repaying their former slaves for the work they had done. In 1784, Jonathan Emerson of Kent County had decided that he wished to pay restitution to some of his father-in-law's former slaves for the years they had worked past the age of eighteen for the women and twenty-one for the men.

Despite the efforts of others to dismantle the practice of slavery, slaveholders felt the need to justify their stand. In Delaware, Thomas Rodney of Kent County led the defense by saying that he was not the only one to believe that "nature found Negroes for slavery." The slaveholders believed that Africans were intended to be nothing more than simple laborers and that "they are never happy but when at it." This attitude went back to the 17th century feeling that Africans were different because they were "black, uncivilized and heathen." However, they were not the only group to be felt only suited for servitude. In the 18th century, some Delawareans thought that the Scots-Irish also stood out and were only suited to the life of an indentured servant.

Most of the Caucasian indentured servants were gone by the end of the Revolution, which made race the dividing line between slave and free men. As more and more questioned the validity of slavery, slaveholders pushed the idea of racism to excuse the institution. To add to the perception that Africans were an inferior race, there were some slaveholders who used the excuse that Africans had to be kept in slavery because white Delawareans and their property would be in danger if they were free.[8]

One of the most famous slaveholders was George Washington. In February 1786, he owned 218 slaves. He was the type of master who did not sell slaves unless they wanted to be sold, which at the time was considered to be humane. At the same time, Washington was conflicted by slavery. These doubts came up in a letter to Robert Morris in Philadelphia in April of 1786. Some Quakers in the city had tried to help a slave escape who belonged to a Mr. Dalby of Alexandria, when he was visiting Philadelphia. Washington was furious that they had tried to free the slave. He felt that the Quakers had not only acted "repugnant to justice so far as its conduct concerns strangers, but, in my opinion extremely impoliticly with respect to the State, the City in particular; and without being able, (but by acts of tyranny and oppression) to accomplish their own ends." Washington felt that, no matter what, the laws of the land should be obeyed. On the other hand, he also said that

> there is not a man living who wishes more sincerely than I do, to see a plan adopted for the abolition of it; but there is only one proper and effectual mode by which it can be accomplished, and that is by Legislative authority; and this, as far as my suffrage will go, shall never be wanting. But when slaves who are happy and contented with their present masters, are tampered with and seduced to leave them, when masters are taken unawares by these practices; when a conduct of this sort begets discontent on one side and resentment on the other, and when it happens to fall on a man, whose purse will not measure with that of the society, and he looses his property for want of means to defend it; it is oppression in the latter case, and not humanity in any; because it introduces more evils than it can cure.[9]

While Washington wrestled with his feelings on slavery the determined efforts of the anti-slavery forces finally bore fruit in 1786 when New Jersey outlawed the slave trade. East Jersey had about seventy-five percent of the slaves in New Jersey, with Perth Amboy being the port of entry for the slave trade. The much smaller amount of slaves in West Jersey was affected by the Quaker stance, and also had a greater number of Caucasian settlers, which meant that the need for slaves was much less.[10]

In 1787, about twenty percent of the population of America, 600,000 people, had African ancestry and most of them were slaves. Ninety percent of all slaves in the new country lived in the South. The economy of America lay in the balance of mutual need between North and South. The South needed the North to ship its produce to market and the North needed the goods from the South to trade. They were all in debt, but in different ways. People in the North had national paper, while the South held notes and bonds issued from their own states. The South did not want the Federal government to tax them to help the North pay off their national debts, while the North did not want an increase in taxes to pay off state debts.

Anything that would upset that balance was a matter of concern to both the North and the South. The North was concerned that the South would take over the new government. This fear came from the general belief that the future expansion of the country would take place in the Carolinas, Georgia, and the area that would eventually contain the states of Alabama, Kentucky, Mississippi, and Tennessee. There were those in the North who assumed that this expansion would make the South dominant in population and wealth and a predominant factor of both for the South was slavery.

Congress could have possibly dealt with anything else but slavery. Their stand on slavery was what defined the two sections. James Madison said it on June 30 when he mentioned that the states were divided, "not by their differences in size, but by other circumstances; the most material of which resulted partly from climate, but principally from the effects of their having or not having slaves."[11]

The argument over slavery continued into the Federal Convention in 1787, which had convened in Philadelphia to formally set up the new country. On July 12, one of the issues on the agenda was how slaves would be counted when it came to representation of the various states. General Charles Pinckney of South Carolina moved to change a suggestion from Edmund Randolph of Virginia about having the slaves count as only 3/5 of a white man to have them equal to the whites in representation, the only type of equality they could expect in the Deep South. He thought that it was only fair because the slaves were the laborers and that they "add equally to the wealth, and considering money as the sinew of war, to the strength of the nation." The suggestion of General Pinckney was defeated, with only South Carolina and Georgia voting in the affirmative.

Slavery was again discussed on Tuesday, August 21, when Luther Martin of Maryland proposed to permit a prohibition or tax on the importation of slaves. He believed that since five slaves were to be counted as three free men to determine the number of representatives in Congress, it encouraged slavery.

He thought it was unreasonable and inconsistent with the character of the country to have it written into the Constitution. The debate continued into the next day.

John Rutledge of South Carolina did not see how Section 4, Article 7, encouraged the slave trade. He was not worried about slave insurrections and was willing to exempt the other states from helping against one. The main question to him was whether or not the southern states would join the country. He also said that the northern states should understand that if this issue were left alone, they would see that the increase of slaves would mean an increase of goods they could sell.

Colonel George Mason of Virginia blamed the greed of British merchants for the slave trade. He said that the British government constantly stopped Virginia from ending it. He thought slavery was evil and the trade should be abolished. He said that Maryland and Virginia had already stopped the importation of slaves and North Carolina also did in practice. Colonel Mason said that slavery discouraged the arts and manufacturing and prevented the immigration of Caucasians, which he believed helped the nation to grow. He also feared divine retribution on the nation for allowing slavery to exist. He believed that the federal government had the right to prevent the increase of slavery. The colonel also thought that if the states gave up some of their rights to the national government, there was no reason why they could not give up the right to determine the fate of slavery.

Oliver Ellsworth of Connecticut then said that since he never owned a slave, he could not say how slavery affected the owner's morality as Colonel Mason did. However, if he wanted to look at it from a moral standpoint, they should just abolish slavery altogether. He said that Virginia and Maryland did not need to import slaves since they multiplied to the point that it was cheaper to raise them than to import them. However, in South Carolina and Georgia, it was necessary to import them due to the "sickly rice swamps." He felt that the issue of slavery should be left alone because to ban it would be unfair to South Carolina and Georgia and because as the population increased, there would be enough cheap laborers to make slavery useless.

General Pinckney said to let the states decide for themselves. If they were unable to decide for themselves, there might be problems with getting the states to endorse the Constitution. He also said that if the section stayed as it was, not everyone would sign the Constitution, which meant that they would not join the United States. General Pinckney also expressed another concern. If the imports stopped, Virginia would gain because the value of its slaves would increase and that would not be fair to South Carolina. He thought that more slaves meant more commerce and more money for the Treasury.

James Wilson of Pennsylvania said that if South Carolina and Georgia wanted to get rid of the slave trade in a short amount of time, they could not refuse to join the Union if the tax was passed. As the section of the Constitution was written at the time, all imports were to be taxed. Slaves were exempt from the tax.[12]

John Dickinson, a Quaker from Delaware, thought they should not authorize in any way the slave trade. He did not believe that the southern states would refuse to join because of the slave trade, especially since any ban would not take place right away. Dickinson was prepared to call the Carolinians' bluff because he did not believe that the Deep South would actually leave the other colonies if the slave trade were banned. He believed that most people in South Carolina and Georgia wanted the Constitution and a stronger federal government.[13]

Hugh Williamson of North Carolina said that the law in North Carolina did not directly prohibit the slave trade. They put "a duty of 5 pounds on each slave imported from Africa, 10 pounds on each from elsewhere, and 50 pounds on each State licensing manumission." He also felt that the southern states could not join if the clause was rejected and it was wrong to force them to do it.[14]

On August 24, 1787, William Livingston of New Jersey delivered a report from the Committee of Eleven that they recommended the seventh article of the Constitution should state that the "migration or importation of such persons as the several States now existing shall think proper to admit, shall not be prohibited by the Legislature prior to the year 1800, but a tax or duty may be imposed on such migration or importation at a rate not exceeding the average of the duties laid on imports." The next day, General Pinckney moved to remove the 1800 limit on the movement of slaves and make it 1808. The new date would make the end of the slave trade to be twenty years away from the convention. The motion was seconded, and James Madison rose to argue against the new date. He felt that "twenty years will produce all the mischief that can be apprehended from the liberty to import slaves. So long a term will be more dishonorable to the American character than to say nothing about it in the Constitution." The motion was brought up for a vote and the date was changed, with only New Jersey, Delaware, Pennsylvania, and Virginia voting against.

Gouverneur Morris did not let this change go unchallenged. He suggested that the clause read that the "importation of slaves into North Carolina, South Carolina, and Georgia shall not be prohibited." He thought that this change would be fair to the states which would be affected and, concurrently, let it be known that this part of the Constitution was created to make these states happy. Apparently, if Morris could not keep the end of the slave trade at 1800, he wanted to make sure it was known whose fault it was that the slave trade was allowed to continue for another eight years.

Colonel Mason did not object to the term *slave*, but he did not like naming the three states in case it offended them. Roger Sherman of Connecticut disagreed with writing the word *slave* in the Constitution and preferred a more vague term such as had been used previously. It was agreed and Mr. Williamson stated that he was against slavery, but he would prefer to deal with it if it meant that South Carolina and Georgia would not be excluded from the Union. The motion was withdrawn and Mr. Dickinson wanted the clause to be focused on the states that had not yet banned the slave trade. The phrase was changed to the "migration or importation of such persons as the several States now existing shall think proper to admit, shall not be prohibited by the legislature prior to the year 1808."

The wrangling continued on the terminology, because the importation of slaves was not the only thing affected. It was the taxing of imported inanimate objects that was a concern. Sherman did not like the part that made men to be property because they would be taxed as slaves. Colonel Mason suggested that not taxing would be the same as putting a bounty on importing slaves. Nathaniel Gorman of Massachusetts thought that Sherman should consider this duty as a discouragement of the slave trade. However, Sherman believed that such a small duty would not be the discouragement of the slave trade, but another source of revenue. James Madison thought that it was wrong to put into the Constitution the idea that men could be property. Reasoning that slaves were property did not hold up because slaves could not be consumed. The clause was finally amended to putting a duty on "such importation not exceeding ten dollars for each person."[15]

Williamson had previously stated that he would rather have slavery in the country than not have the Carolinas and Georgia. This seemed to be the prevailing opinion at the Constitutional Convention. Whether or not the delegates supported slavery was not the issue in their eyes. Their major function was to turn the former colonies into a cohesive country. If they had to deal with something as odious as slavery to accomplish that mission, so be it. The anti-slavery delegates did what they could to limit slavery and the slave trade so that their states would ratify the Constitution the same way the proslavery delegates put as many protections for slavery into the Constitution so that their states would vote for ratification. The moral complexities that the Quakers and other anti-slavery forces threw into the mix could either be considered an annoyance to the smooth creation of an infant government or a reminder of the immoral compromises they made.

Even though the new federal government tied its own hands concerning slavery, there were others who fought on. The Delaware Friends continued their fight against slavery, led by Warner Mifflin and aided by some of the leading Pennsylvania Friends. They sent many petitions to Delaware's governor decrying slavery. In December of 1785, 204 Quakers signed a petition and seven of that number went to the assembly in January of 1786 to deliver it. The petition stated that the undersigned believed that slaves should be freed and given as much help "as the natural rights of mankind and the injunction of the Christian religion require." The Quakers also believed that attacking the slave trade was the surest way of destroying slavery. In their 1788 memorial that they read to the assembly, they prayed that provisions could be made "for suppressing the slave trade." They continued to send petitions to the House of Assembly throughout the rest of the 1780s and into the 1790s.[16]

If the Friends could not stop the slave trade altogether, at least they could make it more difficult for slavers to operate. In 1788, the Friends were able to convince the state legislatures of Pennsylvania, Delaware, and New Jersey to pass laws prohibiting the outfitting of ships for the transportation of slaves from their states and forcibly taking freedmen to the West Indies.[17]

The Friends also helped to create agencies to continue the fight against slavery. Abolitionist groups were formed in Delaware with the combined help of the Friends and the Methodists starting in 1788 with the Delaware Society for Promoting the Abolition of Slavery in Dover. The Delaware Society for Promoting the Abolition of Slavery and for the Relief and Protection of Free Negroes and Mulattos Unlawfully Held in Bondage and Otherwise Oppressed was formed the next year with the help of the Friends and the Methodists in Wilmington, Delaware, and the support of the Mennonites, Presbyterians, and the African Methodist Episcopalians.[18]

Slavery's hold on the South differed from state to state. The plantation system was not as strong in North Carolina as it was in other states. Out of the 300,000 whites living there in 1790, less than one-third of them owned slaves. However, South Carolina was different. Rice was an important cash crop there, but because it needed artificial flooding along the tidal rivers to grow, the land was not healthy to live around. The plantation owners lived only part of the year there and avoided warmer weather by going to stay at summer homes in the hills or in Newport, Rhode Island. The slaves who did live at the plantations were not so fortunate, and some would contract malaria. Since some of the slaves would die because of this, the owners had to constantly replace them. Therefore, the owners supported slavery to maintain a steady stream of workers. In 1790, out of the 1,600 families who lived in the rural part of the Charleston area, 1,300 of them owned a total of 43,000 slaves. The economic need of the plantation owners and the states they lived in to continue slavery made any attack against the institution subject to swift retaliation.[19]

On February 11, 1790, Quaker delegations from New York and Philadelphia delivered petitions to the House of Representatives against the slave trade. Representative James Jackson from Georgia immediately went on the offensive. He believed that the proposal had no right to be brought before the House. In his opinion, the Quakers were obsessed with curing other people's sins and were questionable patriots due to their pacifist beliefs. James Madison was against Jackson's response; he just wanted the matter to die quietly so that the delicate balance between the North and the South would continue. If Jackson did not complain too much about the petition, Madison felt that the problem would go away. However, if Jackson reacted loudly, as he did, others would take notice of the issue. Madison was right.

William Loughton Smith of South Carolina seconded Jackson's response. He said that these petitions were inconsequential because the Constitution clearly stated: "The Migration or Importation of such Persons as any of the States now existing shall think proper to admit, shall not be prohibited by the Congress prior to the Year one thousand eight hundred and eight." Smith's opinion was that it was illegal for Congress to end the slave trade because of the Constitution, so the point was moot. The members of Congress who were also at the Constitutional Convention knew that if that statement had not been placed into the Constitution, then it would not have been passed by some of the southern states. Bringing up this issue again would only bring about the same anger that was a part of Jackson's reaction to the petition. Jackson also believed that the abolition of the slave trade was only the first part of the Quakers' plan. In his opinion, the next step would be the complete abolition of slavery.

Madison believed that Jackson was overreacting. He suggested that the petition be placed in a committee, there to die a natural death. He also believed that if Jackson continued to rail against the petition, then it would get the attention the Quakers wanted.

The next day, another petition arrived in the House from the Pennsylvania Abolition Society.[20] The Pennsylvania Abolition Society was formerly the society founded by Anthony Benezet in 1775 which had been revived by James Pemberton and Benezet in 1784. The majority of its members were Quakers, but its membership was not exclusive to them.[21] Their petition requested, as Jackson feared, the abolition of the slave trade and slavery. It also challenged the excuse that Congress should not do anything about slavery. It was their opinion that the "general welfare" clause of the Constitution permitted Congress to abolish slavery and the slave trade. However, it was the signature of the society's president that destroyed any hope of burying the petition. When Benjamin Franklin fixed his name to the document, it brought the question out into the open and a debate, lasting four to six hours, occurred that day.

Thomas Scott of Pennsylvania spoke first for the petitioners. He said that the Constitution did put limits on what could be done about the slave trade. However, nothing was said about ending slavery. Jackson was next, with the argument that slavery was God's will. He followed it up by saying that slavery was necessary for economic reasons and that "rice cannot be brought to market without these people."

Elbridge Gerry of Massachusetts felt that it was not the fault of the southern states that they had slavery. He felt that the first settlers had pushed them into it and that the northern states should try to rescue them from it. He thought that it was a political and moral duty to help the South free itself from slavery. He believed that the Quaker petitions were not traitorous, but "as worthy as anything that can come before this house." He thought the money necessary to buy the slaves from the South should come from a national fund set up from the sale of western lands.

John Page of Virginia brought up a point that preyed on the minds of slaveholders and their supporters. He believed that the Deep South states should not try to censor talk of slavery or the slave trade. His concern was that once word got back to the slave quarters throughout the country that Congress would not even consider the petitions, the slaves would have no hope of freedom and there would be slave insurrections.

James Madison thought that it was acceptable to talk about slavery and the slave trade even though Congress could not do anything about the issue. They could, however, enact legislation about slave expansion in the Western Territory. Congress voted and agreed to discuss it.[22] A motion was made and seconded to refer both petitions to a committee for consideration. It was agreed to study the petitions by a vote of forty-three to eleven.[23]

The Congress was in the middle of a debate on the assumption of state debts on March 8 when Thomas Hartley of the Pennsylvania delegation presented a committee report on the anti-slavery petitions presented by the Quakers and the Pennsylvania Abolition Society. Massachusetts had a Revolutionary War debt of more than five million dollars. If the assumption bill was passed, the debt would be out of their hands. There were rumors that New England and South Carolina would leave the Union unless the bill was approved. Those states having financial troubles wanted this bill passed so badly that their aggressive stand made many southerners angry. Some of them were saying that they wondered why the country should stay together if their interests were so far apart. It was in this atmosphere that the Quaker petition appeared.[24]

The committee prepared to submit its report to Congress. There were complaints from the members of the Deep South states that the subject was being brought up again. William Smith complained that the anti-slavery supporters who packed the galleries looked like "evil spirits hovering over our heads." James Jackson made threatening faces at the Quakers gathered to watch and called them lunatics. He then began a harangue so muddled and angry that reporters in attendance had trouble writing down his words.[25] The tirades pushed back their report until March 16.

On the day the report was due, George Washington received a visit from Warner Mifflin,

> one of the People called Quakers; active in pursuit of the Measures laid before Congress for emancipating the Slaves: after much general conversation, and an endeavor to remove the prejudices which he said had been entertained of the motives by which the attending deputation from their society were actuated, he used arguments to show the immorality—injustice—and impolicy of keeping these people in a state of slavery; with declarations, however, that he did not wish for more than a gradual abolition, or to see any infraction of the constitution to effect it. To these I replied, that as it was a matter which might come before me for official decision I was not inclined to express any sentiments on the merits of the question before this should happen.[26]

On March 16, the report on the Quaker petition came before the House. Fisher Ames of Massachusetts had first thought that the petition drew attention away from the financial plan they had been working on. However, when the debate became ugly, he changed his mind. He was furious that the South attacked the Quakers and the eastern states. Ames felt that the House deserved all of the criticisms it received because "language low, indecent, and profane has been used ... in short, we have sunk below the General Court in the disorderly moment of a bawling nomination of a committee."[27]

The "language low, indecent, and profane" started with Jackson of Georgia. He was the first speaker to respond to the report and spent two hours expressing his contempt for the idea of ending the slave trade. He was baffled that Congress would allow "shaking Quakers" to dictate the will of the country. He also mentioned the Sectional Compromise at the Constitutional Convention, declaring that the slave trade would continue for another twenty years. The Quakers were, in his opinion, asking Congress to go back on that promise, which was the pact that convinced the Deep South to enter the Union. He also felt that if slavery was wrong, then it was the fault of the British. He asked what would be done with the slaves if they were freed. In his opinion, they would either be relocated or integrated into American society. Relocation was too expensive and integration would mean that there might be interracial marriages. Slavery was 'a necessary evil" and until someone could come up with a solution, the subject of emancipation should be dropped.

However, the one person who was the catalyst for this subject haunting Jackson and the other proslavery forces was Benjamin Franklin. He was certainly no stranger to the Quakers or the anti-slavery movement. On Franklin's first day in Philadelphia, he had followed a group of Quakers into their meeting house and, since he had been up all night, he had fallen asleep. They were kind to him by only awakening him when the services were over. Another Quaker later that day pointed him toward a safe place to spend the night.

Before Franklin had changed his mind about slavery, he had kept two slaves, George and King, as his personal servants.[28] Even though he had owned slaves, Franklin had been connected with the antislavery movement for many years. In 1729, he published antislavery tracts for the Quakers. Between the 1750s and the 1770s, he gave support to Anthony Benezet and other Quaker abolitionists. He also spoke out against the belief that slaves were inferior to the whites. He never really pushed hard for the abolition of slavery until he became president of the Pennsylvania Abolition Society in 1787. He had intended to introduce a proposal at the Constitutional Convention to call for the inclusion of a statement of principle that would condemn the slave trade and slavery. Several northern delegates and a member of the Pennsylvania Abolition Society talked him out of it because they feared that it would cause the Sectional Compromise to fall apart, which would then convince the southern members of the Convention to walk out.[29]

One of the major questions concerning the slaves was what should be done once they were freed. Franklin's answer was to educate them. The Society and Franklin published their plan to get public support[30] in November of 1789. They felt that slavery was "an atrocious debasement of human nature." To just set them free would not be good enough. It was their idea to "instruct, to advise, to qualify those, who have been restored to freedom, for the exercise and enjoyment of civil liberties, to promote in them habits of industry, to furnish them with employments suited to their age, sex, talents, and other circumstances. And to procure their children an education calculated for their future situation in life." This idea was offered to "promote the public good, and the happiness of these our hitherto too much neglected fellow-creatures."[31]

Back at Congress, Smith tried to discredit Franklin's stand by saying that "even great men have their senile moments." The Pennsylvania delegation took this as a personal insult and rose up in fury to defend their most famous citizen. In their opinion, his stand against slavery was not the ramblings of a senile old man. It meant that "the qualities of his soul, as well as those of his mind, are yet in their vigour." It also showed that Franklin could still "speak the language of America, and to call us back to our first principles."

Scott of Pennsylvania was also furious at the insult and attacked the constitutional defense to slavery that the Deep South states used. He felt that the Constitution was a written document, not a collection of unwritten agreements. Nothing was written about slavery. His opinion was that "if Congress should at any time be of the opinion that a state of slavery was a quality inadmissible in America, they would not be barred ... of prohibiting this baneful quality."

Even though Franklin spoke for the end of the slave trade, there were other major political figures who did not. John Adams and Alexander Hamilton, both outspoken critics of slavery, said nothing during the debate. George Washington, like Hamilton, felt that the debate was an embarrassing and possibly dangerous problem that needed to be handled as quickly as possible. Jefferson also stayed quiet, but James Madison did speak. Madison felt that the topic had to be removed from the light of day because it could potentially cause the disillusion of the country. He was also concerned about the fate of his own state because there was a fear in Virginia that if the slaves were emancipated, the Virginia economy would be destroyed. Madison wanted the question to go away, but the reaction of Jackson and his supporters changed that.[32]

In a letter he wrote to Benjamin Rush on March 20, 1790, Madison told him how the anti-slavery petitions

> have employed more than a week, and are still before a Committee of the whole. The Gentlemen from South Carolina and Georgia are intemperate beyond all example and even all decorum. They are not content with palliating slavery as a deep-rooted abuse, but plead for the lawfulness of the African trade itself—nor with protesting against the object of the Memorials, but lavish the most virulent language on the authors of them. If this folly did not reproach the public councils, it ought to excite no regret in the patrons of Humanity and freedom. Nothing could hasten more the progress of those reflections and sentiments which are secretly underminding the institution which this mistaken zeal is laboring to secure against the most distant approach of danger.[33]

William Maclay, a senator from Pennsylvania, also wrote in his journal about the reaction toward the Quaker petition. He felt the House had

> certainly greatly debased their dignity, using base, invective, indecorous language; three or four up at a time, manifesting signs of passion, the most disorderly wanderings in their speeches, telling stories, private anecdotes, etc. I know not what may come of it, but there seems to be a general discontent among the members, and many of them do not hesitate to declare that the Union must fall to pieces at the rate we go on. Indeed, many seem to wish it.[34]

Even though Franklin was, in fact, very old and would be dead within three weeks, he proved that he was still more than capable of defending both himself and his beliefs. In a satire dated March 23 and published two days later in the *Federal Gazette*, Franklin blasted Jackson's speech "in Congress against their meddling with the Affair of Slavery, or attempting to mend the Condition of the Slaves." He wrote that it reminded him of a speech "made about 100 Years since by Sidi Mehemet Ibrahim, a member of the Divan of Algiers." The imaginary Ibrahim was being challenged by a sect called Purists to bring about the abolition of piracy and slavery. Ibrahim defended his enslavement of Christians in much the same language as Jackson, saying that if "we forbear to make slaves of their People, who in this hot Climate are to cultivate our Lands? Who is to perform the common Labours of our City, and in our Families?" Ibrahim also argued that if the Christians were set free, they would be "too little disposed to labour without Compulsion, as well as too ignorant to establish a good government." He also said that God gave them the entire world and all it contained, "who are to enjoy it of Right as fast as they conquer it." The conclusion was that the "Doctrine, that Plundering and Enslaving the Christians is unjust, is at best problematical: but that it is in the Interest of this state to continue the Practice," and the petition was rejected.[35]

Apparently, Dr. Franklin was closer to the truth in his satire than he knew. On the same day that Franklin wrote his last article, the mood toward the petitions was not as receptive as it had been. Several of the northern members who had supported the Quakers changed their minds. Ames of Massachusetts was not pleased that the "southern gentry have been guided by their hot tempers, and stubborn prejudices and pride in regard to southern importance and negro slavery." At the same time, he also felt "ashamed that we have spent so many days in a kind of forensic dispute—a matter of moonshine." Ames, who had voted in the affirmative to put the Quaker petition into a committee for consideration, ended up voting against placing the report in the Journal of the House because he believed that it was "highly exceptionable and imprudent" to state constitutional opinions in the records of the House.[36] Jackson thanked Ames for once again working toward a conciliatory spirit. John Pemberton, one of the Quaker petitioners, sat in the gallery and wondered if a deal had been made.

The details of the report would come later. It had seven resolutions which covered the question of whether or not Congress had the right to abolish slavery. The House then reviewed the report and trimmed it to three resolutions. These resolutions made it unconstitutional for Congress to act against slavery until 1808. The vote was put into the record by a vote of 29 to 25.[37]

Whether or not a deal had been made did not change the fact that those of African descent still needed help, and there were people willing to do just that. Thomas Harrison was a Quaker tailor and member of the Pennsylvania Abolition Society. His shop became a combination of information center and resting place for escapees. He would assign cases of escapees wanting their freedom to the Acting Committee and negotiate with slave owners to avoid legal action.[38] In one such case in 1791, Mrs. Susanna Budd agreed to take one hundred and twenty pounds in exchange for manumitting her slave Pero. Any money Pero earned would be given to Harrison and then transferred to Mrs. Budd at a rate of four pounds a month until Pero had bought his freedom. Harrison also set up the same arrangement for the freedom of Rudolph Boice in 1792. Boice had escaped from Baltimore and went to Philadelphia. Harrison and William Lane, another member of the Pennsylvania Abolition Society, arranged with William Moore, the slave owner, so that Boice would pay him "forty five pounds, for his full Freedom, Liberty, from Bondage in three Equal Payments." To secure the payment, a mortgage was put on Boice's house.[39]

In 1792, Fisher Ames sponsored a petition against slavery that Warner Mifflin had brought to Congress. The representative from Delaware was not in attendance, so Ames introduced it. A representative from North Carolina complained about the subject of slavery being brought up by Mifflin, whom he categorized as a "fanatic, who, not content with keeping his own conscience, undertook to become the keeper of the conscience of other men." He also said that he did not want the petition to be even placed into the Journal of the House. Ames defended Mifflin and his petition by saying that every citizen in the country had the right to petition Congress. However, Ames also believed that the federal government was unable to do anything about the situation. A South Carolina representative also upheld a citizen's right to petition the government, but he also thought that the petition was "a mere rant and rhapsody of a meddling fanatic, interlarded with texts of Scripture and concluded with no specific prayer." He followed up this statement with something that sounded like a veiled threat. He said that he believed that it was dangerous to continue to present petitions like this to Congress because their continued presence might make the southern states nervous and jeopardize the standing of the slaves. Whether or not the threat was real that the South might want to leave the Union because of the slavery issue is open to debate, but the petition was rejected. The only victory that Mifflin received was that the petition was allowed to remain in the House's records.[40]

As entrenched as slavery was in the new country, two events were about to make it harder for anyone fighting against it. A young man named Eli Whitney graduated from Yale in 1792 and moved to Georgia to take a job as a private tutor on a plantation in Georgia owned by Catherine Greene, the widow of General Nathanael Greene. Once there, he realized that the southern planters were having a terrible time making cotton profitable. The long-staple cotton that was easy to separate from its seeds could only be grown near the coast. The inland cotton had green seeds that were so sticky that it took one worker a full day to produce one pound of useable cotton. The tobacco industry was in a decline due to a combination of oversupply of the product and soil exhaustion. Therefore, the creation of a technique to make growing cotton profitable was important to the southern plantation owners.

Mrs. Greene discussed with Whitney how a comb goes through a person's hair and wondered if the same technique could be used for seed removal on the cotton. Whitney, who always had a knack with machinery, set to the problem and, months later, came up with the cotton gin. He created a small version that could be operated by hand as well as larger versions that could be powered by horses or water. In a letter to his father, Whitney claimed, "One man and a horse will do more than fifty men with the old machines."

Whitney's claim that one man and a horse could do the work of fifty men was, unfortunately for those who fought against slavery, true. While the cotton gin reduced the need of laborers to remove cotton seeds, it created a far greater need for manpower in picking cotton. Growing cotton became a very profitable business and there was an increased need for slaves, which, in turn, made slavery even more entrenched in the South.[41]

The second occurrence that further cemented slavery's power was the passage of the Fugitive Slave Act of 1793. This law permitted slave owners to cross state lines to recapture their slaves and bring them before a local magistrate or federal court to prove that they did own the person they had captured. The law did not make provisions for protection under the writ of habeas corpus or the ability to testify in their own behalf. Professional slave hunters were not always particular about whom they kidnapped, and sometimes the wrong person was captured and taken to the South.[42]

The ironic thing about the law was that the origin of it was to help an African American. In May of 1791, Thomas Mifflin, the governor of Pennsylvania, was petitioned by the Pennsylvania Abolition Society to help a man named John Davis, who had been kidnapped by three Virginians and taken to Virginia and enslaved. In June, Mifflin contacted the governor of Virginia, Beverley Randolph, to request the extradition of the three Virginians. Randolph sent the request to James Innes, Virginia's attorney general. Innes believed that Virginia had no legal right to arrest the men. He then sent the report to Randolph, who sent Mifflin his refusal in July to extradite the men. His defense of not complying with Mifflin's request was that Davis was a fugitive slave. Mifflin asked President Washington to intercede. The President then asked Congress to create legislation to regulate interstate extradition and fugitive slave retrieval. The resulting law not only allowed kidnapping, but it also enacted a $500 fine on anyone who tried to interfere with the capture of a fugitive slave. It also allowed a slave owner to sue for injuries suffered by the escape of the slave. The injuries might include loss of the slave, any physical injuries to either the slave or slave owner, and the cost of retrieving the slave. Therefore, anyone trying to help someone escape from slavery was risking not only arrest but also financial ruin.[43]

The Fugitive Slave Act of 1793 was not the last look at slavery for Congress. In January of 1794, the New England Friends were able to speak with President Washington and he agreed to introduce their memorial against the slave trade to the Senate. On January 21, 1794, he presented the memorial without either supporting or rejecting it.[44] Petitions from the Society for Promoting the Abolition of Slavery, which had just had their convention in Philadelphia on January 1, and the Providence (Rhode Island) Society for Abolishing the Slave Trade were added to the Quaker petition and the three were looked at together on February 17.[45] The anti-slave-trade memorials were also looked at by the House on the same day, and they passed a bill making it illegal for an American citizen to be a part of the foreign slave trade. By March 21, the Senate passed a bill that made it illegal to conduct the slave trade from America to foreign countries, and President Washington signed it the next day. The penalties for breaking this law were that the ship involved in the slave trade would be seized, any person involved in the crime would be liable and pay a fine of $2,000, and the captain and crew of the ship would have to pay a $200 fine per slave.[46] This bill proved that even though Congress passed the Fugitive Slave Law the year before, there were some men in Congress, as well as President Washington, who were willing to listen to those who were fighting slavery. They were also even willing to lend a hand in fighting the slave trade themselves if they thought that there would not be dire consequences from the southern members of Congress.

The Friends did not just depend on Congress to fight slavery. In New Jersey, the Gloucester County Society for the Abolition of Slavery began in Burlington on May 2, 1793. It was not a Friends organization, even though the clerk, Joseph Whitall, and the treasurer, Samuel Mickle, were both Quakers. During their November 23, 1793, meeting, James Cooper reported that care was extended to a slave owned by Isaac Burroughs, Jr., who had promised to manumit him the following Christmas. James and Paul Cooper were assigned to the case and if the slave was not freed at that time, they were to take legal action against him to ensure that the manumission took place.[47]

By 1795, the Philadelphia Yearly Meeting reported "No slaves among us."

The Friends did more than just set free their slaves. They also tried to help them assimilate into society. They helped to educate the ex-slaves and gave a small plot of land to each one so that they could support themselves.[48] That was also one of the goals of the Abolition Society. In their October 20, 1795 meeting, they read the missive from the yearly meeting and discussed how to educate former slaves and how they would pay for it out of their funds. They also mentioned three Africans: Dinah, Hester, and Hannah, who were freed by the will of John Mickle. It was thought that they were being held against their will. One of them was in Salem, New Jersey, and another was in Philadelphia. The Society was going to look in on them. By April of the next year, they were still checking on how African children would be schooled. However, they had answers on what happened to Dinah, Hester, and Hannah. Hannah was being held by James Miller in Gloucester County. Dinah and Hester were in Philadelphia and under care.

During their meeting of September 2, 1796, the society reported a census taken on those of African descent in Gloucester County. Of the 350 living there, 47 were householders and daily laborers, 2 were mechanics and a shoemaker, 29 were slaves, and the rest were free women, young men and children. It was also reported that many of them "are Industrious, of orderly lives, and reported a very useful part of the community in the several neighborhoods where they live."[49]

The Quakers continued to not only free their slaves, but also to give them a start in their new lives. Isaac Burrough of Newton Township, Gloucester County, New Jersey, bequeath his slave Tabb to his wife Martha in 1796 until Tabb became thirty years old. Burrough also gave to his man Robert "the house where he lives and one acre of ground and thirty pounds, also ten pounds for each of his sons to be applied by my executors to their schooling, and my negro man Stephen shall be and they are hearby [*sic*]declared free to all intents and purposes immediately after my decease."[50]

The Friends did not give up on their appeals to Congress on behalf of those still held in bondage as well as those already freed. On November 30, 1797, the Friends sent a memorial from the Philadelphia Yearly Meeting held two months before and it was read in the House. It stated that "a number of persons of the African race, who were set free by members of the religious society of Quakers in the state of North Carolina, have been reduced into cruel bondage under the authority of existing or retrospective laws." It was ordered that the memorial be sent to a committee to be examined and a report be sent to the House.[51]

The rejections of the abolition of slavery continued, but the petitions continued as well. At the Philadelphia Yearly Meeting on November 15, 1799, yet another petition against slavery was written. In it, the Friends stated that they were "religiously engaged to call the attention of the people to a subject, which for a long course of years hath exercised our society and many of other religious denominations, that of keeping our fellow men of the African race in slavery." The petition also asked "our fellow citizens at large to unite, in the spirit of meekness and wisdom in promoting this good cause, believing it will be acceptable to that just and holy Being who created all nations of one blood." The petition received the same reaction as the previous ones.[52]

In 1796, St. George Tucker, professor of law at the University of William and Mary, had proposed a gradual abolition of slavery in Virginia. The proposal, which was made up of several lectures that he had given at the university, was published in Philadelphia. He felt that the abolition of slavery was "an object of the first importance, not only to our moral character and domestic peace, but even to our political salvation." He also stated that while America "hath been the land of promise to Europeans, and their descendants, it hath been the vale of death to millions of the wretched sons of Africa."[53] The proposal was not passed, but in 1800, a slaveholder's worst fears were realized in Virginia when an alleged slave rebellion was discovered. Gabriel, a free blacksmith, confessed that the plan was to take over "the whole of the country where slavery was permitted." He also said that all Caucasians were to be killed, except for Quakers, Methodists, and Frenchmen. Hundreds were arrested, many with little or no evidence against them. Out of this number, twenty-six were executed even though no one had been hurt. The backlash hurt both slaves and free people in the South. Voluntary manumissions in Virginia were banned except when there was prior approval. Newly freed slaves had to flee the state or risk being enslaved again. In North Carolina, slaves could only be freed with proof of meritorious service, which was determined by receiving a license from the county court and posting a two-hundred-pound bond to guarantee that the ex-slave would live in a lawful manner. Free people had to travel with authorization or risk arrest, a fine, or be sold into slavery. They could also be enslaved if they failed to pay their taxes or a fine. They were also barred from creating schools or coming together in a meeting if Caucasians felt threatened by the meeting. Anyone known to oppose slavery was considered a troublemaker. They were not allowed to become members of a jury that were deliberating a case brought by a slave who claimed that he had been freed. These developments caused some free people to flee the South. In particular, by 1800, more than nine percent of the population of Philadelphia was of African descent. They may have fled the South to escape trouble, but that did not mean that trouble was not waiting for them in places like Philadelphia. Fortunately, there were people there who were willing to help in spite of the government's inaction toward slavery.[54]

7. Legal Help In and Out of Court

Those of African descent were not the only ones migrating to make a better life. In 1787, a sixteen-year-old farm boy from Deptford, New Jersey, named Isaac T. Hopper arrived in Philadelphia. Hopper went to the city to learn a trade from his uncle, a tailor who had made clothes for George Washington and Benjamin Franklin. He did learn to be a tailor, but he also developed a set of skills for a completely different type of vocation.

Soon after he arrived, Hopper met an enslaved sailor who had jumped ship to regain his freedom. The sailor, named Joe, had been seen by a sea captain who was at Hopper's uncle's house on business. The captain told Joe to wait at the uncle's house until the next ship to Bermuda set sail. When Hopper met him, Joe was sitting in the kitchen with tears running down his face. The tears made Hopper want to help Joe, so he said, "Tell me truly how the case stands with you, I will be your friend; and come what will, you can feel certain that I will never betray you." Joe then admitted that he was a runaway slave. Hopper did not want to send the man back to slavery so he asked a neighbor if he knew of anyone who could help. The neighbor told Isaac about a Quaker named John Stapler who lived in Bucks County, Pennsylvania. Stapler was known to be "a good friend to colored people," so Joe was given a letter of introduction and directions on how to find him. Hopper later heard that the sailor arrived safely and that he was able to get a job. Joe spent the rest of his life there and there was "none to molest or make him afraid." It was Hopper's first foray into assisting escapees, but it was certainly not his last.

Isaac Hopper became a Quaker when he was twenty-two, and one of the reasons that he and others like him were kept busy with assisting escapees was the way the laws were written. Philadelphia had many runaways passing through and the slave laws were created in a way that made it difficult for someone to be found innocent. If a man was arrested as a fugitive slave and freed for lack of proof, the magistrate who heard the case received no money. However, if a man was found guilty of being an escaped slave, the magistrate would receive five to twenty dollars. This kept the Pennsylvania Abolition Society busy, and Hopper became an active member. He also was one of the overseers of the school for those of African descent started by Anthony Benezet. For several years, Hopper taught adults at the school several nights a week. He soon became well known as someone to go to for help.

In 1797, a wealthy family from Virginia came to Philadelphia to spend the winter. They had a slave named Charles Webster, who worked for the family as a coachman and waiter. Webster went to visit Hopper several weeks after the family's arrival. He asked Hopper if he was free due to now living in Pennsylvania. Hopper replied that Webster would have to live in Pennsylvania for six months with his master's knowledge and consent to be considered free under Pennsylvania law. Webster was afraid that his master might know about the law and return him to Virginia before the six months were up and informed Hopper that he was "resolved never to return to Virginia." Hopper said that his master might not know about the law or might have forgotten about it, so Webster should sit tight and wait the six months. If the master began packing or started talking about returning to Virginia, Webster should immediately contact Hopper.

Six months to the day that Webster arrived at Pennsylvania, Webster's master came to him and said: "Charles, grease the carriage-wheels, and have all things in readiness; for I intend to start for home tomorrow." Webster did as he was told without protest and as soon as he was done, he went to see Hopper, who assured him that he was a free man by law. Despite this, he was very nervous and felt that he was still in danger. Hopper told him to return to his master until the next day and if he was arrested, send one of the hotel servants to fetch Hopper.

The next day, Webster went back to see Hopper, who then took Webster to William Lewis, a highly respected lawyer who never took a fee from anyone wanting to escape slavery. Lewis heard Webster's story and wrote a polite note to the Virginian informing him that Webster was no longer a slave according to the laws of Pennsylvania and that any attempt to stop Webster from leaving would be illegal. Lewis then told Hopper to go visit the Virginian before Webster delivered the note.

Hopper found the Virginian at home and told him that Webster was a free man. The Virginian was furious and began berating Hopper about sticking his nose in where it did not belong. Hopper answered him by saying: "If thy son were a slave in Algiers, thou wouldst thank me for tampering with him to procure his liberty. But in the present case, I am not obnoxious to the charge thou hast brought; for thy servant came of his own accord to consult me, I merely made him acquainted with his legal rights; and I intend to see that he is protected in them."

Later in the day, after Webster showed the Virginian the note from Lewis, he offered to hire Charles to drive his carriage home. Webster refused because he knew that doing so would be very dangerous for his newfound freedom. The Virginian, seeing that his attempt to trick Webster did not work, became angry and demanded that Webster give him his clothes because they were his property since Webster no longer was. The former slave then took off his clothes and turned to leave the house naked. The Virginian, incensed, grabbed Webster, dragged him back, and demanded that he put his clothes back on. Webster once again did as he was told and walked away, never seeing his former master again. Webster eventually married, built a home, and had fourteen children, who received their education at the school founded by Anthony Benezet.[1]

The Gloucester County Society for the Abolition of Slavery was also involved with education for children as well as freedom from slavery. At their half-year meeting on October 31, 1796, their records state, "Thomas Stokes produced receipt for the payment of one pound two shillings and 3 pence for the schooling of two Black Children of Charles Chesters. The Treasurer is directed to pay the same when called upon."[2] By 1800, there were 49 members of the abolition society in the county of Gloucester in New Jersey. Among their members were John Gill, Isaac, Joseph, and Samuel Mickle, and Joseph Whitall.[3]

In August of 1800, an incident occurred that brought about unexpected freedom. Two American ships, the *Phebe* and the *Prudent*, delivered 135 African men, women and children to the Lazaretto Quarantine Station outside of Philadelphia. The ships had been captured by the U.S. Navy vessel *Ganges* in violation of a recent law that banned American vessels from being a part of the slave trade. The Africans were taken to the Lazaretto station to be given clothing, food and medical care. Richard Peters, a federal judge, granted them their freedom, gave them all the last name of Ganges, and asked the Pennsylvania Abolition Society to assume custody of them. The Society did so and arranged for them to be indentured as servants in and around Philadelphia so they could learn the skills needed to survive in America. Thomas Harrison arranged for one girl, Mary Ann Ganges, to be "Apprentice to Thomas Egger of the City of Philadelphia, Quarantine Master, to learn the Art, Trade, and Mystery of Housekeeping." She would also be taught "in the trade and Mystery of Housewifery" and she would be provided with "sufficient Meat, Drink, Wearing apparel, Lodging and Washing, fitting for an Apprentice, during the said term of nine years" and would be taught "to read and write and when free, to have two suits of apparel one whereof to be new."[4]

The Quakers in New Jersey had another way to help African Americans become more independent and have greater freedom from the threat of slave catchers. They sold small tracts of land to people who had either escaped slavery or had been manumitted. These tracts of land eventually became independent towns, such as Springtown in Cumberland County, New Jersey, on the northern end of Greenwich Township, which was created around 1800. Two other towns that came about the same way were Lawnside in Camden County, which had also been known as Snowhill and Free Haven,[5] and Timbuctoo in Burlington County. These towns also had something else in common: they later became stops on the Underground Railroad.[6]

Between one half and three-quarters of all the African Americans who lived in the North were free in 1800.[7] However, the threat of slavery could hang over someone who was already free as well as an escapee. In March of 1801, a Captain Dana booked passage on a ship sailing from Philadelphia to Charleston, South Carolina. He went to the house of a free woman and told her that he had a suit of clothes that was too small for his son. He said that if the clothes fit her son properly, he would give them to him. He then said that he wished to take the boy back to his quarters to let him try the clothes on. The woman agreed and the boy went off with the captain. Instead of going to his quarters, the captain took the boy to the ship and had the captain of the ship hold him against his will. Just before the ship was to sail away, a violent storm came up and it was necessary to moor at a wharf. Later, a man at the wharf heard a child crying and went to investigate. He found the cook of the ship and asked him about the crying. The cook told the man that Captain Dana brought a boy onboard and that the boy said that he had been stolen from his mother. The man sent a note to Isaac Hopper, who immediately contacted a policeman. Hopper and the policeman then went to the wharf and questioned the captain of the ship. He claimed that all hands were ashore and that he was alone on the ship. Hopper then asked for a light so that he could search the ship. The captain refused and said that his word should have been enough for them. Hopper then grabbed an axe and said that he would break down the door unless he was allowed to enter. The captain allowed Hopper and the policeman to search the ship and they found the cook and the boy. The constable took everyone into custody and they all went to the mayor's house.

It was still raining when they arrived at Front Street, the home of Mayor

Inskeep, at midnight. The mayor was informed that Isaac Hopper desired to see him. Once the Quaker was taken upstairs to the mayor's chambers, Hopper told the mayor what had happened. He then requested that the mayor issue a verbal order to place the captain and the cook in jail to await trial. Mayor Inskeep refused because he thought that it was "a matter of too much importance to be disposed of in that way. I will come down and hear the case." It turned out that the captain of the ship was an old friend of the mayor's. His friendship with the accused clearly did not affect the case, because the mayor ordered the captain to appear for trial the next morning. If he did not appear, the captain would have been fined three thousand dollars. The cook was placed in jail for the night as a witness and the boy was sent home with Hopper, who promised to produce him the next day for the trial.

Hopper found the boy's mother and the three of them went to see the mayor the following day. During the hearing in the mayor's office, the captain of the ship protested his innocence. He claimed that he knew nothing of the situation and that he was merely taking care of the boy at the request of a passenger. When he was told that he would be expected to appear at the next court to face charges of kidnapping, the captain became frightened and told them where Captain Dana could be found. Captain Dana was then captured and taken to Hopper's house. The kidnapper flew into a rage, protested his innocence, and swore vengeance against anyone who had dragged him into this situation. His protests meant nothing because when he went to trial, he admitted his guilt and claimed that he did it because he needed money. He was freed on a $1,500 bond and the child was never bothered again.

In 1801, Hopper had an occasion to keep another child from being separated from his mother. Wagelma was a ten-year-old who was apprenticed by his mother to a Frenchman in Philadelphia. The man was planning to take his family by ship to Baltimore and then to France. He put Wagelma on a ship bound for Baltimore without receiving the permission of his mother, as Pennsylvania law stated. The boy's mother had no idea that he was leaving until the ship had already sailed. She was frightened that her son could be sold into slavery in Baltimore or sent to the West Indies and sold there. Even if this did not happen, she was afraid that she would never see him again, so she contacted Isaac Hopper for help.

Hopper hurried to the wharf at sunrise to find that the ship had already sailed. He mounted a horse and rode three miles south to Gloucester Point in hopes of catching the ship. There was a ferry at the point owned by a widow who was a friend of Hopper. He told her the story and she ordered one of her ferrymen to take Hopper to the ship, which was just coming into view. They hurried and were able to come alongside the ship. The captain assumed that

Hopper was a passenger and ordered his men to help Hopper on board. Once on the ship, the Quaker told the captain his business. Hopper then went to the man and informed him that when he took the boy, he was in violation of Pennsylvania law. Since he had six to eight friends with him, the Frenchman decided that he did not need to obey the law. Hopper went to the captain and asked him to place Wagelma on the ferry, which was still following alongside the ship. The captain did not want to get involved, but Hopper pulled out a copy of the laws that applied to the case. The captain realized that Hopper had the law on his side and had the boy placed on the ferry.

Wagelma made it safely onto the ferry, but the Frenchman and his friends had other ideas for Hopper. They grabbed the Quaker and attempted to throw him overboard, but he was able to get a grip on the coat of one of the men. They beat his hand with canes and were able to loosen his grip on the man's coat. However, the determined Quaker grabbed another man's coat and hung on. In the meantime, the ferryman was able to maneuver his boat under Hopper and he dropped into the ferry. They made it back to the shore and Hopper and Wagelma returned to the Quaker's home, where the boy's mother was waiting.[8]

Congress did not feel that they had the right to abolish the slave trade until 1808, but it did not stop them from changing existing laws about African Americans. On January 18, 1802, the House defeated an amendment to the 1793 Fugitive Slave Law which required African Americans to show a certificate of freedom when they sought employment.[9] This helped African Americans to get jobs, but it did not protect them from other dangers.

There was a practice among those who bought slaves called "buying them running." This expression meant that speculators would purchase slaves who had already run away at a much lower than market value and then try to catch them. The risk was that they might not be able to find them. In April of 1802, Joseph Ennelis and Captain Frazer, both of Maryland, came to Philadelphia to find slaves they had bought in this risky manner. They seized a man by the name of William Bachelor, a sixty-year-old free man, and claimed that they owned him. The two men had brought with them an African American who swore before a magistrate that Bachelor was a slave, but had escaped. The three accusers seemed so respectable that the magistrate wrote out an authorization for them to take Bachelor to Maryland.

As they walked out of the magistrate's office, they passed Dr. Finley, a man who was a friend of Bachelor's. Finley argued for Bachelor's freedom with Ennelis and Frazer, but to no avail. The doctor then ran to Isaac Hopper's house and, almost out of breath, told Hopper: "They've got old William Bachelor, and are taking him to the South, as a slave. I know him to be a free man.

Many years ago, he was a slave to my father, and he manumitted him. He used to carry me in his arms when I was an infant."

Hopper asked where they were and Finley informed him that they were headed toward Gray's Ferry. He went after them and caught up with the party about a half mile from the Schuylkill River. The Quaker approached Ennelis and politely informed him that there had to have been a mistake because Bachelor was a free man. Ennelis pulled out a pistol and told Hopper that they were legally within their rights to take Bachelor, and he said, "I will blow your brains out if you say another word on the subject, or make any attempt to molest me."

Hopper stood his ground and said,

> If thou wert not a coward, thou wouldst not try to intimidate me with a pistol. I do not believe thou hast the least intention of using it in any other way; but thou art much agitated, and may fire it accidentally; therefore I request thee not to point it toward me, but to turn it the other way. It is in vain for thee to think of taking this old man to Maryland. If thou wilt not return to the city voluntarily, I will certainly have thee stopped at the bridge, where thou wilt be likely to be handled much more roughly than I am disposed to do.

Hopper was finally able to talk the men into going back and seeing the magistrate who originally declared Bachelor a slave. Dr. Finley and others testified on his behalf and Bachelor was set free. It was also decided to charge Ennelis with attempting to take Bachelor forcibly out of the state and into slavery. When Hopper went with two constables to deliver the warrant to Ennelis, he was found writing with a pistol on either side of him. As soon as they had entered the room, Ennelis picked up a pistol and threatened to use it on them unless they left. Hopper warned him that the men with him were "officers, and have a warrant to arrest thee for attempting to carry off a free man into slavery. I advise thee to lay down thy pistol and go with us. If not, a sufficient force will soon be brought to compel thee." With that, Ennelis agreed to go with the officers. His resolve to go quietly did not last very long. As they were going to the jail, Ennelis argued with one of the officers and hit him in the face with a cane. The officer hit him back and knocked him down. The Quaker intervened, helped Ennelis to his feet and said, "Thou hadst better take my arm and walk with me. I think we can agree better."

Ennelis stayed at his hotel during the investigation. Many testimonials to his character came from Maryland and Virginia, and Ennelis' lawyer showed them to Hopper, hoping that the charges against his client would be dropped. Hopper said that he had no power to do that, but he did know that the abolition society had only prosecuted Ennelis to make a point to anyone who might try to take away the freedom of a free man. He also informed Ennelis that the abolition society would agreed to drop the charges if Ennelis would pay all court costs. He agreed with the deal and soon both Bachelor and Ennelis were free.

The bane of every person running away from slavery was the slave catcher. In July of 1802, David Lea came to Philadelphia to hunt runaways. Several days after his appearance, Lea seized a man who he claimed was the slave of a Nathan Peacock of Maryland. The man admitted that Lea was correct about his identity and he had left because he did not want to be a slave anymore. His friends did not want him separated from his wife and children, so they asked Peacock if they could buy his freedom. Peacock set a high price for his freedom, and the escapee had to stay in jail until the conclusion of the incident. Isaac Hopper was called in and, when he arrived, asked Lea if he had any business in Philadelphia. Lea answered no. Hopper then asked him if he had any money and received the same answer. The Quaker then said to the magistrate in charge of the proceedings that Lea was a stranger in town with no visible means of support and by "his appearance, there is reason to conclude that he may be a dangerous man. I would suggest whether it be proper that he should be permitted to go at large." Lea became very evasive in his answers to the magistrate, so he too was placed in jail until the court was again in session.

When he arrived at the jail, Lea objected to being searched. His objections ignored, Lea was found with more than fifty advertisements for runaway slaves in his pockets. The advertisements showed the real reason he was in Philadelphia. As Lea sat in jail, Isaac Hopper went to see him. During the conversation that followed, Hopper found out that Lea was to receive forty-five dollars for returning the man to Peacock. The Quaker then told Lea that if he would pay forty-five dollars to Peacock to help pay for the man's freedom, Lea could go free as well. The slave catcher agreed and paid the money. Unfortunately, the deal to set the escapee free fell through because Peacock wanted too much money. Hopper wanted to return Lea's money to him, but Lea refused. Apparently, he had a change of heart about slave catching. He only wanted three dollars to cover his expenses to return home. He also wrote out a document that stated: "I request Isaac T. Hopper to pay the money received from the order, which I gave him upon Nathan Peacock, to the managers of the Pennsylvania Hospital, or to any other charitable institution he may judge proper."

It was not long afterward that Lea received his release from jail. The escapee was not so lucky. The law sent him back to Maryland, but that did not last long. He escaped again and returned to live in Philadelphia. This time, he was able to stay because his freedom was able to be purchased at a lower price.[10]

The efforts of all those who fought against slavery in New Jersey finally bore fruit in 1786 when the slave trade in that state was abolished. By 1804, the New Jersey legislature voted to gradually abolish slavery. It declared that all children born of slaves after July 4, 1804, were free after they served as apprentices to their mothers' masters. The female children were to stay until their twenty-first birthday and the male children until their twenty-fifth birthday. The New Jersey Society for Promoting the Abolition of Slavery helped to enact the legislation. They believed in the concept of gradual emancipation because they thought that it had a better chance of success than trying to force complete and immediate emancipation on the state.

There was an abandonment clause to the 1804 law that helped slave owners. A master had to provide for the children of female slaves for one year. After that time, he could abandon them to the public overseer of the poor. They could then be declared paupers and bound out of service. This would force the state to pay their new master, usually their former master, three dollars a month for maintenance. It became so expensive for the state that the clause was repealed in 1811.[11]

The mindset in Congress was that there was nothing they could do about the slave trade until 1808. This unbending attitude discouraged the anti-slavery forces on any reforms until then. However, not everyone in Congress had given up on fighting the slave trade. George Logan, a doctor and senator from Pennsylvania, had been removed from his meeting in 1791 when he joined the local militia. He had joined as a civic duty and when his militia was called up to fight in the Whiskey Rebellion, he resigned. However, he continued to go to meeting with his wife and lived by the Friends' beliefs. On January 24, 1804, Senator Logan requested permission to read a memorial in Congress against slavery. Once again, slavery's defenders went on the attack. James Jackson of Georgia, William Cocke of Tennessee, and Robert Wright and Samuel Smith of Maryland demanded that the memorial not be read in the Senate. As far as they were concerned, the Quakers did not have slaves and had no right to complain about slavery. They also felt that the mere discussion of slavery would immediately drop the value of slaves in the South and would also encourage bloody slave rebellions like the recent one in Santo Domingo. However, the hysteria toward the memorial did not extend to all the Senators. John Quincy Adams of Massachusetts defended Logan's right to read the memorial. James A. Bayand of Delaware and Jesse Franklin of North Carolina also wanted the petition to be read. After a three-hour debate, Logan was free to read a petition from the American Convention for Promoting the Abolition of Slavery. The Society, made up mostly of Quakers, had just finished their annual meeting in Philadelphia and they wanted Logan to read their petition.[12] It was their wish that "such laws may be enacted as shall prohibit the introduction of slaves into the territory of Louisiana, lately ceded to the United States."[13]

Just because Senator Logan won the right to read the petition, it did not mean that the controversy was over. The next day, the Senate discussed it as an amendment to the bill that would decide how the government of Louisiana would be set up. Jackson of Georgia mentioned that slaves must be allowed to enter Louisiana because crops could not be grown without them. John Smith of Ohio disagreed with that statement by saying that he had "spent considerable time there—white men can cultivate it." The debate went on for a week, with some of the southerners becoming angry and even going so far as to subtlety hint at secession if they did not get their way.[14] Finally, on January 30, 1804, the Senate, by a vote of 21 to 7, made it illegal to

> import or bring into the said territory, from any port or place within the limits of the United States, or cause to, or procure to be so imported or brought, or knowingly to aid or assist in so importing any slaves ... from any port or place without the limits of the United States.... And no slave or slaves shall directly or indirectly be introduced into said territory, except by a person or persons removing into said territory for actual settlement and being at the time of such removal bona fide owner of such slave or slaves, and every slave imported or brought into the said territory, contrary to the provisions of this act, shall thereupon be entitled to and receive his or her freedom.[15]

While Congress wrangled with the slavery question, others had to deal with it on a more personal level. In August of 1804, Ben, a slave of Pierce Butler of South Carolina, came to the abolition society for help. The thirty-six-year-old Ben was born into slavery and worked for Mr. Butler's family his entire life. Ben had lived most of the previous eleven years in Pennsylvania. Butler was planning to take him back to South Carolina, but Ben did not want to go because his wife was very sick and he did not want to leave her. The Society believed that Ben was legally no longer a slave and proposed to apply to Judge Inskeep for a writ of habeas corpus. Isaac Hopper was assigned to deliver the writ to Butler.

When he arrived at Butler's house on Chestnut Street, he was informed that Butler was at dinner. Hopper agreed to wait for Butler to finish his dinner before discussing his business. After dinner, Butler appeared and Hopper served him the writ. Butler read the paperwork and said, "Get out of my house, you scoundrel!" Hopper pretended that he did not hear him. Butler again screamed at him to leave. Hopper again feigned deafness and said, "This paper on the walls is the handsomest I ever saw. Is it French or English?" He then very slowly headed for the door. Butler bellowed that he was "a citizen of South Carolina. The laws of Pennsylvania have nothing to do with me. May the devil take all those who come between masters and their slaves." Thinking that Hopper was truly deaf, he walked up to the Quaker and screamed into his ear.

Hopper did not react to the punishment to his ear and as he reached the doorway, he turned to Butler and said "Farewell. We shall expect to see thee at Judge Inskeep's."

On the day of the hearing, the sight of Hopper at Judge Inskeep's was enough to send Pierce Butler into another outburst of fury. He grabbed a copy of the Bible and said that he was willing to swear that he would not sell Ben even if he was offered fifteen hundred dollars. He also said that he was as honorable a man as anyone could find. Hopper countered by saying that Butler was "not even just. Thou hast already sent back into bondage two men, who were legally entitled to freedom by staying in Philadelphia during the term prescribed by law. If thou hadst a proper sense of justice, thou wouldst bring those men back, and let them take the liberty that rightfully belongs to them." Butler apparently did not appreciate the words of the Quaker because Butler told him that if he "were in a different walk of life, I would treat your insult as it deserves." Hopper was a pacifist, but he was not a coward. He calmly replied that he would "consider it no honor to be killed by a member of Congress; and surely there would be neither honor nor comfort in killing thee; for in thy present state of mind thou art not fit to die." Butler then told the judge that he thought Hopper was either deaf or crazy because of his actions. The judge smiled and said that Butler must not "know Mr. Hopper as well as we do."

During the trial, a lawyer was found for Ben, but Butler defended himself. He claimed that he was just a visitor to Philadelphia and that the only time Ben stayed in the state for any length of time was when Congress was in session. Southern congressmen were permitted to keep their slaves with them in Pennsylvania for as long as they liked. Butler later admitted that he returned from Congress to Philadelphia with Ben on January 2, 1804, and they remained until August 3. Ben's lawyer countered the argument by stating the law was created for the time when Congress convened in Philadelphia. However, Congress no longer met in Philadelphia and the argument was no longer valid. The judge agreed and Ben was set free. This was not the last time Ben had dealings with Butler. Ben had gone to work for Isaac W. Morris, who lived several miles from Philadelphia. One day soon after the trial, Ben went into Philadelphia on business and was seized by a U.S. marshal. Butler had filed suit against Ben and bail was set at two thousand dollars. Isaac Hopper and Thomas Harrison paid the bail and the trial was before the Circuit Court of the United States. Butler had hopes of winning the case because the judge, Bushrod Washington, was a slave owner. The case was heard in October of 1806. However, Judge Washington was not the only judge hearing the case. Richard Peters also presided, and eventually Ben was set free and never bothered by Butler again.[16]

The courts could be used to do more than defend people from slavery. Thomas Harrison and Isaac Hopper would sue the owners of Pennsylvania ships who were illegally involved with the slave trade. In 1804, they took the Pennsylvania owners of two ships, the *Eliza* and the *Sally*, to court. The *Eliza* picked up six slaves in Antigua and sold them in Havana. The *Sally* picked up 100 slaves in Gambia and sold them in St. Thomas. In 1805, they also brought legal action against the owners of the brig *Tyrphrena*, which took twelve slaves to Havana and sold them.[17]

There was the rare occasion where a slave owner actually went to see Isaac Hopper to receive help in getting his slave back. In 1805, a slave owned by a Colonel Hopper of Maryland ran away with his family to Philadelphia. The escapee rented a house on Green's Court and lived there for several months. Colonel Hopper learned where he was and came to Philadelphia. He then contacted Richard Hunt, a constable who also worked as a slave catcher. The colonel obtained a warrant and he and Hunt went to the man's home. The escapee had just returned home from work and was setting down to dinner when Colonel Hopper and Hunt barged into his home. Thinking quickly, he leaped up, threw his arms around the colonel's neck and cried out: "O, my dear master, how glad I am to see you! I thought I should like to be free; but I had a great deal rather be a slave. I can't get work, and we have almost starved. I would have returned home, but I was afraid you would sell me to the Georgia men. I beg your pardon a thousand times. If you will only forgive me, I will go back with you, and never leave you again."

Colonel Hopper was so surprised that he did forgive the escapee. He was ready to dismiss Hunt when the escapee asked him to stay for a few minutes. He told the colonel that he had a little money and he wanted to buy his master something to drink. He came back directly with some gin and proceeded to give both the colonel and Hunt as much gin as they could drink. He knew that both men liked their liquor and so, while he talked on and on about Maryland, he kept filling their glasses. It was not very long before both men were unconscious on the floor. The escapee then packed up his family and went to hide in New Jersey.

When Hunt and the colonel woke up, they found an empty house. They spent several fruitless days searching for the escapee and his family. Finally, the colonel went to see Isaac Hopper. He complained to the Quaker that he had been fair to the escapee, had given him a good home, and what he got for it was a dirty trick played on him. He followed up his complaints by asking for Hopper's help in finding the escapee and promising to treat them as if the escapee and his family were his own children.

Isaac Hopper said to the colonel that if "the man were as happy with thee as thou hast represented, he will doubtless return voluntarily, and my assistance will be quite unnecessary." He also told the Colonel that he would do everything in his power to keep the family free. The Colonel wanted to know if Hopper had seen the escapee and Hopper answered that he had gone to him "when he left his own house in Green's Court and I gave him such advice on that occasion, as I thought proper. Thou art the first slaveholder I ever met with bearing my name. Perhaps thou hast assumed it, as a means of gaining the confidence of colored people, to aid thee in recapturing the objects of thy avarice." The Colonel realized that he would not get any help from Hopper. A week later, he became ill and died. The escapee stayed in Philadelphia and was never bothered again.[18]

Even those in power felt helpless in dealing with the slavery issue. Thomas Jefferson wrote to his friend George Logan on May 11, 1805, on his feelings about slavery. He told Logan that he had "most carefully avoided every public act or manifestation on that subject. Should an occasion ever occur in which I can interpose with decisive effect, I shall certainly know and do my duty with promptitude and zeal."[19]

Harrison and Hopper were certainly men who operated promptly and with zeal in helping others escape slavery. In 1805, James Lawler was a slave to a Mr. McCalmont of Delaware. The thirty-year-old Lawler escaped and lent himself out to a farmer in New Jersey. Several months later, Lawler discovered that several runaways who lived in the area had been captured and returned to the South. He was afraid that the same fate awaited him. Therefore, he wanted to find a person who could buy his way out of slavery and he would bind himself to that person for a set amount of time to repay the debt. Lawler went to the farmer to ask for advice and he suggested that Lawler talk to Isaac Hopper.

Hopper wrote to McCalmont and inquired how much it would cost to buy Lawler his freedom. Instead of writing back, McCalmont came to Philadelphia with a merchant who lived in town. The merchant told Hopper that McCalmont was a respectable man who treated his slaves very well. He also said that Lawler would be much better off living with McCalmont and asked Hopper to help them find Lawler. Hopper doubted that James would have agreed with the idea that he was better off a slave and that even "if I had no objection to slavery, I should still be bound by every principle of honor not to betray the confidence reposed in me. But feeling as it is well known I do on that subject, I am surprised thou shouldst make such a proposition to me."

This did not discourage the two men. They went to see Harrison. Instead of the polite refusal they received from Hopper, they were met by the ironic Harrison who told them that he knew "that slaves sleep on feather beds, while their master's children sleep on straw; that they eat white bread, and their master's children eat brown."

McCalmont, realizing that he would never get Lawler back, then told Hopper that he would be willing to free Lawler for one hundred and fifty dollars. A Mr. John Hart, who was a druggist, came up with the money. Someone asked Hunt if he was afraid that Lawler would run away before working off his debt. Hunt replied that he was not afraid because he planned to "tie him by the teeth." What Hunt meant by that was that he planned to feed Lawler well.

Apparently Hunt kept his word, because Lawler was happy in his new position. A year or two later, Lawler asked permission to visit McCalmont and the servants who worked for him. Hunt agreed and loaned him a horse. Lawler arrived at McCalmont's home and went into the kitchen to visit with his friends. When McCalmont returned home, he saw the fine horse in front of his home and thought that it was an important man coming to visit. He was surprised to see Lawler in his kitchen. They spoke pleasantly to each other and both enjoyed the visit. As Lawler prepared to leave, McCalmont informed him that the only thing he did not like about the visit was that seeing Lawler on a fine horse would now make his other slaves dissatisfied. Lawler returned to the Hunts and served out his bonded time. When the time was up, Lawler stayed with them as a hired hand.

Another adventure involving Isaac Hopper and Thomas Harrison was with a man named William Anderson, a slave in Virginia. When he was twenty-five, Anderson and two other slaves went to Philadelphia. Anderson told his master that he wanted to go to Philadelphia to see if he could do something for himself. Several months later, his master sold him while he was still away (called "sold them running") to Joseph Ennelis. The new owner went out and got a warrant and a policeman and went to Philadelphia to find the three slaves.

Ennelis tried for several days to find the three men, but was not successful. He then went to Hopper and Harrison for help. He offered to sell the three men cheap if the two Quakers would help him find them. Hopper refused to help Ennelis and advised him "to go home and obtain thy living in some more honorable way; for the trade in which thou art engaged is a most odious one. On a former occasion thou wert treated with leniency; and I recommend a similar course to thee with regard to these poor fugitives."

Ennelis offered to sell the three men for two hundred and fifty dollars and Hopper agreed. A few days later, Anderson went to Hopper's home and asked for advice. He told Anderson that Harrison had bought him and his two friends. Hopper also said that Anderson should go and find the other two and work out how he would pay Harrison back. He did go see Harrison and offered to become an indentured servant to pay him back. The bad news was that he could not find the other two men. Anderson did become a servant to Jacob Downing and served his time faithfully. Downing treated Anderson well and Anderson thought highly of Downing. At the end of his time, Anderson received one hundred and twenty-five dollars. He then sought out Harrison to give him the money and ask the Quaker if he had ever heard anything of the other two men. Harrison had not, and Anderson felt bad about Harrison losing one hundred and twenty-five dollars. He offered to indenture himself again to pay the rest of the money, but Harrison said he "hast paid thy share, and I have no further claim upon thee. Conduct as well as thou hast done since I have known thee, and thou wilt surely prosper." Anderson did just that, but the two other men were never seen again.

Even though some Quakers were vigorously fighting against slavery, it did not mean that all of them felt that those of African descent were equal to Caucasians and wanted to socialize with them. David Maps and his wife were two of the very few Quakers of color at the same meeting that Isaac Hopper belonged to. At the yearly meeting held in Philadelphia, they came with other members to Hopper's home to have dinner. Hopper's family was wondering if the other members would object to eating with the Mapses. Hopper handled the situation by going out to his guests and saying: "Friends, dinner is now ready. David Maps and his wife will come with me; and as I like to have all accommodated, those who object to dining with them can wait till they have done." Everyone walked in together.[20]

John Parrish, a Quaker from Philadelphia, had been working against slavery for fifty years. His attacks against slavery included presenting anti-slavery petitions to various government officials and monitoring the activities of domestic and international slave traders. His passion against slavery started when he was a young man in Maryland, where he witnessed such "scenes of degradation" that he devoted the rest of his life to helping stamp out slavery.[21] He published an essay in 1806 entitled "Remarks on the Slavery of the Black People," which was directed toward local, state, and federal governments as well as slave owners. He implored the state governments to abolish the domestic slave trade and wanted the federal government to immediately end the African slave trade and not wait for the 1808 deadline. He was a firm believer in gradual emancipation, the way the Friends did it among themselves. He feared that if action was not taken against slavery, the country would face the wrath of the Lord.[22]

Parrish was not the only one who feared the wrath of the Lord in regard to slavery. The Philadelphia Yearly Meeting of 1806, as well as the 1755 meeting, denounced slavery among its members as an "enormous national evil" and stated that the Friends should "discourage it by all the justifiable means in their power; it being obvious that wherever it prevails it tends to corrupt the morals of the people, so as not only to render them obnoxious to the displeasure of the Almighty, but deaf to his warnings, and insensible and regardless of his impending judgments."

The Friends were also instructed to influence those who owned slaves to be kind to them, give them religious training, and provide them with the education they would need to be productive members of society. They were also to help "the black people as are at liberty, in the education of their children, and common worldly concerns."[23]

With the end of 1806, came the end of Congress dragging their feet on the question of importing slaves. The House worked on a bill to prohibit bringing slaves into the country. President Thomas Jefferson showed his support for this bill by giving a message to Congress on December 2, 1806 stating he recommended that they should remove the country "from all further participation in those violations of human rights which have been so long continued on the unoffending inhabitants of Africa."[24] On December 29, they worked on amendments to the bill, and on December 31 they voted on the changes. They removed the word *slave* and said that anyone after December 31, 1807 found transporting

> or cause to be transported or brought into the United States, or the territories thereof, any negro, mulatto, or person of color, contrary to the true intent and meaning of this act, every person, or persons so offending, shall be deemed guilty of a high misdemeanor, and being thereof convicted before any Court having competent jurisdiction, shall suffer imprisonment not more that ten, nor less than five years.

They passed the changes by a vote of 63 to 53. Congress voted again on January 8, 1807, to pass it on to a select committee, which it passed by a vote of 76 to 46. Finally, on March 2, 1807, President Jefferson signed into law the bill prohibiting the importation of slaves into the United States after December 31, 1807.[25]

Jefferson mentioned how he felt about the end of the importation of slaves in answer to a letter sent to him by Quakers. On November 13, 1807, he replied that whatever had convinced

> our forefathers to permit the introduction of personal bondage into any part of these States, and to participate in the wrongs committed on an unoffending quarter of the globe, we may rejoice that such circumstances, and such a sense of them, exist no longer. It is honorable to the nation at large that their legislature availed themselves of the first practicable moment for arresting the progress of this great moral and political error.

Even though the law applied to the entire nation, it only affected South Carolina. All of the other states had already banned importing slaves from Africa. In fact, South Carolina had reinstated the foreign slave trade in 1804. An article in the *Charleston Courier* from January 1, 1808, announced the ban and also stated the amount of slaves who were brought into the state from 1804 to the present. In 1807 alone, 15,676 people were taken from Africa, bringing the total for the four-year period to 39,310.[26] Another step had been taken against slavery, but the fight was far from over. However, the Friends were soon to have a far more immediate problem that would have serious ramifications not just in their anti-slavery actions but also affect their entire society.

8. The American Colonization Society and the Schism

Now that the slave trade was illegal, those against slavery were looking into new ways to force the complete abolition of slavery. Elias Hicks was a Friend who was a member of the New York Yearly Meeting. He spoke out against slavery while on preaching tours of the South and in 1811, published an essay entitled Observations on the Slavery of the Africans.[1] The essay not only made a case against slavery, it also pushed an idea to fight it. Hicks wanted people to boycott any products made with slave labor. His reasoning was that if "we purchase the commodity, we participate in the crime. The slave dealer, the slaveholder, and the slave driver are virtually the agents of the consumer, and may be considered as employed and hired by him, to procure the commodity." He also believed that a boycott of merchandise made by slave labor would "have a particular effect on the slaveholders, by circumscribing their avarice, and prevent their heaping up riches, and living in a state of luxury and excess on the gain of oppression: and it might have the salutary effect of convincing them of the unrighteousness and cruelty of holding their fellow creatures in bondage." He thought that if "the people of the United States, and the inhabitants of Great Britain, withdraw from a commerce in, and the use of the produce of slavery, it would greatly lessen the price of those articles, and be a very great and immediate relief to the poor, injured, and oppressed slaves, whose blood is continually crying from the ground for justice."[2]

Others preferred a more direct approach to fight slavery. Thomas Garrett was born on August 21, 1789, and raised in a Quaker household on a farm near Upper Darby, Pennsylvania. His father taught him the trade of tool maker, but in 1814, he began his career as an abolitionist. He had returned home one day and discovered that an African American woman who worked for his father had been kidnapped. There were wagon tracks leading away from his home and Garrett noticed that one of the wheels left an unusual pattern. Garrett followed it from Upper Darby to the navy yard near Philadelphia. From there, he was able to track them to nearby Kensington through inquiries and was able to free the woman. The experience greatly affected Garrett and he eventually became one of the most important members of the Underground Railroad in Delaware.[3]

Another idea that abolitionists, Friend and non–Friend alike, were considering was the idea of removing those held in slavery from society altogether. The American Colonization Society was created in 1817 for the purpose of sending free people of color to Africa. The idea had its supporters and detractors from the very beginning, even between the races. There were some African Americans who liked the idea of emigrating to Africa, while others wanted to stay and fight against slavery in America. Some Caucasians supported the society due to the belief that African Americans would be happier in Africa than in America due to the racism they would have to deal with, while other Caucasians saw shipping people to Africa as a way of doing some ethnic cleansing. There were others that saw it as an opportunity to spread Christianity to Africa through those emigrating there.[4]

The use of a colony to remove former slaves had been considered years before. Thomas Jefferson had suggested it in 1773, and in 1811 he said that he felt "nothing is more to be wished than that the United States should themselves undertake to make such an establishment on the coast of Africa." Four years later, a petition was sent to Congress requesting that unsettled land in the West be put aside for "all those negroes and mulattoes who have been, and those who may hereafter be, emancipated within the United States; and that such donations, allowances, encouragements, and assistance be afforded them as may be necessary for carrying them thither and settling them therein."[5]

Someone who had doubts about the entire process was President James Madison. On June 1, 1814, he discussed colonization with Jesse Kersey, a Friend from Chester, Pennsylvania. He said that he "thought of the plan of removing the slaves to Africa as contemplated by Paul Cuffee; but many objections had occurred against it. He had also thought of their being colonized: but in this, difficulties also presented. In fact, difficulties would present in every plan that could be taken up." He said the only probable method that he could see "to remedy the evil,—would be for the different States of the Union to be willing to receive them; and thus they would spread among the industrious and practical farmers, and their habits, education and condition."[6]

The Paul Cuffee mentioned in the letter was a Massachusetts Quaker whose father was a slave and his mother a Native American. He owned his own ship and had a crew made up entirely of free men. Cuffee believed that his people would never be completely accepted in the United States and thought that living in Africa would be the best possible solution. Therefore, in 1811, he sailed to Sierra Leone to observe the conditions of the English colony there. He liked what he saw and went to Liverpool to speak to the colony's sponsors. They encouraged him to go out and find people who would be interested in relocating to the colony. In 1816, he took thirty-eight people from Boston to Sierra Leone, most of whom he carried for free. They were welcome in the colony. When Cuffee returned to America, he was swamped with requests from people who wished to go.[7] On December 5, 1816, Robert Finley wrote to Cuffee a few weeks before he organized the American Colonization Society. He asked Captain Cuffee for information on Sierra Leone and asked whether there were any other places in Africa that could be used for colonization. He also told Cuffee that "the great desire of those whose minds are impressed with this subject is to give an opportunity to the free people of color to rise to their proper level and at the same time to provide a powerful means of putting an end to the slave trade and sending civilization and Christianity to Africa." On January 8, 1817, Cuffee responded to the letter by recommending the Cape of Good Hope to Finley as a suitable place for a colony.[8] The letter was the last action Cuffee committed for colonization because he died later that year.[9]

Finley, a Presbyterian minister from New Jersey, believed that colonization was the best bet that former slaves had to be happy and thrive. He thought that everything

> including their color, is against them; nor is there much prospect that their state can ever be greatly ameliorated, while they shall continue among us. Could not the rich and benevolent devise means to form a colony on some part of the Coast of Africa, similar to the one at Sierra Leone, which might gradually induce many free blacks to go there and settle, devising for them the means to get there, and of protection and support till they were established? Ought not congress to be petitioned to grant them a district in a good climate, say on the shores of the Pacific Ocean? Our fathers brought them here, and we are bound if possible to repair the injuries inflicted by our fathers. Could they be sent to Africa, a three-fold benefit would arise. We should be cleared of them; we should send to Africa a population partially civilized and Christianized for its benefits; our blacks themselves would be put in better condition.

The idea had support in the South as well. Charles Mercer, a Virginia slaveholder, had his own reasons for supporting deportation to either Africa or the northwest section of America, called then the North Pacific. In 1817, he spoke in front of the American Colonization Society. He said that in his state, slaveholders were not permitted to manumit their slaves because it was believed that the slaves were unable to conduct themselves properly. They feared that freed slaves would "sally forth from their coverts, beneath the obscurity of night, and plunder the rich proprietors of the valleys. They infest the suburbs of the towns and cities, where they become the depositories of stolen goods, and, schooled by necessity, elude the vigilance of our defective police."

On December 21, 1816, a public meeting was held in Washington, D.C., to discuss the idea of African colonization. Among those present were Henry Clay, Francis Scott Key, the writer of the Star Spangled Banner, and Judge Bushrod Washington, George Washington's nephew. At the meeting, they passed resolutions to form a society to deport freed slaves to either Africa or somewhere else; to petition Congress to grant them land to create this colony; and to create rules and regulations for the society. On January 1, 1817, the American Colonization Society had its first annual meeting and Bushrod Washington was elected its first president. Membership was open to every citizen of the United States. The annual dues were one dollar, and a lifetime membership could be obtained for thirty dollars.

The problem with the American Colonization Society was that not everyone was on the same page as to why they supported African colonization. Some of the members sincerely felt that it was the best chance any freed slave had of happiness. Others wanted the freed slaves to disappear because they feared that the ex-slaves would cause slave revolts and an increase in crime. There were others who felt that it would help end slavery because slave owners would be more likely to free their slaves if they had a place to send them. They also felt that the former slaves would never be able to assimilate with Caucasians.[10] Even the Friends, who worked as hard as any group to fight the slave trade and end slavery, were as slow as other religions at incorporating freed slaves as members. The Philadelphia Yearly Meeting had agreed in 1796 to allow membership to anyone regardless of color. However, marriage between Quakers of different races was rare. Friends meeting houses also had an area called "Negro benches" where the freed slaves sat away from the other members.[11] The American Colonization Society was not the ultimate solution to the slavery question, but it was another attempt, at least on the part of some, to right a wrong.

The anti-slavery movement in Delaware continued to work on the Delaware legislature and made progress through their persistence. In 1786, a petition signed by 204 Quakers asked for the immediate emancipation of all Delaware slaves. It was rejected, but the next year, a bill did get through the legislature banning the export of slaves from Delaware to other states. This law also allowed property rights and the right to legal recourse to all freed slaves in Delaware. In 1793, the assembly had passed a law prohibiting the kidnapping of freed slaves with the intention of returning them to slavery. In 1816, another law was passed that stated that any captured runaway slaves had to be taken before a judge and put into jail. An announcement of the capture was then required to be placed in a Wilmington newspaper for six weeks and if no one claimed the slaves, they were set free. The law also declared that a fine of fifty dollars a day would be placed on anyone caught hiding or employing a runaway slave without the master's permission.[12] It was another attempt to placate the proslavery forces that only added another bandage to the gaping wound that was slavery.

The slavery issue was about to come back to the forefront of America's political attention with the admission of Missouri to the country. In 1819, some members of Congress wanted the slaves who were already there to be free and make Missouri a free state. The proslavery forces wanted Missouri to come in as a slave state. Others did not want the admission of Missouri to be tied to the slavery question. Maine also wanted to become a state during this time, and its acceptance into the Union was linked to the fate of Missouri.[13] The resulting arguments forced the United States again to compromise on the slavery issue. In March of 1820, the Missouri Compromise was created to solve, not only the problem of whether Missouri would come into the Union as a free or slave state, but also of keeping the Union together. The states that allowed slavery were afraid that if Missouri came into the Union as a free state, the balance of power in Congress would revert to the anti-slavery states. If this were to be the case, the proslavery states felt that they should leave the Union to protect their ability to continue slavery, which they felt they needed to support their economy. The compromise allowed Maine to come in as a free state and Missouri as a slave state, thus keeping the number of slave and free states equal. The compromise further stated that in the land bought in the Louisiana Purchase north of thirty-six degrees and thirty minutes latitude, "slavery and involuntary servitude, otherwise than in the punishment of crimes, whereof the parties shall have been duly convicted, shall be, and is hereby, forever prohibited." It also stated that if anyone "escaping into the same, from whom labour or service is lawfully claimed, in any state or territory of the United States, such fugitive may be lawfully reclaimed and conveyed to the person claiming his or her service."[14]

This compromise did not come easily. The fight before the compromise was so bitter that Elihu Embree, a Quaker abolitionist from Tennessee, declared: "Hell is about to enlarge her borders and tyranny her domain."[15] Another Quaker, Representative Thomas Forrest of Pennsylvania, spoke in Congress against allowing slaves into the Missouri Territory by saying that "the Constitution, so far as slavery may be inferred from it, is nothing but the creature of compromise" and that it was done "to prevent disunion; it was a dereliction of the first principles upon which the independence of our country was achieved; it was an acquiescence in the bondage of those of our fellow-men in whose services their possessors conceived they had a property." He found it distressing "to hear members of one side of the House, or those who are opposed to restriction, use such language against their fellow-members on the other side, as does not comport with their dignified standing on this floor." He finished his speech by admitting that he was a Quaker and thanking the members of Congress from Virginia and Kentucky for saying that Pennsylvania's standing in the Union was due "to the exemplary conduct of the people called Quakers. Would to God we were all Quakers; there would be less strife, more harmony and brotherly love among us; and if we were to follow their precepts and emulate their virtues, we should do as they do." His speech did not help; the compromise went through.[16] However, not everyone believed that the compromise would save the Union. Thomas Jefferson was also upset by the anger displayed during the debate and believed that its bitterness revealed a greater problem. He wrote in a letter to Congressman John Holmes on April 22, 1820, that to him, it was "like a firebell in the night" and that he believed that it was "the knell of the Union. It is hushed, indeed, for the moment. But this is a reprieve only, not a final sentence. A geographical line, coinciding with a marked principle, moral and political, once conceived and held up to the angry passions of men, will never be obliterated, and every new irritation will mark it deeper and deeper."[17]

Even though the laws of the country was still trying to protect slavery, there were people who were just as determined to fight against it. Daniel Gibbons was a Quaker born in December 1775 who lived near Lancaster, Pennsylvania. His father was a judge who was against slavery and used his position to help those who tried to achieve freedom. Once, a slaveholder brought a man before him and claimed that he was his slave. The slaveholder did not have any proof that the man was his slave and the elder Gibbons set the man free. The slaveholder tried to argue with the judge, but the judge told him that keeping quiet and behaving himself was the only way he was going to stay out of jail for contempt of court.

As Daniel Gibbons grew up, he too adopted the antislavery attitude of his father. His father lived in Wilmington, and Daniel spent his summers with relatives in Lancaster and the winters in Wilmington going to school. While he was an apprentice to a Friend in Lancaster County to learn the tanning business, Daniel injured himself so severely that he had difficulty walking for the rest of his life. This injury did not stop him from helping escapees.[18] Daniel and his wife Hannah helped hundreds of fugitives starting in 1813 from their farm near Bird-in-Hand in Lancaster County. They kept detailed records of their work until the Fugitive Slave Law came into effect in 1850. With the passage of the law, they destroyed their records in fear that they would be used against them in court.[19]

Daniel Bonsall, who had been raised by Gibbons, wrote a letter covering Gibbons' contribution to the antislavery cause in 1821. He mentioned that Gibbons was

> a friend to the colored people, and often hired them and paid them liberal wages. His house was a depot for fugitives, and many hundreds has he helped on their way to freedom. Many a dark night he has sent me to carry them victuals and change their places of refuge, and take them to other people's barns, when not safe for him to go. I have known him start in the night and go fifty miles with them, when they were very hotly pursued. One man and his wife lived with him for a long time. Afterwards the man lived with Thornton Walton. The man was hauling lumber from Columbia. He was taken from his team in Lancaster, and lodged in Baltimore jail. Daniel Gibbons went to Baltimore, visited the jail and tried hard to get him released, but failed. I would add here, that Daniel Gibbons' faithful wife, one of the best women I ever knew, was always ready, day or night, to do all she possibly could, to help the poor fugitives on their way to freedom.

Another man active in helping escapees was William Wright. He lived in Adams County, Pennsylvania, and came by his abolitionist opinions not only from his Quaker beliefs, but also from his uncle, Benjamin Wright, and his cousin, Samuel B. Wright, who were both members of the Pennsylvania Abolition Society. His uncle and cousin were involved, much like Isaac Hopper, in lawsuits helping to win freedom for those who had escaped from slavery.

In 1817, he married Phebe Wierman, who was Hannah Gibbons' sister. William and Phebe became involved in the Underground Railroad two years later. The very first person they helped was a man named Hamilton Moore. He had run away from the Baltimore area and his master came after him. Wright and Phebe's brother, Joel Wierman, were able to rescue Moore and send him to Canada.

In November 1828, Phebe went out to her back porch and saw a man who had no hat, coat, or shoes. The man asked if her husband was at home because he was looking for work. Wright was not at home, but Phebe realized that the man was an escapee and invited him in to wait for her husband. Wright soon returned home, and the man told him that he was from Hagerstown, Maryland. He had been taught the blacksmith trade and he was required to keep a record of all the work he did for the week. He did not know how to write, so he created a system of marks and symbols to keep track of how many horse shoes he put on or how many wagon wheels he fixed. One day, he looked into his master's record book and noticed that whenever the number five and the number one were added together, the total was six. He practiced this number until he could write it down and use it in his records. When his master saw the number, he asked him how he learned to write it and he told him. The master became angry and said: "I'll teach you how to be learning new figures." He then threw a horseshoe at him.[20]

The escapee, who later took the name of James W.C. Pennington, finally became convinced to flee because of an incident at the home of his master in Maryland. The master was carefully watching the movements of his family with the aid of another slave. His mother became angry at the slave and told him he ought to be ashamed of himself. The master heard of this and warned her that if she ever spoke to his "confidential servant" again, he would whip her. Pennington knew the temperament of both his mother and his master and realized that a confrontation was coming. He thought about it for four days and decided to escape.

He struggled with the decision to escape because of

> the two great difficulties that stood in the way of my flight: I had a father and mother whom I dearly loved, I had also six sisters and four brothers on the plantation. The question was, shall I hide my purpose from them? Moreover, how will my flight affect them when I am gone? Will they not be suspected? Will not the whole family be sold off as a disaffected family, as is generally the case when one of its members flies? But a still more trying question was, how can I expect to succeed, I have no knowledge of distance or direction—I know that Pennsylvania is a free state, but I know not where its soil begins, or where that of Maryland ends? Indeed, at this time there was no safety in Pennsylvania, New Jersey, or New York, for a fugitive, except in lurking places, or under the care of judicious friends, who could be entrusted not only with liberty, but also with life itself.

Pennington decided not to tell his family and left on a Sunday, the only day of the week that a slave was allowed to rest. The only food he took was a piece of bread. He wanted to go to Pennsylvania, but the only guide he had was the North Star. After three days, his only sustenance the bread, a few apples, and some water, Pennington came upon a toll gate. The only occupant was a twelve-year-old boy. He asked the boy how to get to Philadelphia and was pointed in the right direction. A mile later, he came upon a young man driving a wagon filled with hay. The man asked him if he was a free man and Pennington said yes. The man surmised that Pennington was not a free man and advised him to stay off the main roads because slave catchers were in the area. He then advised Pennington to go to an old man who would help him on his way. The next day, Pennington happened upon an old woman who directed him to William Wright's home. When he was invited to come in and have something to eat and get warm, Pennington felt that the invitation, given "with such an air of simple sincerity and fatherly kindness, made an overwhelming impression upon my mind. They made me feel, spite of all my fear and timidity, that I had, in the providence of God, found a friend and a home."

Wright hired him to cut wood and he also taught Pennington how to read and write. Pennington stayed with the Wrights for six months, but left because he feared that his former master might be looking for him. He left Wright's house to go to Daniel Gibbons and from there to Chester County, Pennsylvania, where he stayed with another Quaker family for seven months. While there, he continued to read and educate himself, but he wanted to continue his formal education. He went to New York, where he became a born-again Christian. His next stop was New Haven, Connecticut, where he worked as a janitor at Yale University while he studied there. He then went to Heidelberg, Germany, where he became a doctor of divinity. He never forgot the kindnesses that William and Phebe Wright showed him, so when he came back to America, he visited them and gave each of them a present. He moved to Florida and preached and opened schools for freed African Americans. He died in 1870.[21]

The American Colonization Society had not given up on their idea to colonize Africa. In 1827, they went to Congress to ask for support in their efforts. They were having a difficult time raising enough money to send people to their colony in Liberia and support them once they arrived. Even though the society had been very careful to not show any preference on the slavery issue, the proslavery forces in Congress went on the attack and denied the society any support.[22]

The Colonization Society was not the only society to have troubles in 1827. Elias Hicks not only spoke out against slavery but also other things within the Friends that he thought were wrong. He believed that some of the wealthier members were getting too close to what he called "the world" and feared that the Friends were becoming just another Protestant religion. Friends were interacting with other religions in their business dealings and he thought that this closeness with other religions was infesting the Friends with un–Friend-like ideas. He could see that Friends were not dressing as plainly as they did previously and were developing closer relationships with ministers from other religions. He also had a different way of dealing with the Bible and his belief in Christ than other Friends. He believed that Jesus became the Christ because he was the only person to live totally in the inner light that is in everyone and that he was what everyone else tried to attain. However, he also believed in the virgin birth. Hicks also said that he loved reading the Bible, but its greatest value was as a guide to the inner light.

Some Friends thought Hicks' beliefs were strongly based in traditional Quaker beliefs, but others were outraged. The battle within the Friends between the years 1819 and 1827 led to what was called the "great separation." It began in the Philadelphia Yearly Meeting, the center of the American Quaker movement. This clash also brought to light other problems with the Friends organization. The opponents of Hicks, who were called the Orthodox Friends, were the more financially successful Friends and lived in the cities. On the other hand, the Hicksites, as those Friends that supported Hicks came to be called, lived in the rural areas and were not as swept up in the Industrial Revolution that was growing in America.

The Orthodox Friends put forth their beliefs on Jesus to counter what the Hicksites were promoting. As far as they were concerned, Jesus was the Christ at birth and redeemed humanity by his death on the Cross. This made salvation available to all people. However, they did agree with Hicks that the Bible should not be put ahead of the inner light.

These disagreements, along with the personal animosity between Hicks and two Philadelphia elders, Jonathan Evans and Samuel Beetle, who took the Orthodox approach, finally came to a boiling point in April 1827. Hicks' supporters were frustrated by the lack of what they considered fair treatment by the Orthodox leadership of the Philadelphia Yearly Meeting. They decided to turn their backs on the meeting and set up their own meeting. Approximately two-thirds of the meeting followed the Hicksites, which not only affected the Philadelphia Meeting, but also Friends across the country, since Philadelphia was considered the focal point of the entire Friends movement in America. There were now two Philadelphia Yearly Meetings, and the rest of the society had to choose sides. The London Yearly Meeting sided with the Orthodox Meeting. The American Meetings were not so clear cut in their support. Virginia, North Carolina, and the vast majority of New England went with the Orthodox, but New York and Baltimore went almost completely with the Hicksites. The Ohio Yearly Meeting was split in half, and twenty percent of the Indiana Yearly Meeting went with the Hicksites.

Pacifist attitudes went out the window and name-calling soon followed. The Orthodox opinion of the Hicksites was, in the eyes of one Orthodox minister, that the movement was "the great leviathan, the monster of human reason and human wisdom, who is endeavouring to lay waste the atoning blood of Jesus Christ." A Hicksite reporter in Philadelphia wrote that, to him, it was plain that it was "the natural tendency of orthodoxy to subvert every important principle of Quakerism."[23]

The split continued for many years, but the Quakers slowly drifted back together, officially ending the schism in 1955. However, much damage had been done, and it made the practice of speaking out against the social ills of their times that much harder for them. It did not stop them, but a new generation of non–Quaker abolitionists came into their own during this time of upheaval. These abolitionists felt that the persistent but respectful approach to fighting slavery that those like the Quakers used was not enough to end slavery. They, unlike the Friends, had no compulsions toward using a blunt-force attack. Many Quaker leaders turned away from that attitude and discouraged other Friends from being involved. They even went so far as to admonish and even disown members whom they thought were too involved in the movement. The fight against slavery continued, but until the end of the Civil War, the Quakers involved in the anti-slavery movement were individuals and not the entire Quaker community.[24]

9. Other Avenues Explored

In the 1820s, the American Colonization Society had hopes of transplanting former slaves to Africa. By 1830, the reality was not as hopeful. Even though the society had famous members such as Henry Clay, James Madison, John Marshall, and Benjamin Lundy, the society was only able to transplant 1,421 people to Liberia.[1] They had been able in the past to receive support from those who believed that colonization was a way to ensure emancipation, as well as the proslavery forces who thought that it was a good thing to send the freed slaves to Africa so they would not influence those in slavery. It was only a matter of time until these polar opposite opinions would clash and members would leave. The drop in membership placed the society in serious financial trouble. In an effort to save themselves, the society sent a Philadelphia Quaker, Elliot Cresson, to Great Britain in an attempt to raise funds to continue their mission.

At first, Cresson had success in Britain. He pushed the anti-slavery focus of the society, as well as the "civilizationist principle." This idea, which English anti-slavery supporters used in the West Indies and Africa, was summed up in a flyer that Cresson distributed. The flyer stated that the

> great objects of the society were the final and entire abolition of slavery providing for the best interest of the blacks, by establishing them in independence upon the coast of Africa, thus constituting them the protectors of the unfortunate natives against the inhuman ravages of the slaver seeking, through them, to spread the lights of civilization and Christianity among fifty millions who inhabited the dark regions.

Anticolonization supporters began attacking Cresson and the entire idea of colonization. Captain Charles Stuart of England wrote pamphlets that attacked the society and challenged Cresson to public debates. Stuart ridiculed the idea that there could be no emancipation without emigration and that the African population could not be removed from America "without the pretence of a crime against them, to a foreign and barbarous land" and that the idea was an act of "criminal absurdity." Stuart also could not believe that anyone who supported the anti-slavery movement would want to be a part of any movement that substituted "banishment for slavery."

Cresson spent two and a half years in England fighting a losing battle against the abolitionists who rejected the idea of colonization. He was able to raise two thousand pounds and enough support in Scotland to establish a settlement in Liberia called Edina. It was named for Edinburgh, the city that had supported his efforts. However, a former supporter of colonization, William Lloyd Garrison, had arrived in England in the summer of 1833[2] and showed the aggressiveness that horrified the Quakers by attacking Cresson and the Colonization Society. In a letter dated June 4, 1833, he began by writing:

> Sir—
> I affirm that the American Colonization Society, of which you are an Agent, is utterly corrupt and proscriptive in its principles; that its tendency is to embarrass the freedom and diminish the happiness of the colored population of the United States; and consequently, that you are abusing the confidence and generosity of the philanthropists of Great Britain. As an American citizen, and the accredited Agent for the New-England Anti-Slavery Society, I invite you to meet me in public debate.

Cresson never met Garrison for a duel of words, but the attacks from Garrison and others who did not support colonization finally drove Cresson to go home.[3]

William Lloyd Garrison, who later became the editor of the Boston anti-slavery newspaper the *Liberator*, first became interested in abolitionism in 1829 when he met Benjamin Lundy, a Quaker who edited a Baltimore newspaper called the *Genius of Universal Emancipation*. Garrison had moved to Baltimore in order to work with him. At that time, Lundy was pushing for gradual emancipation and voluntary colonization to get rid of American slavery. However, they discovered that the free community in Baltimore completely rejected the idea of colonization. By 1831, Garrison had rejected the idea of colonization, and so did Lundy a few years later.[4]

The American Colonization Society was not the only passive attempt to defeat slavery during this time period. The Free Produce Society was based on the idea of stopping slavery by not buying items made with slave labor. In 1826, Lundy opened a free produce store in Baltimore, featuring items that were not made by the slave system. Soon afterward, a Free Labor Society was started in Delaware.[5] On January 8, 1827, the Free Produce Society of Pennsylvania was established. William Rawle, a non–Friend, was its president and Quakers including Isaac Hopper, James Mott, and Thomas Shipley were involved. On that date, they put together a constitution for the society that stated:

> Whereas there are many persons who, while they deplore the existence of Slavery, indirectly contribute to its support and continuance by using articles derived from the labor of Slaves:—And whereas we are satisfied that, by a proper union of reasonable efforts, articles similar to those which are thus produced, may be obtained by free labor:—And believing that the general use of such articles among us as are raised by Freeman, will gradually establish a conviction on the minds of those who hold their fellow creatures in bondage, that their own interests would be promoted by the increased quantity, and more ready sale, of their produce, resulting from the change of the condition of their Slaves into that of hired Freeman.[6]

The men involved in this enterprise were also active in the Pennsylvania Abolition Society that had earlier disbanded.[7] In 1838, supporters from northern states met in Philadelphia as the American Free Produce Association. They wanted to start production and distribution networks completely divorced from slavery. The association started outlets in Pennsylvania, New York, New England, Ohio, and Indiana.[8] George W. Taylor, another Friend involved in the Free Produce Society, rented a store on the northeast corner of 5th and Cherry Streets in Philadelphia that would stock only goods not made by slave labor. The Free Produce Society wanted to send their free labor cotton away to be processed, but Taylor thought that it was best to have a mill nearby. Therefore, they raised money to place machinery in a water-powered mill located at Doc Run, Chester County, Pennsylvania.[9]

The Free Produce organization promoted Taylor's store with pamphlets and journals, such as the *Non-Slaveholder*, which was published in Philadelphia between 1846 and 1854. The idea was promoted as a nonviolent and legal way to fight slavery. Female abolitionists such as Lucretia Mott urged women to turn away from slave made products and to frequent free produce stores. A Colored Free Produce Society of Philadelphia was established in 1830 and a female counterpart was founded in 1831. African Americans started free stores, such as Lydia White's, which opened in 1830 and continued until 1846. William Whipper started his store in Philadelphia in 1834.[10]

At the same time, the organizers of the Pennsylvania Free Produce Society recruited a Quaker schoolteacher from Wilmington, Delaware, to edit an antislavery newspaper. Enoch Lewis was a good choice to be a part of the paper, called the *African Observer*. He once brought an escaped slave into his mathematics class to discuss his experiences as a slave. In 1803, he tried to rescue a runaway slave from slave catchers. The slave catchers would only release the man if someone would buy him for $400. Lewis agreed to do it and immediately went from the home of one Friend after another, trying to raise the money. He was able to collect $100 and put up the other $300 himself. Lewis' yearly salary at the time was $500.[11]

The problem with the movement was that it was not very profitable. The goods sold at the stores were more expensive than the same items sold at other stores. The quality of the goods was poor and the stores barely broke even.[12] Henry Drinker had tried to turn maple sugar into a substitute for sugar in the 1790s because the latter was grown with slave labor and he ended up losing a fortune. Two other Quaker families tried to grow their own cotton and produced enough to create four or five shirts. The cotton plants died off the following autumn.[13] The movement was also not very popular. By the late 1840s, William Lloyd Garrison, a major force in the anti-slavery movement, was mocking the idea by saying that it was either a distraction from real work or it was nothing more than a salve to the consciences of selfish northerners at the expense of slaves who did not benefit from the effort. The change that Garrison and other abolitionists wanted did not come fast enough, in their opinion, with these types of tactics, and their lack of support killed the American Free Produce Association in 1847.[14]

Abolitionists were not the only ones who thought that the end of slavery was not coming quickly enough. At the end of August 1831, an African American preacher named Nat Turner led a revolt of slaves in Southampton County, Virginia. It was one of the two hundred slave rebellions that occurred between 1776 and 1860. This uprising struck terror in the hearts of slave owners through the South. Turner and his followers went from farm to farm, killing and gathering reinforcements as they went, their number growing to eighty slaves. By the time that the state militia had put down the rebellion, which became known as the "Southampton Tragedy," seventy Caucasians were killed and over one hundred African lives were claimed when soldiers and vigilantes committed reprisals. Turner was captured in Jerusalem, the county seat of Southampton County, and was hanged on November 11, 1831.

In response to the uprising, Virginia's governor, John Floyd, kept information sent to him about anyone who worked for emancipation. Someone from Philadelphia once wrote to Floyd with a warning that "much mischief is hatching here."

The mischief the unknown letter writer was referring to may have been when the leading abolitionists in the country met in Philadelphia on December 4, 1833 to discuss the possibility of a national organization for the anti-slavery movement. The former capital of the nation was a fitting place to hold such a meeting. According to the 1830 census, almost ten percent of the population in Philadelphia was people of color. They were a thriving community who held many craft jobs, such as shoemaking, carpentry and cabinetry, and were involved in the food and service trades such as bakeries, oyster shops, dressmaking, and barbering. Their leaders were James Forten, a sailmaker, Robert Bogle, a caterer, Robert Douglass, a barber, Joseph Cassey and James McCrumnell, grocers, and Cyrus Bustill, a baker. They, like the people in Baltimore, were not in favor of colonization. Forten once said that since four generations of his family had lived in Philadelphia, he had no desire to relocate to Africa.[15] His great-grandfather came to America as a slave, his grandfather bought his own freedom, his father became a sailmaker who died when Forten was young, and he himself went to Anthony Benezet's school.[16]

There were problems that needed to be dealt with before the convention began. The abolitionists could not find a church or hall to meet in because the police announced that due to the emotions tied to their cause, they could not guarantee their safety after dark.[17] A committee of delegates attempted to calm the community down by trying to convince two well respected members of the Philadelphia Friends to be the chairmen of the convention. Both men refused, so the committee turned to Beriah Green, a Presbyterian minister, to become the chairman. There was also a problem about where the delegates were going to stay during the convention.[18] The problems of where the delegates would meet and where would they stay were solved when the African community took the delegates in, boarding most of them in their homes, and the Adelphi, an African society, loaned them the use of their meeting hall.[19] Even with this support, there was still a great deal of tension in Philadelphia. Blunt proof of the anger occurred during the convention. A young man arrived at the door of the building and declared that if he had the chance, he would dip his hand in William Garrison's blood.[20]

The convention was held openly and had many spectators. There were American Colonization Society members, southern medical students, and women in the audience. One of them was Lucretia Coffin Mott, a Quaker lay minister whose husband James was one of the delegates. The sixty-three delegates were from ten states and were dedicated to the idea of "immediate emancipation without expatriation." They also shared a common belief that slavery was a sin and that ideas had to be put forth to create a change. Otherwise, economic considerations would always get in the way of ending slavery.[21]

Lucretia Coffin was born on January 3, 1793, on Nantucket Island, Massachusetts. She was raised to believe that a woman was just as capable as a man. The proof of her parents' beliefs was when her mother ran her father's mercantile business while he was away on a long voyage. This experience convinced her that "the exercise of women's talents in this line, as well as the general care which devolved upon them in the absence of their husbands, tended to develop their intellectual powers, and strengthened them mentally and physically."[22] Her family moved to Philadelphia in 1809, and two years later she married James Mott. It was the "ministry of Elias Hicks and others, on the subject of the unrequited labor of slaves, and their example of refusing the products of slave labor" that interested her in the fight against slavery. She felt the need to

> plead their cause, in season and out of season, to endeavor to put my soul in their souls' stead, and to aid, all in my power, in every right effort for their immediate emancipation. This duty was impressed upon me at the time I consecrated myself to that gospel which anoints "to preach deliverance to the captive," "to set at liberty them that are bruised." From that time the duty of abstinence as far as possi-

The American Anti-Slavery Society was formed in 1833, but the Pennsylvania branch began in 1837. This picture, taken in 1851, shows the Executive Committee as a mixture of Quakers and non–Quakers as well as men and women, which was not a common occurrence in the 19th century. Standing (left to right): Mary Grew, Edward M. Davis, Haworth Wetherald, Abby Kimber, J. Miller McKim, Sarah Pugh. Seated (left to right): Oliver Johnson, Margaret Jones Burleigh, Benjamin C. Bacon, Robert Purvis, Lucretia Mott, and James Mott (Swarthmore College, Friends Historical Library).

ble from slave-grown products was so clear, that I resolved to make the effort "to provide things honest" in this respect.

It was these beliefs that brought her and her husband to the convention.[23]

The delegates created a document stating their principles and linking themselves to the American revolutionary spirit. The new American Anti-Slavery Society dedicated itself to organizing abolition groups across the country. These groups would then sponsor people to pass out information and to "remove slavery by moral and political action." When the draft of their declaration was read to the convention, one of the Quakers used the Friends doctrine that "first impressions are from Heaven" and proposed that the document be immediately adopted. The charter was fine-tuned, and Lucretia Mott stood up in the gallery and recommended that the pledge of faith in the document would have more power if the phrases that declared that they planted themselves firmly on "Divine Truth as the Everlasting Rock" and the Declaration of Independence be transposed. The change was accepted, and Mott noticed that one of the members turned around "to see what woman was there who knew what the word 'transpose' meant."

Garrison became friends with Mott and admired her for being "a bold and fearless thinker." Her husband James was a textile merchant who condemned the cotton industry as immoral. One of Lucretia Mott's mottos was "Truth for authority, not authority for truth." She also quoted II Corinthians 3:6 to Garrison, saying that a minister should be "not of the letter, but of the spirit: for the letter killeth but the spirit giveth life." The Motts dealt with the tension in the Society of Friends for ten years before the society broke off into Orthodox and Hicksite groups. The Motts went with the group formed by Elias Hicks, who was more mystical and radical than the more conservative Friends who went toward a more traditional Calvinism.[24]

Southern opponents of slavery came north to be heard at the convention, in spite of the fact that there was a great deal of suppression of abolitionist actions in the North. The most dedicated anti-slavery operatives who came from the South were Angelina and Sarah Grimké.[25] Sarah Moore Grimké was born on November 26, 1792, and Angelina Emily Grimké was born on February 20, 1805. Sarah was named as her godmother. The Grimké sisters were daughters of a prominent slaveholding family in South Carolina. Their father, John Faucheraud Grimké, was a legislator and judge who believed in people's right to think for themselves. He did not give Sarah and Angelina much in the way of a formal education, but he did allow them access to his library. He prepared his sons for a career in the law by holding debates and he allowed Sarah to participate. Their mother, Mary Smith Grimké, was a loving and affectionate woman who loved to read, usually works of a theological nature. She also allowed her daughters to find their own path. One brother, Thomas Smith Grimké, became a lawyer and a state senator, and helped to organize the American Peace Society and the Colonization Society of South Carolina.

In 1819, Sarah accompanied her father to Philadelphia as he was going there for medical reasons. However, Judge Grimké died on August 8. There was another life-altering event that occurred during this time. As she was returning to South Carolina after her father's death, Sarah met Israel Morris and his wife, a Quaker couple. They became friendly with one another and the Morrises gave her a copy of John Woolman's memoirs. Apparently, it had a great effect on her, because Sarah converted to Quakerism the next year. In 1821, she left Charleston to live in Philadelphia, accompanied by her widowed sister Anna. On May 29, 1823, Sarah was accepted into the Fourth and Arch Street Meeting of the Philadelphia Society of Friends.

In the spring of 1828, Angelina began to go to Friends meetings. The previous October, Sarah had come to Charleston to visit her and decided to convert her to Quakerism. From July to November 1828, Angelina visited Philadelphia. When she returned to Charleston, she was firmly committed to Quakerism and the belief that slavery was wrong. On April 28, 1831, Angelina was also accepted into the Fourth and Arch Street Meeting.[26]

The Friends leaders may have felt that the abolitionist movement was too aggressive, but Sarah Grimké did not feel that way. In 1830, she gave a testimony on why she was against slavery and why she had to speak out about it. She talked about how she had left South Carolina

> to escape the sound of the lash and the shrieks of tortured victims, I would gladly bury in oblivion the recollection of those scenes with which I have been familiar; but this may not, cannot be; they come over my memory like gory specters, and implore me with resistless power, in the name of a God of mercy, in the name of a crucified Savior, in the name of humanity; for the sake of the slaveholder, as well as the slave, to bear witness to the horrors of the southern prison house. I feel impelled by a sacred sense of duty, by my obligations to my country, by sympathy for the bleeding victims of tyranny and lust, to give my testimony respecting the system of American slavery—to detail a few facts, most of which came under my personal observation.

She described in detail the beatings of those who tried to escape slavery, the neglect of older slaves, and in one incident, traveling in South Carolina and seeing "a human head stuck up on a high pole. On inquiry, I found that a runaway slave, who was outlawed, had been shot there, his head severed from his body, and put upon the public highway, as a terror to deter slaves from running away." Seeing these things and hearing of more acts of barbarism made her determined to speak out against slavery, even if the Friends hierarchy feared the consequences.[27]

Another delegate came at the invitation of Garrison. In late November 1833, William Lloyd Garrison went to visit John Greenleaf Whittier, a New Jersey Friend and one of the best known poets of the time. Garrison informed him that he had been chosen to be a delegate to a convention scheduled to be held in Philadelphia in December to form the American Anti-Slavery Society. Garrison had been the one to first convince Whittier to speak out against slavery. Whittier was a shy man and had no desire to travel. The only reason he became well known as a poet was that his sister had sent his work out to be published without his knowledge. Before he became an abolitionist, he thought that becoming one meant that he would have to give up his careers as a newspaper editor, an up-and-coming politician, and a poet.

Whittier later wrote about when he first looked at the sixty-two delegates assembled at the Adelphi Building on 5th Street, below Walnut Street, and saw that they were:

> mainly composed of comparatively few young men, some in middle age, and a few beyond that period. They were nearly all plainly dressed, with a view to comfort rather than elegance. Many of the faces turned toward me wore a look of expectancy and suppressed enthusiasm; all had the earnestness which might be expected of men engaged in an enterprise beset with difficulty and perhaps with peril.[28]

Whittier also noted that with only a few exceptions, the convention

> was composed of men without influence or position, poor and little known, strong only in their convictions and faith in the justice of their cause. To onlookers our endeavor to undo the evil work of two centuries and convert a nation to the "great renunciation" involved in emancipation must have seemed absurd in the last degree. Our voices in such an atmosphere found no echo. We could look for no response but laughs of derision or the missiles of a mob.
>
> But we felt that we had the strength of truth on our side; we were right, and all the world about us was wrong. We had faith, hope, and enthusiasm, and did our work, nothing doubting, amidst a generation who first despised and then feared and hated us.[29]

The sixty-two delegates to the convention were made up of, among others, three of African descent, several Unitarians, a dozen evangelical ministers, and twenty-one Friends.[30] One of those was Isaac Hopper, who was considered for thirty years to be a "protector of the free colored people of Philadelphia, and whose name was whispered reverently in the slave cabins of Maryland as the friend of the black man."[31]

Whittier wrote years later about the convention. He remembered the early gray morning when, with Samuel J. May, our colleague on the committee to prepare a Declaration of Sentiments for the convention, I climbed to the small "upper chamber" of a colored friend to hear [William Garrison] read the first draft of a paper which will live as long as our national history.

He also wrote about when he saw "the members of the convention, solemnized by the responsibility, rise one by one, and solemnly affix their names to that stern pledge of fidelity to freedom."[32]

The declaration of sentiments that came from the convention tied their struggle against slavery with the struggle for freedom of the Founding Fathers. It stated that the way the Founding Fathers fought was with "physical resistance—the marshalling in arms—the hostile array—the mortal encounter. Ours shall be such only as the opposition of moral purity to moral corruption—the destruction of error by the potency of truth—the overthrow of prejudice by the power of love—and the abolition of slavery by the spirit of repentance."

They also believed that the free states had an obligation to rid the country of slavery and that they

> are now living under a pledge of their tremendous physical force, to fasten the galling fetters of tyranny upon the limbs of millions in the Southern States; they are liable to be called at any moment to suppress a general insurrection of the slaves; they authorize the slave owner to vote for three-fifths of his slaves as property, and thus enable him to perpetuate his oppression; they support a standing army at the south for its protection and they seize the slave, who has escaped into their territories, and send him back to be tortured by an enraged master or a brutal driver. This relation to slavery is criminal, and full of danger: IT MUST BE BROKEN UP.

They vowed to organize branches of their society, if they could, "in every city, town and village in our land." They declared to "send forth agents to lift up the voice of remonstrance, of warning, of entreaty, and of rebuke," as well as to "circulate, unsparingly and extensively, anti-slavery tracts and periodicals." They wanted to "encourage the labor of freemen rather than that of slaves, by giving a preference to their productions." They summed up their position by stating that they would do everything they could to overthrow "the most execrable system of slavery that has ever been witnessed upon earth" and to "secure to the colored population of the United States, all the rights and privileges which belong to them as men, and as Americans—come what may to our persons, our interests, or our reputation—whether we live to witness the triumph of Liberty, Justice and Humanity, or perish untimely as martyrs in this great, benevolent, and holy cause."[33]

Four women were in attendance during the creation of the Anti-Slavery Society. Lucretia Mott, Lydia Maria Child, who later wrote a book about Isaac

Hopper, and the Grimké sisters were not delegates, but were sitting in the balcony. Lucretia Mott was the only one of the four to be invited by the delegates to speak, but they all voted on a resolution at the end of the convention that thanked the women for the strong interest they showed in the emancipation of the slaves.[34]

The Friends did not like to take a public stand against slavery and did not want their members to get involved in anti-slavery associations with non–Friends. They did not have a problem with someone like Lucretia Mott talking in public because among the Friends it was acceptable for women to do so and they allowed them to hold positions of power within their church. Women did, however, have separate meetings and female preachers, and even though they may not have been the major breadwinners of their families, they were skilled fundraisers for their clergy and charitable causes.[35] This type of very public display against slavery would cause Quaker abolitionists like the Motts problems in the future.

The convention had done its job of joining together the foremost abolitionists of the time. It also brought together many people who would eventually become members of a society that would take a more hands-on approach to helping others gain their freedom.

PART III
THE UNDERGROUND RAILROAD

10. Standing Against the Tide

The town of Salem, New Jersey, was a popular place for those who wanted to escape slavery. Many anti-slavery sympathizers lived in the area, there were very few slaves in residence, and there was a greater African American population in proportion to the whole population than in other counties in New Jersey. It was said that when slave catchers came to Salem County to chase escapees, they considered themselves lucky to escape with their lives.[1] Not everybody believed this story, to their regret.

Shortly after daybreak in late December 1835, citizens of Salem were awakened to the sounds of wagon wheels and horses' hooves mixed with the screams of men. Some people who were freshly awakened shouted out: "Fire! Murder! Help!" The real reason for the sounds had nothing to do with fire or murder. The cause was eight men who were naked, chained together in the back of a wagon, and screaming for help. They had been kidnapped and the man responsible was lashing at his horses furiously, desperate to leave town before he was discovered. He did not succeed, thanks to a line of Salem citizens wrapped in blankets, joined by their fully dressed Quaker neighbors, all blocking the street. They had heard the cries for help and came up with the quickest possible solution to stop the kidnappings. The man driving the wagon had no choice but to come to an immediate halt.

The wagon driver and the eight captives were taken out of the wagon and led to the nearby Sherron Hotel to wait for Magistrate Bush to arrive and to sort out what had happened. Bush arrived, and after a short period of time, found the driver, a Mr. Dannenhower, who was a Philadelphia agent for a North Carolina slave owner, guilty of disorderly conduct and breach of the peace. However, before the judgment was passed, someone freed the captives and they went running down the street.

Not only was someone careless about the captives, but they were also careless with the prisoner. During the hearing, Dannenhower pulled out a gun and ran for Bush. Someone grabbed his arm, but the slave hunter pulled out a knife and tried to stab Sheriff English, who had rushed in to intervene. Another man, Joseph Hancock, grabbed a chair and tried to hit Dannenhower, crying out, "Kill the ——; kill him!" What happened after that was not clear. Dannenhower said that he was knocked down, thrown out of the hotel, and robbed. Three witnesses, Joseph Kille, Samuel Clement, and W.G. Beasley, testified that if Dannenhower had been subdued, it was done lightly, and that his pocketbook was taken but returned to him at the jail.

A few hours later, the captives had been rounded up and placed in the jail for their safety. Dannenhower was also being held there until a plan of action could be formulated. The final outcome was that Dannenhower was returned to Philadelphia, where the newspapers made a great deal about his treatment. The men Dannenhower tried to kidnap were set free and were not bothered by Dannenhower again.[2]

Another man who fought to keep those who were free in that condition was Thomas Shipley. He was a Quaker who joined the Pennsylvania Society for the Promoting of the Abolition of Slavery in 1817 when he was twenty. He was also a part of the Anti-slavery Convention in Philadelphia in 1833. Shipley was a strong advocate for the education of African Americans and was long considered their protector and friend. He would leave his business at a moment's notice to help those in their time of need and go to court with them to fight for their rights. All of his arguments were strictly based on the letter of the law, but he also was a sharp questioner in court. If there was the slightest discrepancy in the testimony against whomever he was defending, he would attack that point until the person he was trying to help was freed. This determination to help the African American community was desperately needed in 1835 when he faced his greatest challenge, during the riots in Philadelphia.

Several hundred men marched through the lower part of the city, creating a path of destruction in their wake. They attacked the homes of African Americans and either destroyed or stole what was inside of them. Any person of color they found was attacked as well. The age of the victims did not matter, only the color of their skin. Law enforcement did not rush to their defense, and those who did not support the mob dared not stand in their way for fear that the violence would be turned on them.

Shipley could not stand by and watch the suffering of those he had worked so hard to help. He decided to put on a disguise so that he could mingle among the mob, find out what they were planning to do, and then contact the proper authorities to let them know who the ringleaders were. He went to where the rioters were located and noticed that all they needed to incite them to further violence and destruction was resistance from their intended victims. The rioters had not received any strong resistance at that point, but that was about to change.

A group of African American men had given up on the idea that the police or anyone else was going to come to their aid. At that point, they decided to go to Benezet Hall on South Seventh Street and make their stand. They had a supply of guns and ammunition and were willing to fight to protect their families and homes. The leaders of the rioters heard about it and decided to lead their people to the hall for an attack. Shipley was with them at the time and gathered together information on their leaders and their plans. Determined to stop the violence, Shipley left the mob and ran for the hall. The men were preparing to come out and face their attackers when Shipley arrived. He begged them not to fight fire with fire. Shipley asked them to leave the hall and, when they recognized his voice, they listened to him and left before the mob could arrive. The authorities in the form of the mayor of Philadelphia and his men finally arrived at the hall right after they left. They subdued the mob and, with Shipley's information, were able to arrest the ringleaders.

In December of 1835, Shipley was involved in the trial of Alexander Helmsley, who was in danger of losing his freedom, as were his wife Nancy and their three children. They were arrested in Mount Holly and charged with being runaway slaves. Alexander was claimed by the executor of an estate in Queen Anne's County, Maryland, and his wife and children were being claimed by the family of Richard D. Cooper, also of Queen Anne's County. Shipley felt that the first order of business was to prove that Nancy and the children were actually free. The papers needed to set them free were in Dover, Delaware, so Shipley traveled the ninety-five miles from Mount Holly to Dover to retrieve them without telling the other side what he was doing. He feared that if the opposition knew, they would try to take advantage of his absence. The morning after he left, his whereabouts were questioned. His absence was suspicious because it was unlike him to leave in the middle of a trial. Alexander's lawyers tried to buy some time by going through the witnesses very slowly. The stalling techniques were enough to make the difference. Even though he became ill during his travels, Shipley returned in time and produced paperwork in court to prove that Nancy and the children had been manumitted.

However, Alexander was still in need of help. He needed the signature of the chief justice of New Jersey to move the trial to the Supreme Court of New Jersey so there would be a better chance of a fair trial. The problem was that the judge lived in Newark, which was eighty miles away. Shipley decided to travel there to obtain the paperwork, but he needed a fast way to get to the judge. Fortunately, a friend of Shipley's was heading to Newark in his own vehicle and he offered Shipley a ride. They left in the afternoon, traveled all night, and arrived at daybreak. Shipley went straight to the judge's house and got him out of bed. He apologized for arriving at an early hour, but he explained the situation to Chief Justice Hornblower and said that time was of the essence. The judge was sympathetic and gave Shipley the signature he needed. Shipley then immediately headed back to Mount Holly.

The next day, supporters of Alexander filled the courtroom, including people who knew him as a hardworking and honest man. The judge was ready to pass judgment in favor of the slaveholders when the sheriff entered the courtroom with the paperwork obtained by Shipley. The shocked judge had no choice but to send the case to the Supreme Court for its next session in March.

In the months before the new trial, Shipley was able to collect facts and obtain the services of Theodore Frelinghuysen, a gifted lawyer and fighter for the oppressed. Frelinghuysen presented his case and Chief Justice Hornblower gave his ruling, which was that Alexander was a free man.

Shipley received several threats against himself and his property because of his anti-slavery actions, but he continued his efforts until he contracted a fever and died on September 17, 1836. Many African Americans came to the funeral to pay their respects, even bringing their children to show them the man who "devoted his energies to the disenthralment of their race, and whose memory they should ever cherish with gratitude and reverence." Thousands collected near the Shipley home as his body was taken to the Arch Street Friends cemetery. When the body arrived at the cemetery,

> six colored men carried the body to its last resting-place, and the silent tear of the son of Africa over the grave of his zealous friend, was more expressive of real affection than all the parade which is sometimes brought so ostentatiously before the public eye. In the expressive words of the leading newspaper of the day, "Aaron Burr was lately buried with the honors of war. Thomas Shipley was buried with the honors of peace. Let the reflecting mind pause in the honorable contrast."[3]

Another Quaker who stood up against slavery was William J. Allinson, who lived in Burlington, New Jersey. On August 13, 1836, a man named Colonel Christian came to Burlington and claimed that a farmer, Severn Martin, was actually a slave who had escaped from Christian's plantation in Virginia sixteen years before. Martin worked a farm several miles from the city and was respected for his industry and integrity. Constable Isaac Hancock told Martin that the mayor wanted to see him on a business matter. When Martin arrived at the Steamboat Hotel, Mayor John Larzalere was actually holding court as a county magistrate. Colonel Christian and two men who traveled with Christian testified that Martin was an escaped slave. The only evidence they offered was the testimony of the two men, who were slave hunters, and Christian's description that the slave was "a light colored n____r." Nevertheless, it was enough to place Martin into Christian's custody. Martin tried to fight them, but was overpowered and dragged away to a steamboat. Their plan hit a snag when the captain of the ship refused to allow them on board because he wanted no part of the affair. Martin was then placed into a wagon to be taken away to the South. Allinson, who was a friend of John Greenleaf Whittier, learned of Martin's plight and was determined to help. He headed a committee to raise the eight hundred dollars that Christian had demanded in order to set Martin free. The money was soon raised, in part because the leading citizens of Burlington were descendants of the settlers who came to America to escape persecution and they were determined to set Martin free.[4]

Sometimes there were consequences to helping others escape slavery. In April of 1838, the Supreme Court of New Jersey handed down a verdict against some citizens of Salem County. They were fined one thousand dollars for rescuing a fugitive slave.[5]

On the other side of the Delaware River, in 1838, there was a proposal to amend the Pennsylvania constitution so that free African Americans could legally have their opportunities limited. The predominately Quaker Pennsylvania Abolition Society heard about the attempt and went on the offensive. They hired men who were directed by Charles W. Gardner, an African American Presbyterian minister, to go to Philadelphia and do a private census of all people of color in the city. The plan was to disprove the contention that those of African descent were beggars, criminals, and a general drain on the city. The data was compiled and did prove that the charges were untrue, but the facts were not enough to stop the disfranchisement of the free people of Philadelphia.[6]

Sometimes, standing up against racial discrimination meant something other than trying to smuggle someone away from slavery. Sarah Mapp Douglass came from a successful African American Quaker family in Philadelphia. Her father, Robert, was a hairdresser, her mother, Grace, operated a Quaker millinery shop, and her grandfather, Cyrus Bustill, owned a bake shop next to his daughter's shop. Sarah was a teacher and corresponded with William Lloyd Garrison on anti-slavery issues. In 1835, she met Sarah and Angelina Grimké and they soon became friends. That same year, Angelina noticed that Sarah's mother, Grace Douglass, had never become a member of the Orthodox Arch Street Meeting even though she did attend meetings and wore the traditional Quaker clothing. Mrs. Douglass had her reasons for not joining. There was a separate bench for nonwhites, but Mrs. Douglass instead sat on a bench against the wall. No Caucasian members ever sat near her.

Sarah Douglass also had her own situation about seating arrangements once in New York City. She visited a Quaker meeting there and no one spoke to her but one young woman who asked her: "Doest thee go out a house cleaning?" Sarah replied that she was a teacher. The woman was surprised and proceeded to ignore her. Sarah spent the rest of the meeting in tears.

Two of the people who did not follow this attitude were the Grimké sisters, who were happy to shake up the seating arrangements. When they attended the first Anti-Slavery Convention of American Women in New York City from May 9 to May 12 with Sarah, the sisters, along with the other delegates, sat in the pews of their respective churches which were put aside for nonwhites. Soon afterward, the sisters went to the Arch Street Meeting and sat on the same bench as Grace Douglass. Angelina Grimké also proved that the seating arrangements were not just a one-time thing. Sarah Douglass and her mother were invited to Angelina's wedding to Theodore Weld in Philadelphia in 1837.

In December of 1837, Sarah Douglass wrote a letter to William Bassett, a fellow Quaker and abolitionist, thanking him for a letter he wrote about racial discrimination among the Quakers. In that letter, Bassett mentioned that it was

> allowed that the Negro Pew or its equivalent may be found in some of our meeting houses where men and women brethren and sisters by creation and heirs of the same glorious immortality are seated by themselves on a back bench for no other reason but because it has pleases God to give them a complexion darker than our own.

Bassett had requested information from her on the situation of the Arch Street Meeting. She replied that in her years of experience, there was a bench set apart

> for our people, whether officially appointed or not I cannot say; but this I am free to say that my mother and myself were told to sit there, and that a friend sat at each end of the bench to prevent white persons from sitting there. And even when a child my soul was made sad with hearing five or six times during the course of one this language of remonstrance addressed to those who were willing to sit by us. "This bench is for black people." "This bench is for people of color." And oftentimes I wept, at other times I felt indignant and queried in my own mind are these people Christians. Now it seems clear to me that had not this bench been set apart for oppressed Americans, there would have been no necessity for the oft-repeated and galling remonstrance, galling indeed because I believe they despise us for our color. I have not been in Arch Street meeting for four years; but my mother goes once a week and frequently she had a whole long bench to herself.

Sarah mentioned the experiences of others in her same situation. Knowing that she was in correspondence with Bassett, one of the others affected told her to tell him that the Friends "appointed a seat for our people at the meeting which I attend." The man also said that when someone approached him and told him that a bench was put aside for him, he replied that he would rather "sit on the floor as sit there." Several of the people who spoke to Sarah told her that they no longer attended a meeting. When she asked them why, they replied that they could no longer tolerate the "scorning of those who are at their ease, and the contempt of the proud." Finally, in answer to Bassett's query as to whether the Friends had become more tolerant of non-whites attending meetings, she "unhesitatingly answer[ed] no. I have heard it frequently remarked and have observed it myself, that in proportion as we become intellectual and respectable, so in proportion does their disgust and prejudice increase."

Sarah told Bassett that in Philadelphia there were some Friends "who have cleansed their garments from the foul stain of prejudice, and are doing all their hands find to do in promoting the moral and mental elevation of oppressed Americans. Some of these are members of Anti-Slavery Societies and others belong to the old abolition school." Two of the people she meant were the Grimké sisters. In her opinion, if the rest of the Friends followed their lead, "how very soon would the fetters be stricken from the captive and cruel prejudice be driven from the bosoms of the professed followers of Christ."

Bassett published Sarah's letter about the underlying prejudices in the Friends organization. The Friends did not take this letter quietly or kindly. In 1838, Bassett was threatened with disownment, and later the threat became a reality.[7]

The second National Anti-Slavery Convention of American Women met in the lecture room of Pennsylvania Hall on May 15, 1838. Lucretia Mott and Sarah Grimké were two of the women appointed to be vice-presidents and Sarah Douglass was the treasurer. All three women were also part of the Business Committee. This convention had the distinction of being the last meeting held in Pennsylvania Hall. During the convention, the building was surrounded by a mob that crowded the doors and tried to get in. The Board of Managers passed through the hall to check on the safety of the building and they were impressed that the convention members were a calm, dignified group. Unfortunately, the people who gathered outside were the exactly the opposite.

The attendees found it difficult to listen to the speakers because of the roar of the mob. Angelina Grimké spoke as the mob threw stones at the windows. She addressed what was going on outside by asking:

What is a mob? What would the breaking of every window be? What would the leveling of this hall be? Any evidence that we are wrong, or that slavery is a good and wholesome institution? What if the mob should now burst in upon us, break up our meeting, and commit violence upon our persons, would that be anything compared with what the slaves endure? No, no; and we do not remember them, "as bound with them," if we shrink in the time of peril, or feel unwilling to sacrifice ourselves, if need be, for their sake.

At that point, there was a great noise from outside. She went on and said, "I thank the Lord that there is yet life enough to feel the truth, even though it rages at it; that conscience is not so completely scared as to be unmoved by the truth of the living God." This was punctuated by another outbreak from the mob and confusion in the hall.

The convention adjourned late in the afternoon when the mob assembled. The doors were crowded with the mob and the streets were almost impassable due to the amount of "fellows of the baser sort." However, the women passed through the mob on their way out without showing fear.[8] Fortunately, they all left before the mob put the torch to the hall on the night of May 17. A messenger was sent to ask for help from the police. No help came and the hall burned to the ground.[9]

During this time period, another fight was brewing in Pennsylvania. In February of 1837, Margaret Ashmore, a Harford County, Maryland, slaveholder, hired Edward Prigg, Nathan S. Bemis, Jacob Forward, and Stephen Lewis, Jr., to hunt down Margaret Morgan, who had been a slave of Ashmore's until she escaped in 1832. They went to York County, Pennsylvania, to go before Thomas Henderson, a justice of the peace. They swore that Morgan was a runaway slave and received a warrant for her arrest. William McCleary, a constable for York County, was assigned to bring Morgan and her children before Henderson. McCleary did so, but the judge refused to consider the case. Because of the refusal, Prigg and the others, as stated in *Prigg v. Pennsylvania,*

> did take, remove and carry away the said negro woman, Margaret Morgan, and her children, mentioned in said warrant, out of this state, into the state of Maryland, and did there deliver the said woman and children into the custody and possession of the said Margaret Ashmore. And further say, that one of the said children so taken, removed and carried away, was born in this state, more that one year after the said negro woman, Margaret Morgan, had fled and escaped from the state of Maryland.

The grand jury of Pennsylvania issued a warrant for the arrest of Prigg and the others for kidnapping under the 1826 Pennsylvania law that was "relative to fugitives from labor, for the protection of free people of color, and [to] prevent kidnapping." The law stated if anyone was taken from Pennsylvania "with a design and intention of selling and disposing of, or of causing to be sold, or of keeping and detaining, or of causing to be kept and detained, such negro or mulatto, as a slave or servant for life, or any term whatever," that person or persons responsible for taking them away would be considered guilty of a felony and be fined between five hundred and one thousand dollars. They would also be sentenced to no less than seven years at hard labor, the same as anyone who would be sentenced for robbery.[10]

The governor of Pennsylvania then asked the governor of Maryland to return Prigg and the others to Pennsylvania for trial. The governor of Maryland left the decision to his legislature. They, in turn, said that if the charges would not be dropped, then they wanted the case referred to the Supreme Court. Both sides of the slavery issue saw this trial as very important. The proslavery forces saw the issue as protecting the slaveholders' right to reclaim their slaves from a free state without having to go to court in that state, as well as trying to challenge laws like the 1826 Pennsylvania law which stopped them from doing so. Abolitionists wanted to validate laws like the Pennsylvania law and to ensure the ability of those accused of being runaways to have a jury trial. The trial also affected the Commonwealth of Pennsylvania. It was feared that if states were not allowed to make laws concerning slavery

> for the preservation of their own peace and the protection of their own soil from insult and aggression, arrogate exclusive power for the general government to order and direct how, and by whom alleged fugitive slaves are to be restored to their masters or hired pursuers, and you arouse a spirit of discord and resistance, that will neither shrink or slumber till the obligation itself be cancelled, or the Union which creates it be dissolved.

The final outcome in 1842 was that the 1826 Pennsylvania law was declared by the Supreme Court to be unconstitutional and that Prigg and the others should be set free. The ruling stated that inhabitants of slave states had the right to retrieve anyone who ran away from slavery.[11] The Court said that "the legislation of congress, if constitutional, must supersede all state legislation upon the same subject; and by necessary implication prohibit it."[12]

The problem with this decision was that it made the position of free African Americans in the North somewhat shaky. There was nothing to prevent a slaveholder from coming to the North and claiming that a free man was actually a runaway slave that he owned. Therefore, any man or woman of color needed to be able to prove that they were actually free if they wanted to stay that way. The ruling also made it harder for those who wanted to help anyone in their flight to freedom. It made it harder, but it certainly did not stop them.[13]

In November of 1842, sixteen escapees from Baltimore County, Maryland, arrived in York, Pennsylvania. They were able to get into contact with William Wright, Joel Fisher, Dr. Lewis, and William Yocum, who tried to devise a way to get them on their way without being detected. Yocum was a constable and his profession came in very handy to those trying to escape slavery. He would pretend to hunt the runaways with the slave catchers. In truth, he knew where an escapee really was and he would direct the hunters to the opposite direction, which bought runaways extra time to escape. This particular time, Yocum and a free man named York took each of the sixteen separately to a cornfield that was owned by Samuel Willis near the town of York and hid them under the corn shocks. The next night, Dr. Lewis led them to a place near his home in Lewisburg, York County. They stayed in the area for several days and Dr. Lewis took food to their hiding place. When the searchers left the area to look elsewhere for the escapees, he went to Lewisburg and, with Wright, ferried them across the Conowago River on their horses. The clouds were not always their friends while they were crossing. The clouds would cover and just as quickly uncover the moon, lighting and darkening the river, which was swollen by recent rains, placing them in danger, not of just being discovered, but also of losing their lives in the dangerous river. When all sixteen successfully crossed over to the other side, Wright took them to his house and hid them in a nearby forest until they could continue on into Canada.[14]

This type of action was indicative of a loose formation of people of different races and religious backgrounds who were bound together by their anti-slavery beliefs that eventually became known as the Underground Railroad.

11. The Tracks of the Underground Railroad

The actual origin of the name "Underground Railroad" is not known. Its true beginning is as shrouded in myth and conjecture as stories of the railroad itself. It is definite that the term was not used before 1830, because railroads were not in use before that time. There are several stories that claim to be the origin story, and one of them came from Rush R. Sloane of Sandusky, Ohio. His story was about a slave named Tice Davids who was running away from his master in Kentucky in 1831. When Davids was on the move,

> his master, a Kentuckian, was in close pursuit and pressing him so hard that when the Ohio River was reached he had no alternative but to jump in and swim across. It took his master some time to secure a skiff, in which he and his aide followed the swimming fugitive, keeping him in sight until he had landed. Once on shore, however, the master could not find him. No one had seen him; and after a long ... search the disappointed slave-master went into Ripley [Ohio], and when inquired of as to what had become of his slave, said ... he thought "the——must have gone off on an underground road."[1]

A second possible origin came from several slave hunters who were chasing runaway slaves to Columbia, Pennsylvania. The trail went cold and the runaways were never seen again. No matter how many people the hunters asked or how hard they looked for clues, the escapees could not be found. When they realized that to continue hunting was pointless, the hunters were alleged to say, "There must be an underground railroad somewhere."[2]

Another story concerned Levi Coffin, a leading member of the Underground Railroad. According to the Reverend Calvin Fairbanks, three runaway girls reached Indiana and arrived at Coffin's home with slave hunters close behind them. Thinking quickly, Coffin hid them in his bed. The hunters reached the house and looked in vain for the girls. As they left, one of the hunters said, "That old Quaker must have an underground railroad, for once a slave gets here, he is never seen again."

It may have been called a railroad, but that did not mean that one could buy a ticket and arrive in Canada. The railroad was made up of pockets of people, Quaker and non–Quaker alike, spread out in intervals of ten to twenty miles. This was the distance someone could travel in a night, either by themselves or with assistance.[3] In cities and towns where Underground Railroad activity took place, as opposed to the countryside, people who were a part of the movement were called certain names borrowed from a real railway system to distinguish their jobs. Managers were those people with a great deal of organizational skills. Those who actually led escapees from one point to another were called agents and those people who were not as bold but still wanted to help by contributing money to the agents were called contributing members.[4]

People trying to escape slavery and go to Canada, whether or not they were escorted by members of the Underground Railroad, had one constant means of staying on track, and that was the North Star. They knew that if they followed the star, they would eventually arrive at Canada. The northern neighbor of the United States was a major draw to escapees from the time of the British abolishing slavery in 1834. However, escapees were going to Canada even before that time. During both the Revolutionary War and the War of 1812, the British refused to return the thousands of slaves they freed in the areas of Canada they occupied. They also refused to pay compensation for any slave who escaped to Canada, which made it a very attractive place for escapees to go.[5]

There were three major routes from the South to Canada. The western route went from the western part of the South through Kansas and Missouri to Iowa and Illinois and up through Michigan to Canada. The central route brought fugitives from the South through Kentucky, modern-day West Virginia, and western Maryland to Ohio, Indiana, and Pennsylvania. The eastern route started in the southeast section of the South and went through Virginia, Maryland, and Delaware and up through Pennsylvania and New Jersey to New York, the New England states and finally to Canada.[6]

If an escapee came from Maryland into Pennsylvania, Daniel Gibbons was a man to be trusted to move someone toward freedom. The Friend was not very good at being a physical guide to escapees because he was barely able to walk, but anyone who followed his directions was never captured. He also had a real talent for picking out imposters who claimed to be escapees but who were working for slave catchers. Between 1818 and his death on August 17, 1852, he helped nine hundred people escape.[7]

William Switala, in his book *The Underground Railroad in New York and New Jersey*, breaks the New Jersey section down into different routes. Escapees many times entered New Jersey by crossing the Delaware River or Delaware Bay into the Southern Network. This was the part of southern New Jersey made up of Atlantic, Cape May, Cumberland, and Salem counties. It also included parts of Burlington, Camden, Gloucester, and Ocean counties. This particular network incorporated several different routes through the area. The first one started in Cape May, which is on the southern tip of New Jersey, and where, from 1849 to 1852, Harriet Tubman worked in a hotel every summer to raise enough money to afford to go south to lead people to freedom. From there, there were several branches that took those seeking freedom to a new life. One branch ran northwest to Haddonfield and Snow Hill in Camden County.[8] The land that Snow Hill sat on was originally owned by Ralph Smith, an abolitionist living in Haddonfield. He bought a plot of land around 1840, which he then had surveyed and divided into lots. The lots were sold at a low price to African Americans and the town was called Free Haven. It later changed its name to Snow Hill and eventually became Lawnside.[9] One of the buildings that hid escapees, owned by Peter Mott, a free farmer and pastor of the Mount Pisgah AME Church, still stands today.[10]

The second branch ran from Cape May to the north along the modern-day Garden State Parkway to Somers Point through Mays Landing and then to Egg Harbor City, where the route went west until reaching the city of Camden. Another branch also went to Snow Hill from Cape May, but this one traveled along the eastern shoreline of New Jersey past Somers Point and continued north to Port Republic before turning west and heading toward Camden and Snow Hill. There was another branch that went from Cape May Point and traveled on a road that eventually became the modern-day New Jersey Route 47 to an African American episcopal church in Port Elizabeth that served as an Underground Railroad station. From there, travelers would go to Springtown, near Greenwich in Cumberland County. A final route from Cape May went to Port Norris. The reason for the number of routes coming from the same town was to have alternates in case a particular route was being watched.

A second major route for people coming from Delaware or other southern states originated in Greenwich, New Jersey. The town is situated at the southwest corner of Cumberland County and near the Cohansey River, which is how many escapees entered the city. The AME church had a strong presence in the nearby town of Springtown, and Greenwich contained three Quaker meeting houses.[11] Greenwich itself had a reputation of rebelling against the status quo—it was the site of a tea burning in December of 1774, protesting the British raising the tea tax while the American colonies were still a part of

Great Britain.[12] Fugitives would cross the Delaware Bay from Dover, Delaware, either on their own or ferried across at night. The boats that made the trips announced themselves with signal lights. If those waiting on the New Jersey side saw a yellow light with a blue light on top of it, they knew that fugitives were coming. The escapees would then be taken to Greenwich. From there, people could be taken twenty-five miles northwest on the Greenwich Line of the Underground Railroad to the town of Swedesboro, in Gloucester County. Swedesboro also had a strong Quaker presence and there was an AME church in nearby Woolwich. From there, they went to Burlington County through Evesham Mount and Mount Holly. Another way for travelers to arrive in Camden was to go to Bridgeton, the county seat of Cumberland County, and from there, either travel north to Gloucester County, through Mullica Hill to Woodbury and then to Camden, or, occasionally, they could be placed on a small railway going from Bridgeton to Camden.

Escapees also went across the Delaware River and made their way to Salem, New Jersey, in Salem County and then north to Woodbury. Here, too, the AME Church and the Quakers were strong in the area.[13] The leading Underground Railroad operatives in the area were Abigail Goodwin and her sister Elizabeth. William Still said of Abigail Goodwin that even though the state of New Jersey "contained a few well tried friends, both within and without the Society of Friends ... but among them all, none was found to manifest, at least in the Underground Railroad of Philadelphia, such an abiding interest as a co-worker in the cause, as did Abigail Goodwin." The Goodwin house at 47 Market Street, Salem, New Jersey, was one of the stations for the Underground Railroad. Abigail and Elizabeth were founders of the Female Benevolent Society of Salem, a Quaker organization created to help the less fortunate.

In 1836, Abigail joined the Underground Railroad as a helper, but a year later, she became a superintendent of railroad activity in Salem County. She wrote to a friend and said, "I do feel at least a willing mind to encounter reproach and suffering, almost to advance this great cause." She told another friend that she had "acquaintances in different townships who will assist me, I think as they did last year: but you must not expect a very long list of names. We are poor here in the abolitionist faith; it has not made much progress in our State, particularly in the lower parts of it.... But in the two lower Counties, I cannot insure that anything can be done."[14]

Elizabeth was a strong opponent of slavery, but Abigail was even more so. One friend described the difference between the sisters by saying that Elizabeth "economized greatly in order to give to the cause, but Abby denied herself even necessary apparel, and Betsy has often said that few beggars came to our doors whose garments were so worn, forlorn, and patched-up as Abby's.

Giving to the colored people was a perfect passion with her; consequently she was known as a larger giver than Betsy."[15] The sisters worked together until Elizabeth died in March 1860. Abigail continued helping escapees and later emancipated African Americans until her death in 1867.[16]

Abigail also tried to outfit escapees with clothing, and she would make clothes for them as soon as she was able to raise enough money for material. She felt that they "ought to be fitted out for Canada with strong, warm clothing in cold weather, and their sad fate alleviated as much as can be." Her concerns for escapees went farther than clothes and safe passage to the next safe spot. She also inquired about their education and how they adapted to life in Canada. Occasionally, she would receive a letter from Canada and enjoyed hearing of the progress of those she had helped.[17]

The last starting point for the southern network was in Port Republic, New Jersey. Escapees coming from Maryland and Virginia by ship would travel on the Mullica River and land at Port Republic. They would then continue up the river to Basto and then to Snow Hill.

The Central Network covered the area consisting of most of Burlington, Camden, and Ocean counties and part of Gloucester County. The AME Church and the Quakers were situated in the area as well as in the other networks. The Philadelphia Line of the network went from Philadelphia through Camden to New York. At Philadelphia, escapees would be directed by William Still,[18] the chairman of the Acting Vigilant Committee of the Philadelphia Branch of the Underground Railroad,[19] across the Delaware River to Camden. They would be met by the Reverend Thomas C. Oliver,[20] who was born in Salem and educated in a Quaker school.[21] The Reverend Oliver would then take them to Burlington. One of the safe houses that he used was the pharmacy operated by William J. Allinson.[22] The pharmacist came by his hatred of slavery honestly, since his grandfather Samuel had spoken out against slavery in the 1760s and 1770s. There is an oral history that stated that people trying to escape slavery would hide in the pharmacy's basement. Allinson had opened his pharmacy on the corner of High and Union Streets in 1831 and was a Quaker and a close friend of John Greenleaf Whittier. The poet used to visit the pharmacy and speak out against slavery from its steps.[23]

Another route was between Woodbury and Snow Hill. Escapees would travel from Salem, Swedesboro, or Mullica Hill to Woodbury. Once at Woodbury, travelers had the option of several ways to continue their journey north. The town lay at the junction of roads from Bridgeton, Cape May, Port Elizabeth, and Salem and had both AME churches and Quaker meeting houses in the area. It also was a station for both the Swedesboro and West Jersey Railroads. This gave Underground Railroad workers flexibility in moving people to their destination. African American workers on the Swedesboro Railroad smuggled escapees onto boxcars and shipped them to Camden in this manner.

From Snow Hill, there were two routes north. People coming from Cape May or Port Republic would go to Pennsauken and from there, go to the Philadelphia Line to Bordentown, New Jersey. The other route was to Camden or Evesham Mount. They could reach these towns by going through Haddonfield, which was a suburb of Camden.[24]

One of the places that escapees could rest in Haddonfield was a house called Edgewater. The house was built in 1748, and Thomas Evans, a Quaker, bought it in 1816 and lived there with his wife Abigail and their two sons, Charles and Josiah. Thomas and his wife lived there until 1840 when they moved to 309 Kings Highway. East, also in Haddonfield. Josiah then moved into the house from an adjoining farm with his wife Hannah, four children, and three of Hannah's sisters.

The Evans family would invite Friends to visit after the quarterly meeting at Haddonfield in the spring. It was the custom after the meeting to entertain Friends at the homes of different members. It often happened that thirty to fifty Friends were entertained there. The preparations for this meal would take a week or more.

There were other visitors who did not come at regular times. Both Thomas and Josiah were members of the Abolition Society, and Edgewater was a stop on the Underground Railroad. Escapees were brought from Woodbury and welcomed by Thomas Evans. He would quickly hide them in the hay of his barn or in the attic of his house. They would then be fed in the middle of the night, placed in a covered wagon, and sent to Mount Holly. There was one time when this system did not work smoothly. An escapee named Joshua Sadler whom Josiah Evans was helping was discovered. To cover up the fact that he was helping Sadler escape, Josiah had to buy him. Sadler could have left after the sale was done, but he agreed to stay with Evans until he had worked off the purchase price. When Evans died, Sadler stayed in the area and founded an African American community called Sadlertown.[25]

From Evesham Mount, which later became Mount Laurel, people could continue north through Mount Holly to Bordentown, where that route would merge with the Philadelphia Line to go to New York. Some also came to Evesham Mount from Port Republic. These people would have come through the town of Medford and been helped by Dr. George Haines, a Quaker, and later by Dr. Andrew E. Budd, who bought Haines' house and used it for the same purpose. Once arriving at Mount Laurel, where John Woolman once lived, escapees could either be sent to Bordentown or Burlington, where they could pick up the Philadelphia Line to New York.[26]

Once in Burlington, they were helped by people such as Charles H. Bustill, Emily Bustill, and Joseph Bustill. They were African American Quakers and were mentioned in William Still's book *The Underground Railroad* as being members of the railroad. He wrote of sending "a package of wool" to the Bustills. The "package of wool" was the code for sending escapees to the Bustills, who would then pass them on to the next step toward freedom.[27] Their activism came from Charles and Joseph's grandfather, Cyrus Bustill, who had been freed by his Quaker owner in 1769. The elder Bustill had been taught how to be a baker and operated a bakery in Burlington for many years. He then moved to Philadelphia and founded the Free African Society. He also built and taught in his own free school.[28] Later in life, Charles, Emily, and Joseph became known as the maternal grandparents and uncle of actor and singer Paul Robeson.[29]

There were two other backup routes in the Pennsylvania area to get escapees into New Jersey. The first was from Norristown, Pennsylvania, in Montgomery County, to Yardley, Pennsylvania, which was about thirty miles north of Philadelphia. From there, they would travel across the Delaware River to Trenton. The other route went from Norristown to Bristol, Pennsylvania, and from there directly across the Delaware River to Burlington.[30]

There were other places escapees could go in their quest for freedom. Columbia, Pennsylvania, was a town that had a long history of acceptance toward African Americans. In 1726, John Wright and Robert Barber, both Friends, settled in the area and were joined by another Friend, Samuel Blunson, the next year. Barber and Blunson were slave owners, but eventually their families renounced slavery. The area later became the town of Columbia and the plans for the town were laid out by Samuel Wright, John's grandson, in 1787.[31] It had been named Columbia in the hope that Congress would select it as the new nation's capital. George Washington was for it, but when the vote came up in 1790, it lost by one vote.[32] The lots of the town were sold by lottery, and most of them were bought by Friends from Bucks, Chester, and Montgomery counties and Philadelphia. The Wright family also donated land in the northeast corner of Columbia to the free people in the area, much like the Friends did in Greenwich.

Emancipated people traveled to Columbia to live, and when escapees needed a place to go, they came as well. Slave owners knew this and would hire men to watch the area and arrest any escapees they found. They once paid a man named Eaton several hundred dollars a year to stay in Columbia to look for escapees. Charles Taylor, who drove a stage between Columbia, York, and Baltimore, was also paid to keep watch for any escapees. On the other hand, abolitionists fought the slave catchers in court if they caught anyone, and the free people of Columbia were on guard against them. One time, they caught a slave catcher named Isaac Brooks. They took Brooks through the snow to the back part of town, stripped him, and beat him with hickory sticks. He was never seen in Columbia again.[33]

In Chester County, Pennsylvania, escapees could rest at the home of Dr. Bartholomew Fussell. His family, who were English Friends, had arrived in America at the time of the construction of Philadelphia. He moved to Maryland and taught school while studying the practice of medicine at night. He also opened a Sabbath school to teach the slaves in the area to read so that they could read the Bible. He later returned to Pennsylvania and began to help Thomas Garrett move people north. One of the great joys Dr. Fussell received from his work on the railroad was that he recognized some of the escapees as his former pupils from Sabbath school.

In the same area lived his nieces, Mariann Lewis, Grace Anna Lewis, and Elizabeth R. Lewis. Their mother, Dr. Fussell's sister, taught them at an early age to hate slavery. Their father regretted that he was unable to join any anti-slavery movements due to ill health. The Lewis sisters were under no such restrictions. Grace Anna remembered when she was four or five years old and saw a man named Henry being tied up and carried off into slavery. The terror on his face lived with Grace Anna for her entire life. All three sisters remembered a time when they saw a white handkerchief waved from a back window. It was a signal for a man who was working in the woods to beware of slave hunters. The sisters' home became a depot on the Underground Railroad for escapees coming from Thomas Garrett in Wilmington or from William and Phebe Wright in Adams County, Pennsylvania, when it was unsafe to sent escapees directly to Philadelphia.

All three sisters had gifts that helped them be effective workers for the railroad. Elizabeth was weak in body, but was calm, self-reliant, and intelligent. Mariann was able to come up with quick solutions to problems and Grace Anna was the most physically able of the three and was able to make their plans work.

Moving people from one depot to another was just one part of their job. The sisters also made sure that the escapees had suitable clothes for their journey. If they did not have clothes to fit the travelers, they made them. They got help from neighbors they could trust and formed a sewing circle, which was able to make what they needed quickly. They also received contributions of clothing. At one point, they had three bushel bags filled with clothes. Whatever was left over at the end of the Civil War was sent south to help the newly freed.

They always had to be on their guard because some of their neighbors were against any anti-slavery actions and would spring at any opportunity to harass the sisters. They were also not popular with some people because they were involved with the Temperance Society. In spite of these things, the sisters never lost a passenger on their leg of the Underground Railroad.

Sometimes, an escapee would stay with the sisters until the coast was clear or due to exhaustion or wanting to earn some money before moving on. Whatever the reason, the sisters took care of them. In the fall of 1855, an escapee was in Wilmington, Delaware, when he saw his master on the same northbound train. He jumped from the train and injured his foot badly. He found the Kennett Square, Pennsylvania, abolitionists and they moved him before his foot could heal properly because they were afraid that he would be discovered. The Lewises took him in and nursed him for months. He was fortunate that their cousin, Dr. Morris Fussell, lived nearby and was able to treat him. The following spring, he was finally able to move and escaped to Haiti.[34]

The Delaware routes to freedom led to Pennsylvania and New Jersey. According to William Switala, those seeking freedom would enter Sussex County in southern Delaware from neighboring Maryland. From there, they would make their way north at night, using the major roads to arrive at Camden, Delaware. The trip north would then continue through Dover and Blackbird to Middletown, which was a route that Harriet Tubman used.[35] In Dover, one of the stops was Woodburn, the home of Delaware's governor. It was used during the 1840s and 1850s to help escapees. Supposedly, there was a tunnel that ran from a secret room in the basement to the St. Jones River. From there, they would take boats north along the Delaware River into Pennsylvania and New Jersey.[36]

Odessa, a town not far to the northeast of Middletown, also had several Underground Railroad stations. The Appoquinimink Friends Meeting House was a place where escapees hid, supposedly in the loft. Daniel Corbit, John Alston, and John Hunn were Quakers who worked for the railroad out of Odessa.[37] Corbitt hid his escapees in cabinets on the third floor of his house.[38] Alston, who was John Hunn's cousin and the treasurer of the meeting, wrote a prayer in his diary in 1841 that served as his mission statement. He wrote, "Oh Lord ... enable me to keep my heart and house open to receive thy servants that they may rest in their travels that this house that thou has enabled me to build may be holy dictates unto thee of the pilgrim's rest."[39]

Escapees could then continue northward from Middletown to several towns. The final destination in Delaware was Wilmington, but there were several routes from Middletown. One way was through New Castle first and then to Wilmington. The second was by way of Delaware City,[40] which had a fort off its coast that became one of the largest Northern prisoner-of-war camps in the Civil War.[41] The third route was directly from Middletown to Wilmington. Once in Wilmington, freedom seekers would be guided by the Underground Railroad group run by Thomas Garrett or the AME Church in Wilmington. To continue north, escapees could travel either by foot, in carriages and wagons, by ship, or by rail. They did, however, avoid bridges in their travels because bridges were watched regularly by slave catchers.[42]

The home of Thomas Garrett became known as a place where an escapee could find refuge. When he first began his mission, people in the area were against any form of anti-slavery action. Many people turned their backs on him because he was not shy about expressing his opinions against slavery. His home was under constant surveillance by the police, and Garrett used many secretive means to help escapees. There were times when an abolitionist had to deal with physical intimidation from slavery supporters, but Garrett, being a powerfully built man, did not present an easy target. He worked for many years against slavery and his "firmness and courage slowly won others, first to admire, and then to assist him, and the little band of faithful workers, of which he was chief, gradually enlarged and included in its number, men of all ranks, and differing creeds, and, singular as it may seem, even numbering some ardent Democrats in its ranks."[43]

Another place where escapees could rest was at the Johnson house in Germantown near Philadelphia. The Johnson family were well-known abolitionists who were involved in the American Free Produce Society. They hid escapees in the attic, barns, springhouse, and other outbuildings on the property.[44]

Quaker Thomas Garrett was a major participant in the Underground Railroad. Threats and prosecution did not deter him from helping escapees find freedom (Swarthmore College, Friends Historical Library).

The tracks of the Underground Railroad carried many people to freedom and the chance of a better life. However, the risks to both escapees and workers alike were great. The single greatest threat to the railroad was the passage of a law that was created to help keep the slowly crumbling United States together. This law was the Fugitive Slave Act of 1850.

12. The Compromise of 1850 and the Fugitive Slave Act

The Missouri Compromise of 1820 was designed to solve the problem of bringing into America an equal number of slave and free states. However, twenty-eight years later, the compromise was no longer able to do the job that it was created for. In 1848, the United States had bought California and the modern-day Southwest from Mexico after the Mexican War. The question came up again about how much slavery would be permitted in this new land. The depth of the anger over this battle was made plain in the presidential election of 1848. There was a Free-Soil party that nominated Martin Van Buren as their presidential candidate. Their slogan was: "Free Soil, Free Speech, Free Labor, and Free Men." Van Buren did not win, but he did receive 11 percent of the vote and proved that the country was deeply interested in the outcome of this issue.[1]

The problem came to a boil over how California would be brought into the Union. California had a huge increase in population because of the gold rush of 1849 and had petitioned Congress to be allowed into the country as the next state. The crux of the problem was that it wanted to be brought in as a free state. If this happened, there would be one more free state than slave state. This possibility created a situation that the southern states would not take lying down. If this problem was not bad enough, Congress also had to deal with the claim from Texas that their land extended out to Santa Fe. There was also the problem with abolitionists who were still furious that Washington, D.C., was not only an area that accepted slavery but also the largest slave market in North America. All of these problems were brought to Congress at the same time and threatened to drive the country to the brink of disunion.

Henry Clay, the senator from Kentucky, had put out the fires of the slavery debate in Congress with the Missouri Compromise in 1820. He had helped to save the Union then and was determined to do it one more time.[2] On January 29, 1850, he presented to the Senate his suggestions for a compromise. He felt that it was "desirable, for the peace, concord, and harmony of the Union of these States, to settle and adjust amicably all existing questions of controversy between them arising out of the institution of slavery upon a fair, equitable, and just basis."[3]

Clay may have felt that a compromise was what was needed to settle the issue, but that did not mean that everyone in Congress agreed. In fact, there were some in Congress who did not want a compromise with the same passion that Clay held. The appearance of John C. Calhoun, senator from South Carolina, on March 4, 1850, in the Senate proved just how much he wanted the compromise to be voted down. The sixty-eight-year-old Senator was emaciated and dying when he was assisted to his desk on the Senate floor.

He had come especially to speak out against the compromise. The speech he prepared was forty-two pages long and read by Senator James Murray Mason because he was too weak to read it. In front of a packed gallery, Calhoun's speech attacked Clay's compromise. The sections calling for the abolition of slavery in Washington, D.C., and allowing California to enter the Union as a free state were totally unacceptable to Calhoun and his supporters. He felt that the equilibrium between the North and South had been destroyed and that the sovereignty of the states was on the line.[4]

Congress had split into two groups on this issue. Senator Calhoun and Mississippi senator Jefferson Davis led the proslavery attack. On the other side stood Salmon P. Chase and William Seward, who were firmly against slavery.[5] The debate concerning the issue raged on for eight months. Emotions flared and become so heated that at one point, Georgia representative Robert Coombs exclaimed over a proposed compromise to let the territories decide whether or not they wanted slavery once they became states: "If it should come to pass, I am for disunion."[6]

The seventy-year-old Clay needed help in resolving this issue and received it from a young senator from Illinois named Stephen Douglas.[7] In March, Douglas had spoken about "the self-sacrificing spirit which prompted the venerable Senator from Kentucky to exhibit the matchless moral courage of standing daunted between two great hostile factions, and rebuking the violence and excesses of each, and pointing out their respective errors, in a spirit of kindness, moderation, and firmness." The battle dragged on until the middle of September when Clay and his supporters were able to push through a series of bills that made up the compromise of 1850.[8]

To the first issue of the boundaries of Texas, the state would give up its claim to the disputed land and receive $10 million, which Texas would use to pay off its debt to Mexico. Four territories, Nevada, Arizona, New Mexico, and Utah, would be created without any mention of slavery. The decision to be a slave or free state would be decided by the territories once they applied for statehood. The slave trade in Washington, D.C., would be abolished, but slavery would still be legal. The question of California would be settled by allowing it to come into the Union as a free state. The compromise to make that possible was the Fugitive Slave Act.[9]

The Fugitive Slave Act was only a part of the compromise of 1850. The South was angry that antislavery leaders in the North took every opportunity to speak out against slavery. Southern leaders were also furious that others were helping people as they fled north to escape slavery. This led the South to demand a strong law to stop slave escapes. The first one had passed in 1793, but the South felt that it had too many weaknesses.

One such weakness was the ability of states to enact laws to offset the effects of the 1793 law. In 1826, Pennsylvania abolitionists were able to have a bill put through the legislature which imposed heavy penalties for anyone "who should take or carry away from the State any negro with the intention of selling him as a slave for life." This law was enacted to prevent the kidnapping of free African Americans who lived in the state and selling them into slavery. However, the law was also used to help escapees free themselves from slavery.

The Fugitive Slave Act of 1850 stated that U.S. marshals and deputy marshals who refused to help return slaves would be fined one thousand dollars. If a fugitive was captured but escaped from the marshal's custody, the marshal was liable for the price of the slave. The owner or agent of the owner could either get a warrant from a judge or just grab the fugitive without due process. Also, commissioners would be set up to handle the fugitive slave cases. These men would earn ten dollars for every case where the person being accused of being an escaped slave was found guilty and five dollars if that person was found innocent. This made the entire proceedings wide open for corruption.

The law also made it extremely dangerous for anyone who wanted to help an escapee. Any person convicted of trying to help someone escape slavery or give aid in any way would be fined up to one thousand dollars and placed in jail for up to six months.[10] It also stated that the person convicted of helping a fugitive would also have to "pay, by way of civil damages to the party injured by such illegal conduct, the sum of one thousand dollars for each fugitive so lost as aforesaid, to be recovered by action of debt, in any of the District or Territorial Courts aforesaid, within whose jurisdiction the said offence may have been committed."[11]

The Fugitive Slave Act made the lives of African Americans, both free and escapees, a nightmare. With the little bit of protection that the law allowed now gone, no one of color could be entirely sure of their safety. Twenty thousand people moved to Canada between 1850 and 1860 to free themselves of the constant stress of wondering when someone would drag them to a commissioner. Those who did not move faced the specter of slavery.

The passage of the act created another reaction that was not expected. The general population of the North, which had not been very concerned with the well-being of people of a different color, was now outraged. The act forced the nation to become slave hunters and supporters of an institution that they wanted no part of. People who were ambivalent toward slavery became avowed enemies of it. One such situation occurred in Ohio. Margaret Garner escaped from Boone County, Kentucky, in January of 1856 with her four children and was hidden in a house near Cincinnati, Ohio. Her master was close behind them, and rather than allow her children to be taken back into slavery, she decided to kill the children. She succeeded in killing her favorite child before she was captured. She and her remaining children were taken back to their master. The reaction to this was overwhelming. Rutherford B. Hayes, a future president of the United States, was a lawyer in Cincinnati at the time and he remembered the reaction on his street. His neighbors were proslavery, but afterward, the entire street converted. One of the leaders of the proslavery neighbors came up to him and said: "Mr. Hayes, hereafter I am with you. From this time forward, I will not only be a black Republican, but I will be a dammed abolitionist!"[12]

The Fugitive Slave Law spurred other people to fight against the system. Esther Moore was heavily involved in the abolitionist movement. A Friend who moved to Philadelphia from the Eastern Shore of Maryland, Moore helped hundreds of escapees reach freedom. She worked with the Vigilance Committee of Philadelphia and begged them to notify her "of every fugitive reaching Philadelphia, and actually felt hurt if from any cause whatever this request was not complied with. For it was her delight to see the fugitives individually, take them by the hand and warmly welcome them to freedom."

She had another reason to want to see every fugitive beyond wishing them well. Moore knew that the committee had a difficulty paying for whatever was necessary to move an escapee to the next station. Therefore, sometime after the passing of the Fugitive Slave Act, she put a gold dollar in the hand of every escapee before they left Philadelphia. She felt that they should have one dollar to fall back on, on top of whatever aid that the committee could give. She continued to do this until just before her death on November 21, 1854, at the age of eighty.[13]

The major idea behind the compromise of 1850 was to try to keep the nation together. It did succeed for a time. However, it stirred up passions against slavery not only from abolitionists but also from the average person in the North. These passions continued to grow until the nation was so polarized that something had to give, and what gave was the unity of the country. Until that day, men and women took risks to stand against slavery and sometimes they paid the price.[14]

13. The Penalty for Defiance

The idea of helping those suffering from oppression was one thing when the attempts were successful. However, there were times that the attempts failed and the rescuers were the people who needed help. In 1833, John Kenderdine, a Quaker from Montgomery County, Pennsylvania, was hiding a slave in his home. The master found the escapee and proceeded to take him back to New Jersey, where he lived. On the way, they were overtaken by men determined to rescue the escapee. The rescuers then had the master and the men traveling with him arrested for kidnapping. They were found innocent because they did have a legal right to retrieve the slave. At this point, the ones who tried to stop the seizure were then prosecuted in Pennsylvania in a circuit court on the charges of trespass and false imprisonment. The men in question were all Quakers. The judge found it hard to understand why they had done this since they were "members of a society distinguished for their obedience and submission to the laws." The judge left the amount of damages for the slaveholder and his group to the jury to decide. They, in turn, declared that the penalty to be four thousand dollars.[1] In another case, on April 21, 1838, the Supreme Court of New Jersey gave a penalty of one thousand dollars against men in Salem County, New Jersey, who had rescued an escapee.[2]

Fighting tyranny and injustice was not always risk free or painless. In 1844, Captain Jonathan Walker was working off the coast of Florida when he agreed to transport seven escapees from Pensacola, Florida, to the Bahamas. He was taking them there due to the British ban on slavery. Captain Walker used an open boat for the job and suffered heatstroke as a result. Because of his illness, the boat was captured and the seven were taken into custody. After two trials, Captain Walker was found guilty of trying to help slaves escape. He was sentenced to a fine and a term of imprisonment for each slave he tried to help. He was also required to pay the court cost and was branded on the hand with the letters S.S., which meant slave stealer. Walker's friends paid the fines and he was freed in 1848. He then traveled throughout the North speaking at anti-slavery rallies. John Greenleaf Whittier wrote a poem to celebrate Captain Walker's deliverance from prison and to use his experience to whip up anti-slavery feelings:

> The lift that manly right hand, bold ploughman of the wave,
> Its branded palm shall prophesy "Salvation to the slave."
> Hold up its fire-wrought language that whoso reads may feel
> His heart swell strong within him, his sinews change to steel.[3]

Another sea captain was suffered for his beliefs was Daniel Drayton. Drayton was born in Cumberland County, New Jersey, in 1802, and in April of 1848, his ship, the *Pearl*, was boarded and seventy-five slaves were discovered. He was trying to take them from Washington, D.C., to Philadelphia to freedom. Drayton was charged with forty-two counts and convicted. He was fined ten thousand dollars and spent four years in the Washington jail. Abolitionists put pressure on the government to free him, and in November of 1852, he was pardoned by President Millard Fillmore. He then went to visit Abigail Goodwin in her home in Salem in December.[4]

Those who were active on the railroad were always in fear of being discovered and worried about what people would do with this information if they discovered it. Sometimes, the result was not what was expected. In Chester County, Pennsylvania, the proslavery neighbors of Gravner and Hannah Marsh, Quakers who lived near Downingtown, discovered that the Marshes were workers on the Underground Railroad. The neighbors never turned the Marshes in to the authorities. However, one woman, possibly for her own curiosity, did decide to keep a count on how many escapees passed through the Marshes' home. She kept track for a year, and at the end of that time, she had seen sixty people being helped by the Marshes. The woman, like her other neighbors, never told the authorities about the goings-on so near her home.[5]

Daniel Gibbons was very good at being able to ascertain whether the person at his door was someone trying to gain information on his anti-slavery activities. Once, a man came to his house and said that he was interested in buying a horse. The man gave the impression that he was more interested in information than a horse. This was of particular concern to Gibbons because he did have an escapee working for him. The man noticed him, and when he left, Gibbons sent the escapee away to safety. The next day, a policeman came to Gibbon's house, but he found no one.

Escapees faced another danger beyond discovery. There were some people who were neither abolitionists nor slavery supporters. They would claim that they wanted to help escapees and hire them during busy seasons. When the work was done, they would then tell the escapees that their masters were nearby and they had to run before they were recaptured. They would only pay them a part of the wages they were owed and would either direct them to distant friends to the north or take them partway to their destination and wish them well.[6]

Those who hunted slaves did not always care whether or not the person they captured was a slave or even the person they were looking for. These slave hunters did whatever they thought was necessary to achieve their goal. In the early morning of April 19, 1848, three men broke into the home of Mary B. Thomas, a Friend, of Downingtown, Pennsylvania. They ran upstairs and seized a girl named Martha from her bed. She had been living with the Thomas family for about a year, but that did not matter to her attackers. They carried her down the stairs and pushed Miss Thomas' father aside when he tried to intervene. The girl was shoved into a waiting carriage and taken away. Miss Thomas' father followed the kidnappers to West Chester, but was unable to stop them from escaping with Martha. The Thomas family never saw her again.

In 1813, another kidnapping that had a happier ending occurred in Pennsylvania. A young man had returned to his father's house after being away for a short time and discovered that a woman who worked for the family had been kidnapped. He immediately went after the woman and was able to track the wagon the kidnappers used by the unusual impression one of the wheels made in the road. He followed the wagon from Darby, Pennsylvania, to the Navy Yard in Philadelphia and then to Kensington, where he found the kidnappers. He was then able to secure the release of the woman. From that time on, Thomas Garrett made it his life's work to help any escapee from slavery.[7]

There were times when proslavery people did not mind lashing back at those whom they knew to be abolitionists. On June 21, 1837, James Miller McKim, a former Presbyterian minister, came to Salem, New Jersey, on Abigail Goodwin's urging to talk to Quaker ladies who were interested in helping escapees. He was scheduled to speak at the Salem Court House, but this incurred the wrath of the antiabolitionists. They burned him in effigy and went to Goodwin's house where McKim was staying.[8]

Free African Americans were also victims of slave owners seeking runaways. If they could not find the one they were looking for, then they would grab any person of color and claim that they were the one being sought. These types of abductions finally aroused the anger of the free men in the area of Christiana in southeast Pennsylvania. They created a league of self-protection and their leader was a fugitive slave named William Parker, who harbored runaways at his home. On September 10, 1851, Parker received word from the Vigilance Committee of Philadelphia that a slave owner from Maryland named

Edward Gorsuch had received warrants for the arrest of the two runaways that Parker was hiding.[9] Sarah Pownall, a Friend and the wife of Parker's landlord and neighbor, went to Parker's home that evening and advised him "not to lead the colored people to resist the Fugitive Slave Law by force of arms, but to escape to Canada." He replied that if people of his race were protected by the law that he would not fight. However, he said that "the laws for personal protection are not made for us, and we are not bound to obey them. If a fight occurs I want the whites to keep away. They have a country and may obey the laws. But we have no country."[10]

The next day, Gorsuch, his son Dickerson, his nephew Dr. Pearce, Henry H. Kline, a well-known slave-catching constable from Philadelphia and a group of Gorsuch's friends, broke into the house and demanded the two men. They were able to enter the lower floor of the house, but unable to go to the upper level. One of Parker's friends blew a horn out of a window to call for help. Outside, Gorsuch demanded the return of his slaves. Two men went to a window of the upper floor one at a time to show themselves to Gorsuch and asked him if they were the slaves he was searching for. The slave owner said no and the two men said that they were the only people of color in the house and that they would never be taken alive as slaves.

A short time later, about fifty men arrived at Parker's home after hearing the horn, armed with clubs, guns, and corn cutters, to help Parker. Two Quakers, Castner Hanway, who lived nearby and Elijah Lewis, a merchant, came to see what was going on. Kline ordered them to help retrieve the men in the house that Gorsuch wanted. They refused to do that; however, the Quakers did try to talk with both sides. They suggested to Parker and his men to not go against the law and also asked Gorsuch and his men to leave the area to prevent bloodshed. Dickerson Gorsuch tried to convince his father to leave, but the elder Gorsuch replied that he would "go to hell, or have his slaves."

Hanway and Lewis felt that they were getting nowhere with either side and meant to leave the scene, but one of the people in the house tried to walk out of the door. Gorsuch met him with a gun in his hand and ordered him to go back into the house. The man told him to "go away, if you don't want to get hurt" and pushed Gorsuch aside. Dr. Pearce turned to his uncle and asked if he would "take such an insult from a d——d n____r." Gorsuch's answer was to fire at the escaping man, as did his son and nephew. The men who came to protect Parker opened fire, and when it was all over, the slave owner was dead, his son was seriously wounded, and the fugitives were able to escape.

Kline had backed off a safe distance before the firing had started and was uninjured.[11] Parker protected Dickenson Gorsuch from the anger of his friends and took him into his house until he could be taken to the nearby house of

Sarah and Levi Pownall for treatment. The younger Gorsuch was so moved by the care he received by the Quakers that he swore that if he recovered, he would never again hunt escapees.[12]

At seven o'clock on the morning after, two women came to the house of Joseph Fulton, a Friend. They were frightened and asked if "something could not be done for them; they didn't know what to do, nor where to go to." One of the women was the wife of William Parker. They had managed to escape from their masters and were trying to find a safe place to go. Fulton's daughter, MaryAnn, was determined to help. She told them to go to her carriage and wait for her. Mary Ann then went to the fields to ask her brother for one of their fastest horses so she could help the women escape. He refused her because he was afraid that she would get caught and their property would be confiscated due to the Fugitive Slave Act. Mary Ann was undeterred and so her brother consented to allow her to use a horse called "old blind Nance." He thought she would not risk the trip with a horse with that name, but she took the horse and readied it for the trip.

Mary Ann Fulton decided to travel toward the Caln Friends' Meeting House and ask people on the way whom she trusted if they would hide the women until the officers left the area. She was rejected again and again because they were afraid of getting caught. Finally, with night coming, Mary Ann saw a small African American woman walking toward them. She asked the woman if she knew anyone who would help, and the woman volunteered to hide the fugitives. They were eventually able to arrive in Canada, where they were reunited with their husbands.[13]

This was not the end of the situation. Kline had given a deposition concerning the incident, and warrants for the arrest of all persons involved were issued.[14] The president of the United States became involved and made forty-five marines available to the U.S. marshal in the area. There was a search of the area, and thirty-five African Americans and three Quakers were arrested. The Quakers, Hanway, Lewis, and another man, had surrendered voluntarily. All of the men were not charged with a violation of the Fugitive Slave Law, but they were charged with "wickedly and traitorously [intending] to levy war against the United States."[15]

The abolitionist movement was not very popular in the early 1850s. Many northerners wanted to keep the Union together, so the majority of the people in the North did not actively oppose the Fugitive Slave Act.[16] Even though many people did not support the Fugitive Slave Act, that did not mean that public opinion was universally for anyone standing against slavery. The papers in the area were straightforward in their anger toward the incident. One paper wrote that it was plain to see that the abolitionists are implicated in the Christiana murder. All the ascertained facts go to show that they were the real, if not the chief instigators. White men are known to harbor fugitives, in the neighborhood of Christiana, and these white men are known to be abolitionists, known to be opposed to the Fugitive Slave law, and known to be the warm friends of William F. Johnson [governor of the State of Pennsylvania]. And, as if to clinch the argument, no less than three white men are now in the Lancaster prison, and were arrested as accomplices in the dreadful affair on the morning of the eleventh.

Another paper felt that they did not want

to see the poor misled blacks who participated in this affair, suffer to any great extent, for they were but tools. The men who are really chargeable with treason against the United States Government, and with the death of Mr. Gorsuch, an estimable citizen of Maryland, are unquestionably white, with hearts black enough to incite them to the commission of any crime equal in atrocity to that committed in Lancaster County, Pennsylvania has now but one course to pursue, and that is to aid, and warmly aid, the United States in bringing to condign punishment, every man engaged in this riot.[17]

They were brought before a grand jury held at Independence Hall in Philadelphia in November and December of 1851. Thaddeus Stevens of Lancaster, Pennsylvania, a member of the House of Representatives, was the lead council for the defense. Stevens was determined to win and used some courtroom theatrics to sway the jury. When the African Americans charged were led into the courtroom, they all wore a red-white-and-blue scarf around their necks in support of Hanway. Also, Lucretia Mott was in attendance, quietly knitting.[18] Esther Moore assisted by visiting the prisoners many times and helping them any way she could.[19] Theodore Cuyler, another attorney for the defense of Hanway, in his speech, went on the attack by asking the court if the facts sustained the charges. He said that "three harmless, nonresisting Quakers, and eight and thirty wretched, miserable, penniless negroes, armed with corncutters, clubs, and a few muskets, and headed by a miller, in a felt hat, without a coat, without arms, and mounted on a sorrel nag, levied war against the United States? Blessed be God that our Union has survived the shock."[20] Justice Greer, who presided over the trial, told the jury that to be guilty of treason, the defendants would have to have been trying to effect something of a public nature. A band of fugitive slaves defending themselves from being recaptured, even though they were guided by friends and a death occurred during the ensuing fight, was considered a private matter and not an attack on a nation. The grand jury dropped all charges against the defendants.[21]

The not guilty verdict showed that the passage of the Fugitive Slave Act was not a guarantee that the proslavery forces would have an easy time of fighting anti-slavery proponents. Neither side was willing to concede to the other, and the trial proved that the country could not continue to go on as half slave and half free. Change was coming, and proof of this was that Henry Kline decided that chasing escapees was a very unsafe job and backed away from those activities. Unfortunately for other escapees, that opinion was not shared by others.[22]

After the Christiana incident, special agents armed with warrants and led by proslavery men prowled the area and rampaged through the homes of suspected abolitionists and free men looking for anyone involved with the incident. One posse of men grabbed a man who worked for Thomas Whitson, a Friend, and tried to take him away. Whitson went after the men, and when he caught up with them, asked for his employee's release. They refused, and when one of the posse discovered who Whitson was, they started to curse him and came up to him with a drawn gun. He asked Whitson if he was an abolitionist. Whitson replied that he was and said that he "was not afraid of thy shooting me. So thee may as well put thy pistol down." The man turned to a friend of his and asked if he should still shoot Whitson. His friend said no; "Let the old Quaker go." The next day, Whitson went to a neighbor who had seen his employee several miles away at the time of the riot. The two men went to where the posse had the man under guard and proved that it was impossible for him to be involved in the incident. The posse had no choice but to release Whitson's employee.

Whitson was a member of the Underground Railroad and sent escapees to Lindley Coates, a fellow Friend. Coates, who lived in Sadsbury, Lancaster County, Pennsylvania, was also very careful with his railroad activities after the Christiana incident.[23] He had good reason to be careful, since his barn had been burned down in 1850 because it was known that he helped escapees.[24] Anyone who came to Coates was taken to his cornfield and hidden there. This was done because Coates and his wife expected to have their home searched by the special agents.[25]

Occasionally, someone paid the ultimate price for the freedom of others. In December of 1851, Tom McCreary kidnapped Elizabeth Parker in East Nottingham, Chester County, Pennsylvania. McCreary was known in the area as "a professional slave-catcher" from Elkton, Maryland. He and other slave catchers plied their trade in Chester County, Pennsylvania, because of its closeness to the Maryland border. The man who was called "the infamous McCreary" was very familiar with the area. His kidnapping of Elizabeth Parker and the events surrounding it only proved how he earned that nickname.[26]

McCreary went with several others to the home of Joseph C. Miller, in West Nottingham, where Elizabeth's sister, Rachel, lived. The sixteen-year-old had worked for the Miller family for six years. McCreary came to the door and asked for Mrs. Miller. When Rebecca Miller arrived, McCreary grabbed Rachel and claimed that she was a runaway slave. Mrs. Miller told him that was impossible because she knew that Rachel was born in Pennsylvania and was a free person. McCreary ignored her and dragged Rachel away. Mrs. Miller and her four children screamed for Mr. Miller, who was working outside. He came running and grabbed Rachel's arm, but McCreary pulled out a knife and forced Miller away. McCreary and his men then escaped in a carriage. Miller chased them on foot and caught up with them while they were in an argument with Miller's neighbor, James Pollock, whose wagon blocked McCreary's escape route. Miller again attempted to rescue Rachel, but one of the kidnappers pulled a large knife and threatened Miller with it. The kidnappers took another route and escaped.

The kidnappers went to Perryville, Maryland, to catch the train to Baltimore. Waiting for a train for Philadelphia was Eli Haines, who lived about two miles from Joseph Miller. He knew Rachel and also recognized McCreary. He realized what danger Rachel was in, so he and his traveling companion, a Mr. Wiley, changed their plans and boarded the train to Baltimore to follow Rachel. Haines and Wiley followed Rachel to the holding cells of William Campbell, a slave trader. They then went back to the train station to wait for Miller, whom they assumed would be arriving soon.

Haines and Wiley guessed correctly, because Miller had arrived with William Morris, Abner Richardson, Jesse B. Kirk, and H.G. Coates to help in finding Rachel. They then went to Francis S. Cochran, a Friend, for help. Cochran summoned the police and the group went to Campbell's home. Campbell told them that even though he approved of slavery and the retaking of runaway slaves, he hated kidnapping and kidnappers. Miller identified Rachel and she was taken to the local jail until the legal problems could be worked out. McCreary arrived and was arrested for kidnapping. The Fugitive Slave Law clearly prohibited McCreary's actions, and he had been accused of doing this very thing in the past. A justice of the peace set a court appearance for McCreary on January 7, 1852. Miller and his friends then returned to Cochran's home for dinner.

The Chester County men may have thought that the problem was well in hand, but Cochran knew better. The incident in nearby Christiana had occurred only several months before, and anti-abolitionist feelings were still running high. Miller and his friends were not abolitionists, but they had come into the area and charged a man with kidnapping a woman believed to be a runaway slave. One of the men in Gorsuch's group had made the threat "of hanging the first Abolitionist that they should catch in Maryland."

When they were unable to free Rachel immediately, Miller and his friends decided to return home. Cochran bought their train tickets and had them taken to the station in a roundabout way for their safety. He also told them to stay together and sit in their seats until the train left the station. They arrived safely and took their seats on the train. Before the train left the station, Miller decided to step onto the platform for a smoke, against the wishes of his friends. They followed him to bring him back to his seat, but he was gone. They called his name and stepped out into the crowd to look for him. When they did not see him, they went back to their seats, in fear of their own safety. They talked about the situation and decided that Wiley would continue to look for Miller throughout the train once they got underway because he was the least known of the group and was not directly involved in the affair. They hoped that Miller had reentered the train and was in the wrong car.

Wiley returned to the group at the Stemen's Run station and reported that he was unable to find Miller. They agreed that Kirk and Richardson would return to Baltimore on the next train to search for Miller there. When the others returned, the news of Miller's disappearance aroused the entire neighborhood. Twenty men volunteered to return to Baltimore and find Miller. Before they set off, word came to them that Miller's body had been found hanging from a tree in Stemen's Run, an apparent suicide.

On January 9, the volunteers went to Baltimore to claim the body. Miller had already been buried, and, because it was considered unsafe for the men to claim his body during the day, it had to be dug up at night. He was buried only two feet below ground and place in a cheap box with a too-small lid that allowed dirt to enter the coffin. His friends were able to get a real coffin, and they took him home. They were nearly at the Pennsylvania line when a messenger caught up with them bearing a message. The governor of Maryland wanted to have Miller's body returned to Baltimore for an autopsy.

The postmortem examination in Baltimore was done, in the opinion of Miller's friends, in a circus-like atmosphere. Many in attendance were drinking whiskey and cursing Pennsylvania abolitionists. The examination agreed with the first verdict of suicide and Miller's friends took him home. Once there, two country physicians were permitted to reexamine Miller's body. The doctors who reexamined the body, Hutchinson and Dickey, came to the conclusion that Miller was murdered. His wrists and ankles had unmistakable marks of being bound, and there was a black mark across his abdomen that seemed as if it was made with a rope. The end of his nose looked as if it had been held by some kind of instrument. This news quickly spread and there were demands for another, more through, examination. The newest autopsy not only agreed with the previous one but it also discovered evidence of arsenic in Miller's body. In addition, there was barely two ounces of contents in his stomach and bowels, even though his friends testified that he had eaten a hearty meal at Cochran's home before his disappearance. The theory of what happened to Miller was that he was kidnapped, possibly by McCreary and his friends, stripped, tied up, his nose closed and forced to drink arsenic. He was then dressed and hung from a tree at Stemen's Run because one of the conspirators might have heard Wiley say there that Miller was not on the train and they wanted to make the murder look like a suicide.

McCreary was able to avoid imprisonment in January of 1852 due to insufficient evidence. However, that was not the end of the case.[27] The Friends of West Chester, Pennsylvania, were able to find Elizabeth Parker. She had been sold to a New Orleans plantation owner for $1,900 and the Friends filed a petition for her freedom. The Friends also raised $300 for the legal fees for Rachel. Her day in court arrived with more than seventy people, many of them Quakers from the Chester County Anti-Slavery Society, on hand to testify on her behalf. Only forty-nine of the witnesses were called to the witness stand. McCreary's lawyer gave up due to the onslaught of witnesses on Rachel's behalf and McCreary was indicted by the grand jury in West Chester. He never stood trial because Maryland's Governor Lowe denied the request for extradition. Rachel was declared a free person and the West Chester Friends paid $1,500 to buy Elizabeth's freedom.[28]

Betrayal was a danger anyone involved in escaping slavery had to face. In March of 1857, six men and two women banded together to escape from Maryland to Canada. They traveled for several days and reached Delaware. The escapees did not know that a reward of $3,000 had been placed on their heads. As Thomas Garrett later wrote to his cousin Samuel Rhodes, he was warned to be on the lookout for "six brothers and two sisters, they were decoyed and betrayed, he says by a colored man named Thomas Otwell, who pretended to be their friend, and sent a white scamp ahead to wait for them at Dover till they arrived; they were arrested and put in Jail there with Tom's assistance and some officers."

Otwell had led them to an upper floor of a building that they did not know was a jail. When they saw the bars of the cells, the eight escapees fought back. They went down one flight of stairs and ran into the sheriff's apartment. The sheriff's wife awoke, saw the unexpected visitors, and started screaming. One escapee, Henry Predo, smashed out a window and all of the escapees jumped the twelve feet to the ground. They made their escape as the sheriff fired his pistol at them.[29]

The Dover Eight got away, but that was not the end of the story. The Maryland authorities were furious about the escape and decided to fight back. Samuel Green, a free minister from Dorchester County, was suspected of hiding the Dover Eight. In April of 1857, Green's house was searched for evidence that he helped them escape. The only thing that was found was a copy of *Uncle Tom's Cabin*. It was illegal in Maryland for an African American to own a copy of the book. He was found guilty and, because he was a preacher of some fame, was sentenced to ten years in jail. This verdict was meant as a message to anyone else who wanted to help escapees. One of the people affected by this was Benjamin Ross, the father of Harriet Tubman. He did actually hide the Dover Eight and was afraid that he would be the next one arrested. His employer and former master, Dr. Anthony Thompson, warned Ross that he was probably in danger and advised him to flee. Ross and his wife, Catherine, decided to run, even though they were both free people. Harriet heard about her parents' danger and went to Maryland after them.

Harriet was sure that her aging parents would be unable to travel by foot at night and hide during the day, the way she transported other escapees. So she adapted her style by moving her parents at night by way of a horse pulling a transport that had "a pair of old chaise wheels, with a board on the axle to sit on, another board swung with ropes, fastened to the axle to rest their feet on." She delivered them safely to Thomas Garrett in Wilmington. He gave them enough money to travel by train to Canada, where they were reunited with their children and grandchildren. There were not many escapees as old as Benjamin and Catherine Ross who succeeded in escaping to Canada. They believed that they would only have a few years of freedom, but they were wrong. Benjamin lived for twenty more years and his wife even longer.[30]

Sometimes a worker on the Underground Railroad would be discovered. One time, Harriet Tubman was leading a group of escapees and they arrived in a town just at sunrise in the middle of a rainstorm. She went to the door of a free man who had helped her in the past. She knocked on the door in her usual way, but he did not answer. She tried several more times and finally a white man raised a window of the house and asked her what she wanted. Tubman asked about her friend and the neighbor told her that the man had been kicked out of the house because it had been discovered that he helped escapees. He was not as inclined to help her as her friend had been, and she had to keep her people moving until they could find a safe place to stay.[31]

Not every member of the Underground Railroad was a Quaker and not every Quaker was a supporter of those activities. The Friends did not want to break the law, and those who felt they had to bend the law to help those who tried to escape from slavery were sometimes disowned. Isaac Mendelhall of the Kennett (Pennsylvania) Monthly Meeting was disowned because of his railroad activity. Oddly enough, his wife Diana, who was as involved in railroad activities as her husband, was not disowned.[32]

Many things happened to Thomas Garrett during his career as a member of the Underground Railroad but disownment was not one of them. On August 21, 1858, Thomas Garrett wrote to William Still from Wilmington, Delaware, telling him that it was

> my 69th birthday, and I do not know any better way to celebrate it in a way to accord with my feelings, than to send to thee two fugitives, man and wife; the man has been here a week waiting for his wife, who is expected in time to leave at 9 this evening in the cars for thy house with a pilot, who knows where thee lives, but I cannot help but feel some anxiety about the woman, as there is great commotion just now in the neighborhood where she resides. There were 4 slaves betrayed near the Maryland line by a colored man named Jesse Perry a few nights since. One of them made a confidant of him, and he agreed to pilot them on their way, and had several white men secreted to take them as soon as they got in his house; he is the scoundrel that was to have charge of the 7 I wrote you about two weeks since; their master was to take or send them there, and he wanted me to send for them. I have since been confirmed it was a trap set to catch one of our colored men and me likewise, but it was no go. I suspected him from the first, but afterwards was fully confirmed in my suspicions.[33]

If a person was known to be a part of the Underground Railroad, he or she could count on not being the most popular person in their town. Thomas Garrett had a way of annoying supporters of slavery. One slaveholder whose slave had run away told Garrett that if he ever saw the Quaker in the South that he would shoot him. Garrett answered him by saying, "I think I am going that way before long, and I will call upon thee." True to his word, Garrett was soon in southern Delaware and went to the man's house. He introduced himself and said: "How does thee do? Here I am, thee can shoot me if thee likes." Garrett was not shot, and he gained the man's respect.

Garrett was so well known for his anti-slavery actions that in 1860, there was a resolution in the Maryland state legislature that called for a reward of ten thousand dollars for anyone who could arrest him for the crime of slave stealing. Eventually, Garrett heard of the reward and wrote to the legislature. The seventy-one-year-old man told them that he thought that ten thousand dollars was not enough, and if they offered twenty thousand dollars, he would be happy to turn himself in.[34] The Maryland legislature never responded nor bothered him again.[35]

Garrett was a bold man who went about the business of helping escapees without any thought toward his own safety. However, even his luck almost ran out. In January of 1853, Thomas Garrett wrote to his friend Harriet Beecher Stowe about an incident involving himself and another Quaker who worked with the Underground Railroad. In December of 1846, a family of eight by the name of Hawkins stopped at the home of John Hunn, which was located in Middletown, Delaware. They asked for food and a place to stay for the night and Hunn supplied both. Some of Hunn's proslavery neighbors saw the family and reported them to a constable. In the meantime, Hunn had left his home and went to Middletown for a period of time. After his return, the constable returned with a warrant and asked Hunn for the family. Hunn told him that he did not know where they were. He was actually telling the truth, because when he had left to go to Middletown, Mrs. Hunn led them out of the kitchen and up the staircase. It was there that the constable found them.

Hunn was then arrested and sent to the jail in New Castle, Delaware. The sheriff and his daughter asked Mr. and Mrs. Hawkins about the case. The daughter then wrote to Thomas Garrett to ask him to come to New Castle to prove that the Hawkins family had the legal right to be free. Garrett came and asked for a copy of the paperwork legalizing the seizure of the Hawkins family. He thought there was something wrong with the paperwork and took it, with the entire family, to see Judge Booth, the chief justice of Delaware. Hawkins and his wife admitted that their two oldest boys had been held by Charles Glaudin of Maryland as slaves. They also stated that after the birth of those children, the owner of Mrs. Hawkins, Elizabeth Turner of Maryland, freed her and allowed her to live with Mr. Hawkins, a free man who lived about twenty miles from Mrs. Turner. Almost twelve years had gone by and the Hawkinses had four more children, all born free. The judge examined all of the paperwork and set the entire family free.

It was wet and cold on the day that the Hawkins family was set free. The three-year-old was unable to walk and the youngest child was eleven months old. The family wanted to get back to their home in Wilmington quickly, but they lived five miles away. Garrett went back to the judge and asked him if it was permissible to hire some transportation for the mother and the four youngest children to take them home. Judge Booth answered, in front of the sheriff and Garrett's attorney, that he thought there would be no impropriety to allow that. Garrett then asked the sheriff to find something to take the five Hawkins to their home. This request was granted, but Garrett had not heard the last of this case.

In 1848, Thomas Garrett and John Hunn were brought up on charges in a civil case that they were involved in helping escapees. In particular, they were charged because of arranging for transportation for the Hawkins family. They were both convicted, with Hunn receiving a fine of $2,500 and Garrett a penalty of $5,400.

After the sentence was announced, Garrett asked permission to address the court. He said that since the case against the Hawkins family was dismissed, he had no reason to believe that they were slaves. Then he said that if he

"believed every one of them to be slaves, I should have done the same thing."
He also said that it was his opinion that

> the verdicts you have given the prosecutors against John Hunn and myself,
> within the past few days, will have a tendency to raise a spirit of inquiry through-
> out the length and breadth of the land, respecting this monster evil [slavery], in
> many minds that have not heretofore investigated the subject. The reports of
> those trials will be published by editors from Maine to Texas, and the far West;
> and what must be the effect produced? It will, no doubt, add hundreds, perhaps
> thousands, to the present large and rapidly increasing army of Abolitionists. The
> injury is great to us who are the immediate sufferers by your verdict; but I believe
> the verdicts you have given against us within the last few days will have a power-
> ful effect in bringing about the abolition of slavery in this country—this land of
> boasted freedom, where not only the slave is fettered at the South by his lordly
> master, but the white man at the North is bound as in chains to do the bidding of
> his Southern masters.[36]

He finished his speech by saying: "Judge, thou hast not left me a dollar,
but if anyone knows of a fugitive who wants a shelter and a friend send him
to Thomas Garrett and he will befriend him."[37] After the speech, a young man
who was one of the jurors walked over to Garrett and said: "Old gentleman,
I believe every statement that you made. I came from home prejudiced against
you, and I now acknowledge that I have helped to do you injustice."[38]

Garrett was right on two things. First, the fines were so steep that it did
drive the men into bankruptcy. Fortunately, Garrett had many friends and
they raised enough money to return him to solvency and he continued to work
against slavery until the outbreak of the Civil War.[39]

The second thing was that the ranks of those who hated slavery did grow.
After the passage of the Fugitive Slave Law, many people who had not cared
about the plight of the slave resented being, as Thomas Garrett said, "bound
as in chains to do the bidding of his Southern masters." Another person who
was affected by Garrett and his trial was Harriet Beecher Stowe. She admitted
that she was thinking of the trial while she was creating the character of Simeon
Halliday in her book *Uncle Tom's Cabin*, which certainly fueled the fire in the
slavery issue.[40] This growing discontent in the country did not make the act
of helping escapees any easier. Despite the dangers, Underground Railroad
workers, both Quakers and non–Quakers, continued to send escapees along
the tracks to freedom. To do that, they used a multitude of tricks that kept
escapees moving North and their enemies confused.

14. The Tricks of the Trade

Quakers who were active in the abolitionist movement were in the minority among the members of their society. The Friends in positions of authority were upset by the increasing violence in the abolitionist movement in the mid–1830s and wanted no part of it, so they disciplined and sometimes disowned Friends who, in their opinion, were too involved. The Underground Railroad was certainly a case in point. Conservative Friends were worried about the railroad because any involvement was illegal and had to be kept secret, which was in conflict with their belief in being honest and law-abiding in every aspect of their lives. Those Quakers who were involved in the Underground Railroad felt that slavery was so bad that it was worth it to bend the truth. One Quaker farm couple, when asked if they were harboring runaway slaves, said that "there are no slaves here." They did not recognize anyone as a slave, therefore they felt they were being truthful. Another Friend, who was deaf, hid an escapee in a wagonload of brooms and told his grandson, who was normally his ears, to hide as well. When a federal officer asked him about the escapee, the man could truthfully say that he could not hear a word.[1]

Defying the law of the land to help people gain their freedom was done in many varied ways. Thomas Garrett used to keep a supply of garden tools. He would hand one to an escapee and instruct him to carry it through town, pretending to be a laborer. The escapee would continue on to the bridge that was on the way to the next station and hide the tool under it. Later, the tool would be returned to Garrett so it could be used again for the same purpose.

Another trick used by the Quakers was having an escapee wear the bonnet and dress of a Quaker woman. Joseph G. Walker of Wilmington, Delaware, was approached one evening by a woman who had slave hunters close on her heels. The Quaker had her go into his house and a few minutes later, wearing the clothing of Mrs. Walker, she walked out of the house on the arm of Mr. Walker and made her escape.[2] William Wright put women's clothing on escapees several times and sent them to Daniel Gibbons when they came to his house with slave hunters hot on their trail.[3] Thomas Garrett also placed Quaker garb on escapees and sent them to Kennett Square station masters Moses, Mary, and Samuel Pennock, John and Lydia Agnew, and Mahlon, Mary, Edwin, and Daniel Brosius. They knew that Garrett used Quaker garb often and expected escapees sent by Garrett to be dressed that way.[4]

Underground Railroad workers also used code names to announce the presence of escapees, such as "baggage." They also used passwords to protect themselves. Agents would sign their notes to each other with names such as "William Penn" to show that the note came from a legitimate agent.[5] Other code names used were "load of potatoes," which were escapees hidden under farm produce in a wagon, and "bundles of wood," which were escapees to be expected.[6]

The Lewis sisters also used clothes to camouflage the escapees. They once had an escapee and her son who arrived at their home. The boy was put in girls' clothing and the two of them were accompanied to Canada on a train by a friend of theirs.

An innocent-looking wagon sometimes held more than met the eye. John Vickers, a Friend from Lionville, Pennsylvania, used his wagon to transport escapees to freedom. The wagon looked like it was filled with earthenware when in fact it sometimes conveyed escapees to their next stop on the railroad.[7] It was said that Quaker Samuel Johnson rolled up an escapee in a carpet, put him in a wagon, covered him with straw and took him to a Montgomery County, Pennsylvania, farmer's house.[8]

William Wright also used some trickery to move "luggage." Cato Jourdon, a free man, would bring a group of escapees to Wright, who would then either send them along to Daniel Gibbons or have them shipped to Philadelphia. They would travel in hiding in the false end of a boxcar owned by Stephen Smith and William Whipper, who were free lumber merchants from Columbia.[9]

Harriet Tubman brought three escapees into Delaware, heading for Wilmington. Unfortunately, the authorities knew of their escape and posted rewards for the three and a twelve thousand dollar bounty on Tubman. They needed to cross the Wilmington Bridge to arrive at Thomas Garrett's home. However, the bridge was guarded by police officers, and wanted posters were everywhere. Tubman put the escapees in three separate houses and sent word to Garrett that they needed to cross the bridge. When he found out about their dilemma, Garrett came up with a plan. He hired two wagons and filled them with bricklayers who were paid for their adventure. The bricklayers went across the bridge, acting like they were going for a day of fun. The guards who were watching the bridge let the laughing and singing men pass and expected them to return in the evening. The men did return in the evening, but they were not alone. The escapees were hiding at the bottom of the wagons, with the bricklayers in the seats, still singing and laughing. The guards never suspected a thing, and soon the escapees continued their journey.[10]

Sometimes, helping an escapee was something that happened on the spur of the moment. An escapee from Delaware came up to Daniel Elmer, a Quaker from Bridgeton, New Jersey, and asked him for a job. Elmer accepted the request, and later that day, three men from Delaware came looking for the escapee. They came to Elmer's house and saw the man working in Elmer's back yard. Elmer saw the Delaware men and knew that he had to do something to stop them. He was aware of the law and went to the men, saying that he was willing to turn the escapee over to them just as soon as they could produce the proper paperwork on the escapee. One man agreed to return to Delaware to retrieve the paperwork and the other two stayed to make sure that the escapee did not elude them again.

Meanwhile, Elmer sent word to his cousin, Dr. William Elmer, to ask for his help. The doctor's wife went to Elmer's house and dressed the escapee in a top hat, cane, and pipe so that he could impersonate Daniel Elmer. Mrs. Elmer walked him to the front gate and said loud enough for the men to hear her, "Hurry, Daniel, or William will be gone to bed!" They then walked past the men to her home, where horses were waiting.[11]

Daniel Gibbons also had an occasion where he seized the opportunity to help an escapee. In 1833, he was traveling in Adams County, Pennsylvania, which is near the Maryland border, with Thomas Pearl, who was also involved in the Underground Railroad. They came upon a woman who was in danger of being captured. He stopped, picked up the woman and returned to his home where he could safely send her on her way.[12]

The idea to escape from slavery sometimes came after long consideration, and other times it came suddenly. One time, a woman overheard her master selling her to a slave trader. She immediately escaped and ended up at the home of Caleb C. Hood in Lancaster County, Pennsylvania. She eventually travelled to Massachusetts to live with a son who had escaped before her.[13]

Harriet Shephard was a slave and a mother of five young children. In November of 1855, she had grown fearful that her children might one day become slaves like her and decided on a bold course of action. She stole her master's horses and carriage and used it to help her and her children escape. She also knew of five others who wanted to escape as well and gave them some of the horses she had taken. They escaped from Chestertown, Maryland, and because they were not sure where to go, they stayed on the main roads, and rode through the middle of Wilmington, Delaware, in the carriage with innocent looks on their faces. Against all odds, the ploy worked. Thomas Garrett soon learned about them and sought them out. Once he did, Garrett felt that the escapees had to get rid of the horses and carriages and leave Wilmington as soon as possible. He sent them to Kennett Square, Pennsylvania, then to the Longwood Quaker Meeting House and later to freedom.[14]

Another spur-of-the-moment action to protect an escapee happened in Delaware County, Pennsylvania. A Quaker couple, George and MaLady McCracken, were abolitionists who hid an escapee named Kitty, whom they disguised as their house servant. One day, slave hunters were given a tip that an escaped slave was being hidden there. They arrived without warning to capture Kitty. She managed to escape by slipping through a trap door which led to an outside roof. The roof led to a summer kitchen, and Kitty made good her escape. When the hunters had left, Kitty returned to the McCrackens' home.[15]

Escapees and railroad workers never knew when they might be in danger of discovery. One night, a young female escapee named Tyler came to the home of a Quaker family in Greenwich, New Jersey, and stayed for several months. One morning around dawn, she went to the kitchen to prepare the fire to cook breakfast. She happened to look out of a window and saw her former master in the driveway with two men. She ran upstairs, woke up the Tylers and told them about the men in the driveway. Mr. Tyler told his wife to make up a bundle of clothes for her and he went downstairs to meet the visitors.

Mr. Tyler invited the men into his home and served them coffee. The coffee was part of the plan that had been made while he was still upstairs. He told the men that his wife was ill and he went to the bottom of the stairs and said loudly: "Do you want coffee to be brought up to your room?" This was the signal for the girl to crawl out a small window near the lower roof. Once outside, she was to run to a cornfield where the corn was high enough to hide her. Mr. Tyler's instructions to her had ended with "From the corn field, run to Springtown, and you will be safe."[16]

Anyone who tried to escape slavery took terrible risks, but one of the boldest escapes occurred in 1849. Henry Brown's bid for freedom began in August 1848 in Virginia. His wife and children had been taken from their home and sold to a man from North Carolina while he was out working. Nancy Brown was owned by a man other than the one who owned Brown, but Henry had paid that man fifty dollars so that she and the children would not be sold to anyone else. When he discovered what had happened, Brown went to his master three times to beg him to intercede on his behalf. His owner told Brown that the Methodist minister who bought Brown's family was a gentleman and he did not want to interfere with his affairs.

Brown fell into a depression over the loss of his family that lasted for months. After Christmas, Brown became convinced "that I should be acting in accordance with the will of God, if I could snap in sunder those bonds by which I was held body and soul as the property of a fellow man." He then began to set his mind toward freedom. In January of 1849, he approached a storekeeper in Richmond, Virginia, whom he bought supplies from. Brown believed he was a man of integrity. Brown told him of his situation and said that he would pay the man if he would help him escape. They agreed on $86 and began to work on escape ideas.

None of the ideas appealed to the men, but one day while Brown was at work, he prayed for God to "lend me his aid in bursting my fetters asunder, and in restoring me to the possession of those rights, of which men had robbed me; when the idea suddenly flashed across my mind of shutting myself in a box, and getting myself conveyed as dry goods to a free state." He found a carpenter who was willing to make a box for him to travel in, and the storekeeper wrote to a friend in Philadelphia, asking permission to address the box to him. The friend agreed and Brown, the storekeeper, and Brown's minister quickly prepared a plan. Brown faked an injury and told his master that he needed to rest for several days, which would give Brown a head start if his master decided to pursue him. Then the box was prepared for the express train, with instructions printed on it that stated: "this side up with care." The box itself was

> three feet one inch wide, two feet six inches high, and two feet wide; and on the morning of the 29th day of March, 1849, I went into the box—having previously bored three gimlet holes opposite my face, for air, and provided myself with a bladder of water, both for the purpose of quenching my thirst and for wetting my face, should I feel getting faint. I took the gimlet also with me, in order that I might bore more holes if I found I had not sufficient air. Being thus equipped for the battle of liberty, my friends nailed down the lid and had me conveyed to the Express Office.

The next twenty-seven hours taught Brown just how badly some shipping employees treat shipments. Along with lying on his back as requested, Brown spent some of the three hundred and fifty miles standing on his feet, his face, and in one hour and a half time frame, standing on his head.[17]

In Philadelphia, members of the Pennsylvania Anti-Slavery Society were concerned for the safety of Brown. They had been informed by telegraph when they could expect the box. They sent E.M. Davis, the son-in-law of James and Lucretia Mott, to the Adams Express office to make sure that the delivery was going to their office at 107 North 5th Street. Davis even paid a deliveryman extra to bring the box as quickly as possible. Soon, the box arrived at the society. After the deliveryman left, the door of the office was locked and J.M. McKim, C.D. Cleveland, Lewis Thompson, and William Still opened the box. As Still later recounted, Brown rose "up in his box, he reached out his hand, saying 'How do you do, gentlemen?'" They helped him out and sent him to the home of James Mott and E.M. Davis to recover. He stayed with Still for two days and then headed off to Boston.[18]

Apparently, 1848 was the year for escapees to make outrageous plans for freedom. William and Ellen Croft lived in Georgia, and since they were deep in the South, it was considered almost impossible for anyone to escape to the North for freedom. However, they came up with a bold plan for escape. Ellen was so light-skinned that she was able to pass herself off as a Caucasian woman. Her husband William thought that she could pass as an invalid young man and he would pose as her slave who was traveling with her. In December of

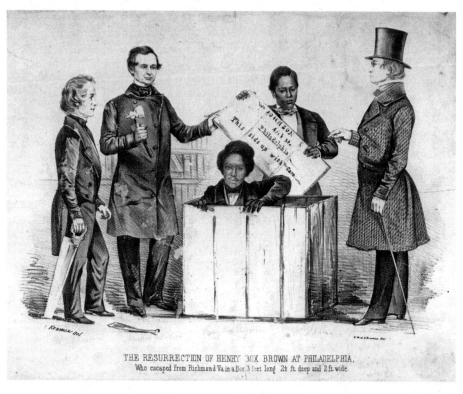

THE RESURRECTION OF HENRY BOX BROWN AT PHILADELPHIA.
Who escaped from Richmond Va. in a Box 3 feet long 2½ ft. deep and 2 ft. wide.

The Resurrection of Henry Box Brown at Philadelphia. Henry Brown emerging from the box that carried him to freedom. His escape from slavery was one of the most audacious on record (Swarthmore College, Friends Historical Library).

1848, they bought the disguise Ellen would need and, like Brown, requested a few days off from their owner so that they could have a head start on anyone who was looking for them. Ellen was then dressed up as a young man. They put a poultice around her face to cover any hint of femininity, as well as to give her an excuse not to engage in conversation with anyone they might meet along the way.

On the night of their escape, they left their home and walked quietly into the street "because we were like persons near a tottering avalanche, afraid to move, to breathe freely, for fear the sleeping tyrants should be aroused, to come down upon us with double vengeance, for daring to attempt escape in the manner which we contemplated."

They took two separate routes to the train station. William took the quickest way in case someone recognized him, and Ellen bought tickets for them. Their fears of being recognized almost came true when Mr. Cray, a friend of Ellen's master, sat on the same seat as Ellen. Mr. Cray tried to engage in polite conversation with her, but she pretended to be hard of hearing and the man soon stopped trying to talk to her and moved to another area to sit.

The train arrived in Savannah and they connected with a steamer to Charleston, South Carolina. Ellen had put her right arm in a sling and William stayed with her to carve her food. During dinner, Ellen was warned not to take her slave to the North in case an abolitionist tried to free him. She also had another man offer to buy William. She said that she could not sell him because she was ill and could not manage without him. The slave trader replied that he could tell "from the cut of his eye that he is certain to run away."

William and Ellen had originally planned to take a steamer from Charleston to Philadelphia, but they had to change their plans because steamers did not run to Philadelphia in the winter. Therefore, they had to improvise and take a steamer to Wilmington, North Carolina. From there, they caught a train to Richmond, Virginia. When they were on the train, a man asked William why they were traveling. William told him that they were going to Philadelphia to get medical attention for his master that he could not obtain in Georgia. The man agreed that William's master would get the proper attention and then gave William "a ten-cent piece and requested me to be attentive to my good master. I promised that I would do so, and ever since endeavored to keep my pledge."

The close calls continued. In Baltimore, an officer informed them that no one traveling with a slave could go beyond Baltimore unless the traveler could prove that they really owned the slave traveling with them. Since they had no such papers, they had to act quickly. Ellen argued that since she had purchased tickets in Charleston to go directly to Philadelphia, she should be allowed to travel on. She made such a scene that spectators started to gather around. Their opinion was that the officer should let the invalid gentleman and his slave move on without being harassed. As the Crofts said a quick prayer for help, the conductor of their train came in and told the officer that they had come in from Washington on his train. Just then, the bell announcing the departure of the train rang. Everyone who had gathered around now stared at the officer. Then, "the officer all at once thrust his fingers through his hair, and in a state of great agitation said, "I really don't know what to do; I calculate it is all right." He then told the clerk to run and tell the conductor to "let this gentleman and slave pass," adding, "As he is not well, it is a pity to stop him here. We will let him go."

The Crofts had spent four days and nights planning their escape and then spent four more days on the run with very little time for sleep. Once they pulled out of Baltimore to Philadelphia, William left Ellen in the first-class section of the train and went back to the section near the luggage cars where slaves stayed during the trip. William decided to rest a little, and while he slept, the train stopped at Havre de Grace, Maryland. The first-class passengers were removed from the train and placed onto a ferry boat which took them across the Susquehanna River. These passengers would then board the train again once they reached the other side of the river. William, being a slave, was left on the train with the luggage and crossed that way. When Ellen did not see him after the passengers were unloaded, she thought that perhaps he had been discovered. She asked the conductor if he had seen William, and the conductor, being against slavery, told her that he "haven't seen anything of him for some time; I have no doubt he has run away, and is in Philadelphia, free, long before now." Ellen asked him to look for William, but the man became furious and told her that "I am no slave-hunter" and stalked off. She then decided to trust that nothing bad had happened to William.

After the train had set off again for Philadelphia, a guard found William and shook him awake. He told William that his master was extremely worried about him and thought he had run away. William immediately went to Ellen to reassure her of his safety. As he walked back to his seat, William found the conductor, the guard, and several other men waiting for him. The guard asked him what his master wanted and William said his master just wanted to know where he was. The guard did not believe him and said that his master thought "you had taken French leave for parts unknown. I never saw a fellow so badly scared about his slave in my life." The guard then said that he wanted to give William "a little friendly advice. When you get to Philadelphia, run away and leave that cripple and have your liberty." William replied that he could not do that. The conductor chimed in and asked him: "Don't you want your liberty?"

William told him that he did, but "I shall never run away from such a good master as I have at present." One of the other men there told the guard to leave William alone and said that "he will open his eyes when he gets to Philadelphia, and see things in another light." The man then gave William a great deal of information that he later used. William also met "a colored gentleman on this train, who recommended me to a boarding-house that was kept by an abolitionist where he thought I would be quite safe, if I wished to run away from my master. I thanked him kindly, but of course did not let him know who we were."

Finally, William saw flickering lights in the distance and he heard someone on the train say that they were coming to Philadelphia. When he heard the announcement, William "felt that the straps that bound the heavy burden to my back began to pop, and the load to roll off. I also looked and looked again, for it appeared very wonderful to me how the mere sight of our first city of refuge should have all at once made my hitherto sad and heavy heart become so light and happy."

The train had barely stopped when William jumped off of the train, collected Ellen, hired a cab, and drove to the boardinghouse that was recommended to him. Ellen sat in the cab, "grasped me by the hand, and said, 'Thank God William, we are safe!' then burst into tears, leant upon me and wept like a child."

The landlord of the boardinghouse was indeed sympathetic to escapees and he introduced them to abolitionists in the area. One of them was Barkley Ivens, a Friend who lived on a farm outside the city. Ivens invited them to stay with him and his family for a few days until Mrs. Croft had recovered from the journey. William said that this offer was "the first act of great and disinterested kindness we had ever received from a white person."

Ivens was a man of dark complexion, and when Ellen first saw him, as he picked them up in a cart, she thought that he was of mixed blood like herself. However, when she found out that he was not, she became very nervous and shy around him. When they arrived at Ivens' farm, even the warm greetings she received from Ivens' wife and daughters did not calm her fears that Ivens would send them back into slavery. Mrs. Ivens offered Ellen tea, and when Ellen replied that they would not be staying long, Mrs. Ivens reassured her that she would not "hurt a single hair of thy head. We have heard with much pleasure of the marvelous escape of thee and thy husband, and deeply sympathize with thee in all that thou hast undergone. I don't wonder at thee, poor thing, being timid; but thou needs not fear us; we would as soon send one of our own daughters into slavery as thee; so thou mayest make thee quite at ease." These words finally calmed Ellen and she began to relax. By the time the Crofts were ready to leave for Boston, they felt like they were leaving their family.[19]

As Shakespeare once said about one man in his time playing many parts, so did the members of the Underground Railroad. One of the more unusual parts occurred in the case of Samuel D. Burris. A free man, Burris was involved with the Pennsylvania Anti-Slavery Society and would go South to lead escapees to freedom.[20] In 1844, his luck ran out. He and John Hunn were arrested for helping several escapees and thrown into jail in Dover, Delaware. They were sued by the owners of the escapees for loss of property and found guilty. Hunn was fined $2,500 and had to sell his farm.[21] Burris was sentenced to be sold either in or out of the state for a period of seven years. The Anti-Slavery Society decided that the only way to save Burris was to raise money and buy him. They decided that known abolitionists such as Thomas Garrett and John Hunn, both friends of Burris, could not go. Therefore, they had to find someone was not known to the slave traders. The Society decided on Isaac S. Flint of Wilmington, Delaware, to buy Burris.

On the day of the sale, Burris was placed on the auction block. Anyone who was interested in buying a slave had the opportunity to examine them before the sale began. Flint watched how the prospective buyers inspected the slaves like they were buying a horse and followed suit. The auction began and a slave trader from Baltimore bid five hundred dollars for Burris. Flint could not let the bidding go too high for fear that he would not have enough money to free his colleague. So he went to the trader and gave him one hundred dollars to stop bidding. The ploy worked and Flint was able to buy Burris. After this experience, Burris swore to never again go south. That did not mean that he stopped working for the rights of his people. In 1852, he moved to California for a better job, but continued to stay appraised of Underground Railroad activities. Also, after the Civil War he worked to raise money to help support the influx of freed slaves into Washington, D.C.[22]

In spite of the difficulties, members of the Underground Railroad continued the fight against slavery, using whatever means necessary, legal and otherwise.

15. Stories of the Underground

One of the by-products of the Fugitive Slave Act was that it made it diffi-cult for future historians to chronicle the stories of the Underground Railroad. When the act was passed, many workers of the railroad destroyed the records they kept on the amount of escapees who were sent to freedom. Robert Purvis of Philadelphia stated that he kept a record of not only the escapees he helped but also those people his colleagues helped. His family was worried that this record could be used against him, so he destroyed it. Daniel Gibbons had begun keeping his own records in 1824, but he too destroyed them after the passage of the act. A friend of William Parker found a large number of letters sent to Parker by escapees around the time of the Christiana incident and they too were destroyed. The timing was excellent because if they had been found during the trial, it would have been disastrous for his defense. However, some records have survived, and along with personal recollections compiled after the Civil War, they allow the stories of the Underground Railroad to come to light.[1] In his book, *The Underground Railroad*, written in 1872, William Still mentioned that he felt that it was not "prudent even now, to give the names of persons still living in the South, who assisted their fellow-men in the dark days of Slavery."[2] The following are some of the experiences of escapees and how certain members of the Society of Friends risked so much to help them.

Daniel Gibbons had started helping escapees in 1797 and continued until his death in 1853. He had a set pattern to help escapees. His family was accus-tomed to hearing a rap on the window at night, which signified someone needed help. The person at the window would be taken into the barn until morning. Then the escapee would be brought into the house, or if there was more than one, brought in one at a time. Gibbons would then quiz the escapees. The first thing he asked them was what their situation was and was their master hard on their trail. If the master were not, Gibbons would get them work. If their masters were nearby, he would take the escapees to the barn or the fields and then send them to the road to Reading, Pennsylvania. Of all the people he helped, only one or two were ever recaptured. Before the Fugitive Slave Act, he would ask them their names, the name of their master, the new name they wanted, and what part of the country they came from.

Many times, a successful escape from slavery was a group effort. One such time was in 1828 or 1829. An escapee was living with Truman Cooper of Sudsbury, Lancaster County, Pennsylvania. One day, he was working in the fields when two slave owners, acting on information they had received, jumped him, tied his hands together, and carried him off. A boy living at the Cooper house saw what had happened and went to the tannery of Thomas Hood to report what had happened. John Hood and Allen Smith, who were nearby, went after the kidnappers. When they caught up with them, the two Friends started a conversation with the slave owners to find out where they were going. They told Hood and Smith that they were going to stay the night at Quigg's Tavern in Georgetown. They took their leave and arrived at Georgetown before the kidnappers. They informed the free population of the situation, who then took up arms and prepared for their arrival. While the kidnappers ate in the tavern, the landlady, Hannah Quigg, untied the captive. The slave owners saw him escaping and tried to stop him. They ran out of the tavern and found a wall of armed free men blocking the road. The slave owners backed down but regained the escapee's trail the next day. He was able to elude them and arrived at Jeremiah Cooper's home. He hid in the woods for a week and Cooper's wife took food to him. At the end of that time, Cooper gave him a suit of his plain clothes and sent him through the railroad and freedom.

In 1835, William Wallace, an escapee, was working in a barn with Jacob Bushong, an abolitionist and Friend. They saw four men on a wagon and two more on horseback coming down the street. Bushong thought that they might be trouble, so he told Wallace to stay out of sight until he found out what they wanted. When he walked up to the men, they asked him if Wallace lived there. It was Bushong's house, so he had no trouble telling the men no. When they pointed at Wallace's house, he did not answer them. The men decided that the silence was a yes to their question, so four of the men went into the house. They tied up Wallace's wife and took her to the Lancaster jail. After placing her in jail, they went to the home of John Urick, a free man, and took his wife to the jail as well. She had originally escaped from slavery with Wallace's wife.

The next day, the two women arrived at Daniel Gibbons' home. When they were asked how they got out of jail, they told him that they had broken out. Gibbons then sent them to the house of his son, Dr. Joseph Gibbons, who

sent them along the Underground Railroad. The story that the women told—
that they had used a knife to break out of jail—seemed odd, so Dr. Gibbons
went to the jailer and asked him how the two women had escaped. The jailer,
"Devil-Dave" Miller, winked and laughed at Dr. Gibbons. Later, it was discovered that Miller had opened the jail door and let them walk free.[3]

According to local oral history, escapees were hidden in the loft of the
Friends Meeting House in Odessa, Delaware. Another story that is more than
oral history happened in Odessa in 1845. The local sheriff was looking for an
escapee named Sam. The sheriff went to the Corbit-Sharp house, which was
built in 1774 by William Corbit, a Friend who made his fortune as a tanner,
to look for the escapee. The lady of the house, Mary Corbit, accompanied the
sheriff in his search. Above the stairway leading to the third floor was a door
behind which was a cubbyhole and inside this small area was Sam. As they
walked up the stairs, Mrs. Corbit hoped that the sheriff would think that the
space was too small to hide a man. They walked steadily up the stairs and the
sheriff continued his search past the cubbyhole. He did not find Sam and left
the house. Years later, Mrs. Corbit told her daughter, Mary Warner, that her
heart was beating so loudly throughout the search that she was afraid that it
would give her away.[4]

In the late 1840s, a man named "Little Sittles" escaped from his master
and ended up at Crosswicks and stayed with Enoch Middleton in Burlington
County, New Jersey. Middleton was known as a bold man who took chances
that other members of the railroad would not take.[5] At one point, he hid thirty
escapees at his home at the same time, and would even move escapees during
the day.[6] Sittles eventually went to Canada, but decided to return to Crosswicks. He found a job at a slaughterhouse across the creek from Middleton's
home. This creek was also the boundary between Burlington and Mercer
Counties. Six months after Sittles' return to New Jersey, someone informed
his former owner of his whereabouts. The master went to Sittles' place of
employment accompanied by the Burlington County sheriff and tried to take
him. Sittles broke free and ran for the creek. He went to Middleton's house
and asked for his help. The Quaker hid Sittles and met the slave owner and
the sheriff at the bridge leading to his property. Middleton rejected the papers
the owner had on Sittles and, even when he was physically threatened, refused
the two men access to his land. Since the sheriff had no jurisdiction on Middleton's property, the two men had to back away. Sittles then went back on
the Underground Railroad and to Canada.[7]

Samuel W. Mifflin came by his resistance to slavery through his family.
His grandfather, John Mifflin, was the first Friend in Philadelphia to obey the
edict to liberate their slaves, and William Wright was his uncle. He grew up

watching different members of his family helping escapees. One time, he saw a man dressed like a woman walk across his yard. The dress only reached the man's knees and Mifflin wondered how he could ever pass as a woman. But once the man got on a wagon, the dress covered his legs and no one was the wiser. Another time when he was young, Mifflin knew of an escapee that his family was hiding in a cornfield. His cousin would go out with his gun and a bag that looked like his lunch. Actually, he was taking food out to the escapee until he could be safely moved.

When he grew up, Mifflin came home one night to discover thirteen escapees sitting in his living room. His older brother had found them wandering in the neighborhood. They stayed in the house for two days because of heavy rains that made the nearby Susquehanna River unsafe to cross. On the third night, they were ferried across the river to Columbia.

After his father's death in 1840, Mifflin took over the house and continued his father's work on the Underground Railroad until 1846, when his job as a civil engineer took him away. He returned two years later and restarted his efforts against slavery.[8]

The Quakers had a reputation among slaves as people who would help those who tried to free themselves. Mary Thomas told a writer from the Federal Writers' Project in 1938 about how her father and grandfather escaped slavery. They suspected that their owner was going to sell them, so they decided to escape. The two men had heard of the Underground Railroad and knew if they were able to go to Baltimore, they could meet with friends who could get them to Philadelphia. From there, the Quakers were known to either let the escapees live in the area or escort them to other people who would get them to Canada. The danger in doing this was that any "slave who went off the farm had to have a pass signed by the master or he would be picked up by a sheriff and put in jail and be whipped." The grandfather was able to read and write, so he was able to create a pass to get them safely on their way. They waited in Baltimore for several days until they were able to meet someone from the Underground Railroad. Mrs. Thomas then said that one night during their escape, her father and grandfather

> were dressed in some calico [?] homespun like a woman and rode to Philadelphia on the back seat of a wagon loaded with fish. In Philadelphia the town was being searched by slave-holders looking for runaway slaves, so the people where they were suppose to stay in Philadelphia hurried them across the river about ten miles.
>
> My grandfather and my father stayed across the Delaware from Philadelphia, helping a farmer harvest his crops, and they built a cabin and soon other escaped slaves from among their former neighbors slipped into New Jersey where they were.

Finally there was almost a hundred escaped slaves in the one spot and because they were free at last and this place was a haven just like the Bible talked about, they decided to stay there and so they got together and called the place Free Haven.

My uncle says that he reached there by hiding in the woods all day and walking at night. So many people came from Maryland that they changed the name of the little village to Snow Hill, which was the name of the town nearest the farms from which all or most of the people had run away from. The post office people made them change the name again and now it is Lawnside, but I was born there sixty-four years ago and I still think of it as Free Haven.[9]

Daniel Gibbons used to send escapees to the home of Jeremiah Moore, another Friend, who lived in Christiana, Delaware. He would give directions to Moore's house by saying that Moore lived at "the first house over the bridge where the public road crossed the railroad." Moore would hide them in one of the upper rooms of his home and when he brought them down for something to eat, he would bolt all of the doors. He would do that because he noticed groups of proslavery men hanging around the woods near his home. The men would also come to his door on other business and blatantly look around the house for traces of escapees.

One day, Abraham Johnson, a slave belonging to a Mr. Wheeler of Cecil County, Maryland, heard that he was to be sold the next day. That night, Johnson, along with his mother, sister, and her child, escaped. They went to Robert Loney, a free man who ferried escapees across the Susquehanna River at night at different places below the town of Columbia. They eventually arrived at Moore's house. Johnson worked for Moore for five years and the others lived nearby. However, by the time of the Christiana incident, they had all moved to Canada.[10]

Molly escaped from a farm in Cecil County, Maryland, but was recaptured in Middletown, Delaware. She escaped from her master again and went to the home of John Hunn. She stayed for a month but decided to move on after seeing many other escapees moving north. Hunn contacted his friend and fellow Quaker Thomas Garrett to see if he could find a place for Molly to live. Garrett found a family in Chester County, Pennsylvania, to take Molly in and she stayed there for six months. It was during this time that the Fugitive Slave Law was passed. Molly heard of several escapees being arrested in Philadelphia and sent back to their owners. This news made her nervous, so she left her home and moved on to Canada for her own safety.

Courage and an ability to quickly react to a problem were certainly needed if someone was involved with the Underground Railroad. In the fall of 1851, four escapees came from Washington County, Maryland, to Adams County, Pennsylvania, and arrived at William Wright's home. Their journey was a hard one and their masters had gone to Harrisburg to search for them. Two of the escapees stayed at the home of Joel Wierman, Wright's brother-in-law, and the others, Fenton and Tom, hid at Wright's. Several days later, Wright, Fenton, Tom, and a crew of carpenters were working on Wright's barn when a group of men arrived. One of them was the owner of the escapees and they were recognized. Fenton and Tom said that they had left their coats in the house and went inside. Wright then brought the owner and his men into his home and spoke with them for an hour about slavery. One of the men then asked Wright to bring the escapees out. He refused, but told them that they could search the house if they wished. They realized that Wright was stalling for time and searched the house and the barn. However, they went past the carriage house without going into it. They did not find the escapees and left. Tom had hidden in the carriage house and Fenton went into the fields. The slave hunters then went to Wierman's home and captured one of the escapees. The others were not found and were able to go to the next stop on the railroad.[11]

Another incident at Wright's house showed the quick thinking that saved more than a few escapees. A large number of escapees arrived at the home, two of them being a mother and a small child, with their masters hot on their trail. All of the escapees were able to be spirited away except for the infant. They were afraid that the child might start crying and give away the others. Wright created a plan in which a young woman who was staying at the house would take the baby to bed with her. When the slave-owners arrived, they were asked to please be careful while searching the house because there was a small child there. When they reached the room where the baby was hiding, they were warned with a "Shh" from the "mother" to not wake the baby. She then pinched the child, which then started to cry, thus convincing the searchers that the story they heard was true. They soon left and everyone, including the baby, moved on.[12]

Abigail Goodwin not only helped escapees move on to Canada but she also raised funds to pay for the cost of helping them. In a letter to William Still in January of 1855, she stated that she had "enclosed ten dollars I have made, earned in two weeks; and of course, it belongs to the slave. It may go for the fugitives ... I am sorry that the fugitives' treasury is not better supplied."[13]

There were times when trying to help an escapee became far more complicated than was originally intended. On July 18, 1855, the American minister to Nicaragua, John H. Wheeler, was leaving Philadelphia by boat for New York City. His slave, Jane Johnson, and her two children, David and Isaiah, were traveling with him. William Still and Passmore Williamson, a Quaker and the secretary of the Pennsylvania Antislavery Society, received information about Mrs. Johnson and her children. The two men went to the boat and arrived before it left. They were given a description of the three people and began to search the boat. Upon finding them, they asked for Wheeler's permission to speak to his servants. Colonel Wheeler refused, but Williamson spoke to Mrs. Johnson anyway. He asked her if she was a slave. When she answered yes, he informed her that because Wheeler had brought her to a free state, she could be set free.

Colonel Wheeler was unable to stop Williamson from speaking to Mrs. Johnson. However, he consistently cut in on the conversation. He first insisted that Mrs. Johnson was going to New York with him to visit friends and that she wanted to go back to the South because she had three other children there and she did not want to be parted from them. He also said that he was going to give Mrs. Johnson her freedom one day. The truth was that Wheeler had realized before Williamson and Still had arrived at the boat that he had made a mistake in bringing Mrs. Johnson with him because of the laws of Pennsyl-

Taken from *The Underground Railroad* by William Still (1872) this drawing shows the rescue of Jane Johnson and her children from their master in 1855 in Philadelphia. Passmore Wilkinson, one of the participants and a Quaker, was taken to court to reveal their whereabouts. Mrs. Johnson's dramatic entrance during the trial brought about his acquittal (Swarthmore College, Friends Historical Library).

vania. He had kept a very close eye on her for fear of something like this happening. Mrs. Johnson also had only one child in the South and he had been sold far away from her. She did not expect to ever see him again. In spite of all of Colonel Wheeler's efforts, she told Williamson that "I am not free, but I want my freedom—ALWAYS wanted to be free!! But he holds me."

Finally, a bell sounded, which indicated that the boat was about to leave. Williamson asked her to come with him. Mrs. Johnson gathered up her children and went with Williamson. Wheeler rushed them and grabbed both Mrs. Johnson and Williamson. The Quaker shook off the slaveholder and the small party moved on. Mrs. Johnson's seven-year-old son cried out "Massa John! Massa John!" as they left, but his older brother and mother were not sorry to leave Wheeler.[14]

A group of free men came with Williamson. As the boat prepared to leave, they came on board and carried Mrs. Johnson and her children to a waiting carriage. Two of them threatened Wheeler, who was in pursuit, not to try to stop them.[15] The younger boy was still whimpering as he sat in the carriage that he was being taken away from Wheeler. His brother told him that he was a fool for crying and that Wheeler would sell him if he ever caught them. The boy immediately stopped crying and the carriage moved on.[16] Williamson had not helped to take the Johnsons off the boat and into the carriage, but that did not give him much protection. Wheeler went to a policeman on the dock for help, but the officer refused to do anything.

Not to be put off, Wheeler then went to the U.S. District Court for a writ of habeas corpus to force Williamson to return the Johnsons. Williamson's response to the court was that the Johnsons had never been in his possession. Judge John K. Kane believed that Williamson was not being forthcoming in revealing what had happened, so he charged the Quaker with contempt of court and put him in jail. On July 31 and again in August, Williamson petitioned the chief justice of the Supreme Court of Pennsylvania for a writ of habeas corpus. He was refused in July and the court was in recess in August.

On October 3, Jane Johnson returned from Massachusetts, where she had escaped to when she left the boat, to appear before Judge Kane with her lawyers Joseph B. Townsend and John M. Read.[17] She entered the courtroom wearing a veil and was accompanied by Lucretia Mott and several others.[18] She told the judge that she had not been in Williamson's custody and had not seen him since leaving the boat. She asked the judge to remove the writ of habeas corpus on her and her children. She also requested that Williamson be released from custody. The court refused to enter the plea. The judge said that Johnson had no rank in the federal court. He said that Williamson was not being punished, he was being held in contempt of court. He also stated that just because a slave owner brought his slave into free territory, it did not mean that the slave was now free.

On November 4, Williamson appeared before the district court and stated that he had not intended to hold the court in contempt or hinder the court from doing their job. He said that he did not produce the escapees in court because he was unable to do so. The court believed him and set him free. Mrs. Johnson and her children stayed free because Wheeler was no longer in the country to request them back.[19]

Just because someone was free did not mean that they were safe from exploitation. In March of 1856, a boy named Anderson lived with his free parents in Mount Holly, New Jersey. He was approached by a man from Hainesport who wanted to hire him to work at his father's farm in West Philadelphia. The two agreed to the terms of employment and they went to Philadelphia. However, the man had other ideas. He took Anderson to Baltimore, where he tried to sell him for five hundred dollars. Anderson was able to escape and contact the Friends in the area. He told them his story and the man was arrested and placed in jail. The Friends then returned the boy to his family.[20]

Sometimes, the way to freedom took a lot longer than originally thought. William Jordan was a slave of Mrs. Mary Jordan, who was married to the governor of North Carolina. They were both hard masters, being stingy with food and clothing, but not flogging their slaves as much as other masters in the area. William was separated from his wife by two hundred miles when his mistress married the governor. He was promised that he would be able to see his wife on certain occasions. Not long after arriving at the governor's plantation, William asked if he could go see his wife. He was told that it was ridiculous to travel two hundred miles to visit his wife and was turned down. It was then that William made up his mind to escape. If he could not see his wife but once or twice a year, then it was worth it to him to either live in a cave or die. He escaped, and for ten months, he did live in a cave. As hard as living in a cave was, William preferred it to living with the governor of North Carolina.

William did have one friend who kept an eye out for a captain who would sail him north. Finally, a Captain Fountain took William north and he met Thomas Garrett. The Quaker gave him a pair of boots and money for passage to Philadelphia. He also gave William a letter dated December 12, 1855, to give to William Still. In it, he told Still that he had been living in the wild for about a year. William eventually made his way to New Bedford, Connecticut, where he felt safer.[21]

The fight against slavery needed money to continue, and the pursuit of it was not easy. On July 30, 1856, Abigail Goodwin wrote to William Still about her fund raising efforts. In her letter, she stated, "I have tried to beg something for them, but have not got much; one of our neighbors, S.W. Acton, gave me three dollars for them. I added enough to make ten, which thee will find inside."[22]

Thomas Garrett sometimes worked with Harriet Tubman in the course of their business with the Underground Railroad. The Quaker felt that "Harriet has a good deal of the old fashioned Quaker about her, she is a firm believer in spiritual manifestations." She told him that she had every confidence that God would always preserve her in her journeys to free slaves and only went on her missions with God's consent. One such incident occurred when Tubman came to Garrett's store in 1856 and asked for him. She told him that God sent her to get money from him. He told her that he "expected thee would want a new pair of shoes as usual when thee hast been on a journey, those I can give that, but thee knows I have a great many calls for money from the colored people and thee cannot expect much money from me." She replied that he could give her "what I need now. God never fools me." Garrett asked her what she needed and Tubman told him the amount she needed to rescue her sister and children. He asked her if she had been to Philadelphia lately. "No, not for several weeks." "Has anyone told thee I had money for thee?" "No, nobody but God." Garrett then gave her the money he was holding for her, which was the amount she needed.

When Tubman went to her sister, she found out that two of the children had been taken from her and lived twelve miles away. Her sister refused to leave without them. She then told Harriet that she was hoping to be able to visit them between Christmas and New Year's Day and that they would try to escape then. Harriet agreed to return at that time and left the area with five escapees.

The masters of three of the escapees were determined to retrieve them. They went to Wilmington and placed handbills around town with a description of the escapees and the offer of a reward for their return. They also placed them at the railway depots and major towns in the area. The bills were a waste of time in Wilmington because the free people of the city ripped them down as fast as they went up. Despite the reward, Tubman was able to take the escapees to Canada.[23]

Thomas Garrett sent another person north who spent a long time in the woods hiding from her master. In June of 1857, Garrett helped a woman who was

the mother of twelve children, one half of which has been sold South. She had been so ill used, that she was compelled to leave husband and children behind, and is desirous of getting to a brother who lives at Buffalo. She was nearly naked. She called at my house on 7th day night, but being from home, did not see her till last evening. I have promised her two under garments, one new; two skirts one new: a good frock with cape; one of my wife's bonnets and stockings, and gave her five dollars in gold, which, if properly used, will put her pretty well on the way.

Garrett thought that she was about sixty or seventy and had escaped to avoid being sold. Her master was rumored to be preparing to sell her, and since four of her children had been sold away from her, she thought she had better escape before it was too late. She spent three weeks in the woods alone with very little food before she found a place of safety.

In November of 1857, Garrett once again helped someone who spent a great deal of time hiding before heading for freedom. He wrote to William Still to inform him that

Captain Fountain has arrived this evening from the South with three men, one of which is nearly naked, and very lousy. He has been in the swamps of Carolina for eighteen months past. One of the others has been some time out. I would send them on to-night, but will have to provide two of them with some clothes before they can be sent by railroad.

After the escapees had arrived in Philadelphia and were cleaned up, the three men were asked how they had arrived. Henry's story is the only one of the three to have survived. He had been a slave in North Carolina when he and his master, Jesse Moore, fell into an argument in August of 1857. Moore, who was drunk, stabbed Henry in the neck with a knife. He then took Henry back to the slave quarters, retrieved his gun, and called to his overseer to bring rope. While the overseer was gone, Henry said to Moore, "Now you are going to tie me up and cut me all to pieces for nothing. I would just as leave you would use your gun and shoot me down as to tie me up and cut me all to pieces for nothing." Moore then told Henry to go. Henry started to go, but Moore "put up his gun and snapped both barrels at me. He then set his dogs on me, but as I had been in the habit of making much of them, feeding them, &c., they would not follow me, and I kept on straight to the woods." Henry stayed in the woods until he could get away.

Thomas Garrett sent six men to Philadelphia in February of 1858. He sent a letter to William Still announcing their arrival. The men were accompanied by a free man, who delivered them to the Philadelphia branch of the Underground Railroad. As with many others who escaped to freedom, one of the escapees, Plymouth, had to leave people behind. His wife and four children were owned by someone other than his master and he was unable, in his eyes, to be either a good husband or father.

Another man who left with Plymouth and the others, Horatio, was misled by his master, a common occurrence among slaves. His master had gone to

Canada, and when he came back, he went out of his way to tell his slaves that "Canada was the meanest part of the globe that I ever found or heard of." He told Horatio and his other slaves that he "did not see one black or colored person in Canada." The master said that he asked what happened to the escapees who reached Canada and said he was told that they were rounded up and shipped off around Cape Horn and sold there. He followed up by saying that "the suffering from deep snows and starvation was fearful." Horatio believed that the stories were lies, but did not tell his master what he thought. The six escapees were able to prove Horatio's master wrong by going to Canada, where nothing bad happened to them.[24]

Another kind of help that escapees received was money. Abigail Goodwin wrote to William Still in February of 1858 that he would find enclosed with her letter a donation of "five dollars for the fugitives, a little for so many to share ... but better than nothing; oh, that people, rich people, would remember them instead of spending so much on themselves."[25] On May 25, she expressed the same concern about money to Still when four escapees arrived at her home with none, "but were pretty well off for clothes." She gave them all that she had, "but it seemed very little for four travelers—only a dollar each—but they will meet with friends and helpers on the way." She was also afraid for them because "it's so cold, and one of them had a sore foot; they will not get away— it's dangerous staying here."[26]

On August 31, 1860, Thomas Garrett was visited by Harriet Tubman and two men she had brought out of Maryland. Garrett paid a man to take the two men to Chester County and gave Harriet Tubman ten dollars to hire a man with a carriage to take the wife of one of the men and their three children to Chester County. Garrett was concerned about the safety of everyone involved because he had heard reports that the roads were more dangerous for escapees in the previous months. At the same time, Garrett believed that Harriet Tubman had "a special angel to guard her on her journey of mercy."

There was very little written about the escapees in William Still's notes except that they were able to reach Canada safely. He did not write in detail about what became Harriet Tubman's last trip into Maryland as a part of the Underground Railroad because of the fear that the information might fall into the wrong hands. When John Brown's papers were found after he died at Harper's Ferry the year before, it served as a warning to the Underground Railroad that proslavery forces might capture any information and use it to attack anyone who helped escapees seek freedom. For the next year, in all of the large cities in the North and the South, proslavery mobs harassed abolition meetings. Therefore, it was considered prudent to not keep detailed records of escapes and who was involved in them.

Another way people struggled to free their fellow man was to buy their freedom. In a letter to William Still, Abigail Goodman informed him that she had sent forty-one dollars to Esther Moore, another Friend abolitionist, for that purpose. Abigail thought that "abolitionists there are all opposed to buying slaves, and will not give anything. I don't like buying them, or giving money to slaveholders either." The money was to go toward buying a family of ten slaves from a slave-holder in North Carolina. He had offered to sell the entire family for one thousand dollars. Abigail did not want to give money to a slave-holder, but she could not resist the idea of rescuing the family.[27]

There were those in the anti-slavery movement who did not like to give money to slave owners, but the point soon became moot because of the Civil War.

16. The Last Fetter Broken

By 1861, Wilmington, Delaware, had become an abolitionist town, but there were still dangers for a blatantly anti-slavery man like Thomas Garrett. He did not fear for his safety, but that did not mean that others were not afraid for him. In that spirit,

> in the dark days of the beginning of the war, which every Wilmingtonian will remember with a shudder, in those days of doubt, confusion, and suspicion, without his knowledge or consent, Thomas Garrett's house was constantly surrounded and watched by faithful black men, resolved that, come woe to them, no harm should come to the benefactor of their race.[1]

Abigail Goodwin continued to raise money for the abolitionist cause in spite of the war. She wrote to J. Miller McKim in answer to his request for funds and stated that she was sending her "usual donation and much wish to oblige you by obtaining what I can from others... That I am afraid will be very little. It seems useless to ask anybody: money is so hard to get.... This terrible war consumes so much. Our state has a $100,000 tax to raise, which will make the people poorer than ever; and so many beggars here."[2]

The Civil War was a devastating event in America's history, but it did lead to some profound changes. On September 23, 1862, Abigail Goodman wrote to William Still about recent events concerning slavery. She mentioned that she had

> read the President's proclamation of emancipation, with thankfulness and rejoicing; but upon a little reflection, I did not feel quite satisfied with it; three months seems a long time to be in the power of their angry and cruel masters, who, no doubt, will wreak all their fury and vengeance upon them, killing and abusing them in every way they can—and sell them to Cuba if they can. It makes me sad to think of it. Slavery, I fear, will be a long time in dying, after receiving the fatal stroke.[3]

Abigail Goodwin was not the only person who was not pleased with Lincoln when it came to slavery. By 1862, abolitionists were no longer treated with contempt. Many members of Lincoln's Republican Party felt that the fate of the nation depended on the destruction of slavery. They felt that if the rebellion was put down and slavery was allowed to continue, it would be like a cancer in the country that would spread and eventually cause another rebellion. On the other hand, the Democratic Party wanted peace either by negotiations or by military action against the Confederate armies. They felt that the Union armies would be demoralized if they thought that they were fighting for the end of slavery and not the end of a rebellion.

On July 22, 1862, Lincoln told his cabinet that he wanted to issue a proclamation of emancipation. His decision was based, not only on a wish to end slavery, but also on a more pragmatic belief that if the slaves in the South were free, it would cripple the rebellion. Lincoln asked his cabinet for their opinions, and Secretary of State Seward advised Lincoln to wait until a major Union victory occurred to release the proclamation. Seward's thought was that if he released it at that time, it would be construed "as the last measure of an exhausted government." Lincoln agreed with the idea and put the proclamation aside. The victory he needed happened at the Battle of Antietam on September 17, 1862.[4]

The Emancipation Proclamation, which went into effect on January 1, 1863, did not affect the entire divided country. It only applied to any state that left the Union, and there were exceptions to those states. Any part of the Confederacy that had been returned to Northern control was exempt. What it did affect in the North was the ability of men of African descent to fight in the war. They were permitted to join the Union army and navy and they seized the opportunity. By the end of the war, almost 200,000 men had fought for their own freedom.[5]

Just because the Emancipation Proclamation had been enacted, that did not mean that slavery was finished. Winlock Clark had been sold for a period of seven years in January of 1864. Clark wanted to enlist in the Union army and he sought out Thomas Garrett for advice. Garrett sent him to Philadelphia to see William Still so that "no land sharks shall get any bounty for enlisting him; he has a wife and several children, and whatever bounty the government or the State allows him, will be of use to his family." At the end of the letter he gave Clark to give to Still, Garrett wondered, "Am I naughty, being a professed non-resistant, to advise this poor fellow to serve Father Abraham?"[6]

On April 8, 1864, the Senate passed the Thirteenth Amendment, which would end slavery forever in America, by a vote of 38 to 6. The road for the amendment to be passed in the House was a little harder. However, on January 31, 1865, the Thirteenth Amendment was passed by a vote of 119 to 56.[7] When the Speaker of the House announced the final vote,

the announcement was received by the House and by the spectators with an outburst of enthusiasm. The members on the Republican side of the House instantly
sprung to their feet, and, regardless of parliamentary rules, applauded with cheers
and clapping of hands. The example was followed by the male spectators in the
galleries, which were crowded to excess, who waved their hats and cheered loud
and long, while the ladies, hundreds of whom were present, rose in their seats
and waved their handkerchiefs, participating in and adding to the general excite-
ment and intense interest of the scene. This lasted for several minutes.

It was then suggested that the House should adjourn for the day in honor of
"this immortal and sublime event." It was voted on and passed.[8] The very next
day, Boston lawyer John Rock, an African American, was presented for admission to practice in front of the Supreme Court and was sworn in by the chief
justice. On that same day, President Lincoln sent the amendment out to the
states to be ratified, which was done on December 18, 1865. Of the states that
did not ratify the amendment, two of them were New Jersey and Delaware.[9]

Whether or not every state ratified the 13th Amendment, slavery was
finally removed from America and Abigail Goodwin was able to see the fruits
of her labors. She took ill in early 1866 and finally, as William Still wrote, she
had "seen with joy, the desire of her heart, in the final emancipation of every
bondman in the United States, she departed in peace, November 2, 1867, in
the 74th year of her age."[10]

When the war ended, the Kennett Monthly Meeting decided to invite
back the Friends they had disowned because of their anti-slavery activities.
Slavery was done and no longer considered a disturbing element. The disowned
Friends accepted the invitation and were brought back in without the acknowl-
edgment that was usually expected of returning Friends.[11]

Dr. Bartholomew Fussell, a Friend from West Chester, also saw the end
of slavery. He was one of the signers of the Declaration of Sentiments of the
American Anti-slavery Society in Philadelphia in 1833 and was able to attend
the last meeting of the Pennsylvania Anti-Slavery Society. Even though fighting
slavery was important to Dr. Fussell, he also was a believer in the equality of
the sexes. He wanted to open up the study of medicine to women and in 1840,
he first taught a group of women. In 1846, he began to plan for a college for
the medical education of women. Eventually, the Woman's College in Philadelphia was created. He continued with his work for equality until his death in
1870.

Thomas Garrett died on January 24, 1871. Even though the war was over
and the slaves were free, he continued to work for social reform. Before his
last illness, Garrett was concerned with women's rights, and his last public
appearance was as the president of a woman suffrage meeting in Wilmington.

His funeral was plain, as was the custom of the Friends. At three o'clock, the funeral procession started from his home to the Friends Meeting House in Wilmington. His remains were carried "by the stalwart arms of a delegation of colored men, and the family and friends of the deceased following in carriages with a large procession on foot, while the sidewalks along the line, from the house to the meeting-house, more than six squares, were densely crowded with spectators."

The meeting house was packed and just as many people were outside. Lucretia Mott was there, and normally she did not believe in doing eulogies. However, she looked out at the crowd, two races together in their respect for Garrett, and decided that talking about his accomplishments was the proper thing to do. Others also spoke, including William Howard Day. He said that he did not feel like paying a tribute because "his grief was too fresh upon him, his heart too bowed down, and he could do no more, than in behalf of his race, not only those here, but the host the deceased has befriended, and of the whole four millions to whom he had been so true a friend, cast a tribute of praise and thanks upon his grave."[12]

Those who took fate in their own hands and escaped or even just attempted to escape slavery wanted the same thing as the Society of Friends wanted in the 17th century. They wanted to live their lives on their own terms. The prevalent theory of many Caucasians living in America in the 17th through the 19th centuries was that those in slavery deserved to be slaves or were better off being slaves. The Friends had a different opinion. Even though many Quakers did not want to fully integrate their religion, they were among the first to understand that slavery was wrong and to fight against it.

The Friends' opinion of slavery was influenced by their own interpretation of God's will. It is also possible that the experiences of the founding members of the Society of Friends allowed the following generations of Friends to understand how the repression of fellow human beings was immoral. The Quakers were in the forefront of the fight against slavery and the slave trade, both with legal means, such as petitioning the federal government numerous times, and illegal means, such as the Underground Railroad. The Railroad, because of the Fugitive Slave Acts of 1793 and 1850, was an illegal enterprise. To the leaders of the society, it was wrong to go against the law of the land. However, many Friends, as well as members of the Methodist, Baptist, Episcopalian, and AME churches and other individuals, risked their reputations, fortunes, and lives to end what those in a position of power seemed reluctant or unable to do. The combination of these different voices brought about a social change that ended a shameful chapter in American history.

Appendix

I. The 1688 Protest Against Slavery at the Germantown Monthly Meeting.[1]

This is to ye Monthly Meeting held at Richard Worrell's.

These are the reasons why we are against the traffick of men-body, as followeth.

Is there any that would be done or handled at this manner? Viz., to be sold or made a slave for all the time of this life? How fearful and faint-hearted are many on sea, when they see a strange vessel,—being afraid it should be a Turk, and they should be taken, and sold for slaves into Turkey. Now what is better done, as Turks doe? Yea, rather is it worse for them, which say they are Christians; for we hear that ye most part of such negers are brought hither against their will and consent, and that many of them are stolen.

Now, tho they are black, we can not conceive there is more liberty to have them slaves, as it is to have other white ones. There is a saying, that we shall doe to all men like as will be done ourselves; making no difference of what generation, descent or colour they are. And those who steal or robb men, and those who buy or purchase them, are they not all alike? Here is libety of ye body, except of evil-doers, wch is an other case. But to bring men hither, or to rob and sell them against their will, we stand against. In Europe there are many oppressed for conscience sake; and here there are those oppressed wh are of a black colour.

And we who know that men must not comitt adultery,—some do commit adultery, in others, separating wives from their husbands and giving them to others; and some sell the children of these poor creatures to other men.

Ah! Doe consider well this thing, you who doe it, if you would be done at this manner? And if it is done according to Christianity? You surpass Holland and Germany in this thing. This makes an ill report in all those countries of Europe, where they hear off, that ye Quakers doe here handel men as they handel there ye cattle. And for that reason some have no mind or inclination to come hither. And who shall maintain this your cause, or pleid for it? Truly we can not do so, except you shall inform us better hereof, viz, that Christians have liberty to practice these things.

Pray, what thing in the world can be done worse towards us, than if men should rob or steal us away, and sell us for slaves to strange countries; separating housbands from their wives and children. Being now this is not done in the manner we would be done at therefore we contradict and are against this traffic of men-body.

And we who profess that it is not lawful to steal, must, likewise, avoid to purchase such things as are stolen, but rather help to stop this robbing and stealing if possible. And such me ought to be delivered out of ye hands of ye robbers, and set free as well as in Europe. Then is Pennsylvania to have a good report, instead it hath now a bad one for this sake in other countries. Especially whereas ye Europeans are desirous to know in what manner ye Quakers doe rule in their province;—and most of them doe look upon us with an envious eye. But if this is done well, what shall we say is done evil?

If once these slaves (wch they say are so wicked and stubborn men) should joint themselves,—fight for their freedom,—and handel their masters and mastrisses as they did handel them before; will these masters and mastrisses take the sword at hand and war against these poor slaves, like, we are able to believe, some will not refuse to doe; or have these negers not as much right to fight for their freedom, as you have to keep them slaves?

Now consider well this thing, if it is good or bad? And in case you find it to be good to handel these blacks at that manner, we desire and require you hereby lovingly, that you may inform us herein, which at this time mever was done, viz, that Christians have such a liberty to do so. To the end we shall be satified in this point, and satisfie likewise our good friends and acquaintances in our natif country, to whose it is a terror, or fairful thing, that men should be handeld so in Pennsylvania.

This is from our meeting in Germantown, held ye 18 of the 2 month, 1688, to be delivered to the monthly meeting at Richard Worrell's.

[Signed by:] Garret henderich
Derrick u de graeff
Francis daniell Pastorius
Abraham up Den graef

II. The Fugitive Slave Act of 1793.[2]

An Act respecting fugitives from justice, and persons escaping from the services of their masters.

Be it enacted, &c., That, whenever the Executive authority of any State in the Union, or of either of the Territories Northwest or South of the river Ohio, shall demand any person as a fugitive from justice, of the Executive authority of any such State or Territory to which such person shall have fled, and shall moreover produce the copy of an indictment found, or an affidavit made before a magistrate of any State or Territory as aforesaid, charging the person so demanded with having committed treason, felony, or other crime, certified as authentic by the governor or Chief Magistrate of the State or Territory from whence the person so charged fled, it shall be the duty of the executive authority of the State or Territory to which such person shall have fled, to cause him or her to be arrested and secured, and notice of the arrest to be given to the Executive authority making such demand, or to the agent of such authority, appointed to receive the fugitive, and to cause the fugitive to be delivered to such agent when he shall appear; but if no such agent shall appear within six months from the time of the arrest, the prisoner may be discharged; and all costs or expenses incurred in the apprehending, securing, and transmitting such fugitive to the State or Territory making such demand, shall be paid by such State or Territory.

Sec. 2 And be it further enacted, That any agent appointed as aforesaid, who shall receive the fugitive into his custody, shall be empowered to transport him or her to the State or Territory from which he or she shall have fled. And if any person or persons shall, by force, set at liberty, or rescue the fugitive from such agent while transporting, as aforesaid, the person or persons so offending shall, on conviction, be fined not exceeding five hundred dollars, and be imprisoned not exceeding one year.

Sec. 3 And be it also enacted, That when a person held to labor in any of the United States or in either of the Territories on the Northwest or South of the river Ohio, under the laws thereof, shall escape into any other of the said States or Territory, the person to whom such labor or service may be due, his agent or attorney, is hereby empowered to seize or arrest such fugitive from labor, and to take him or her before any Judge of the Circuit or District courts of the United States, residing or being within the State, or before any magistrate of a county, city, or town corporate, wherein such seizure or arrest shall be made, and upon proof to the satisfaction of such Judge or magistrate, either by oral testimony or affidavit taken before and certified by a magistrate of any such State or Territory, that the person so seized or arrested, doth, under the laws of the State or Territory from which he or she fled, owe service or labor to the person claiming him or her, it shall be the duty of such Judge or magistrate to give a certificate thereof to such claimant, his agent, or attorney, which shall be sufficient warrant for removing the said fugitive from labor to the State or Territory from which he or she fled.

Section 4 And be further enacted, That any person who shall knowingly and willingly obstruct or hinder such claimant, his agent or attorney, in so seizing or arresting such fugitive from labor, or shall rescue such fugitive from such claimant, his agent or attorney, when so arrested pursuant to the authority herein given or declared; or shall harbor or conceal such person after such notice that he or she was a fugitive from labor, as aforesaid, shall, for either of the said offences, forfeit and pay the sum of five hundred dollars. Which penalty may be recovered by and for the benefit of such claimant, by action of debt, in any Court proper to try the same, saving moreover to the person claiming such labor or service his right of action for or on account of the said injuries, or either of them.

Approved, February, February 12, 1793

III. The Fugitive Slave Act of 1850.[3]

Section 1

Be it enacted by the Senate and House of Representatives of the United States of America in Congress assembled, That the persons who have been, or may hereafter be, appointed commissioners, in virtue of any act of Congress, by the Circuit Courts of the United States, and Who, in consequence of such appointment, are authorized to exercise the powers that any justice of the peace, or other magistrate of any of the United States, may exercise in respect to offenders for any crime or offense against the United States, by arresting, imprisoning, or bailing the same under and by the virtue of the thirty-third section of the act of the twenty-fourth of September seventeen hundred and eighty-nine, entitled "An Act to establish the judicial courts of the United States" shall be, and are hereby, authorized and required to exercise and discharge all the powers and duties conferred by this act.

Section 2

And be it further enacted, That the Superior Court of each organized Territory of the United States shall have the same power to appoint commissioners to take acknowledgments of bail and affidavits, and to take depositions of witnesses in civil causes, which is now possessed by the Circuit Court of the United States; and all commissioners who shall hereafter be appointed for such purposes by the Superior Court of any organized Territory of the United States, shall possess all the powers, and exercise all the duties, conferred by law upon the commissioners appointed by the Circuit Courts of the United States for similar purposes, and shall moreover exercise and discharge all the powers and duties conferred by this act.

Section 3

And be it further enacted, That the Circuit Courts of the United States shall from time to time enlarge the number of the commissioners, with a view to afford reasonable facilities to reclaim fugitives from labor, and to the prompt discharge of the duties imposed by this act.

Section 4

And be it further enacted, That the commissioners above named shall have concurrent jurisdiction with the judges of the Circuit and District Courts of the United States, in their respective circuits and districts within the several States, and the judges of the Superior Courts of the Territories, severally and collectively, in term-time and vacation; shall grant certificates to such claimants, upon satisfactory proof being made, with authority to take and remove such fugitives from service or labor, under the restrictions herein contained, to the State or Territory from which such persons may have escaped or fled.

Section 5

And be it further enacted, That it shall be the duty of all marshals and deputy marshals to obey and execute all warrant, or other process, when tendered, or to use all proper means diligently to execute the same, he shall, on conviction thereof, be fined in the sum of one thousand dollars, to the use of such clamant, on the motion of such claimant, by the Circuit or District Court for the district of such marshal; and after arrest of such fugitive, by such marshal or his deputy, or whilst at any time in his custody under the provisions of this act, should such fugitive escape, whether with or without the assent of such marshal or his deputy, such marshal shall be liable, on his official bond, to be prosecuted for the benefit of such claimant, for the full value of the service or labor of said fugitive in the State, Territory, or District whence he escaped: and the better to enable the said commissioners, when thus appointed, to execute their duties faithfully and efficiently, in conformity with the requirements of the Constitution of the United States and of this act, they are hereby authorized and empowered, within their countries respectively, to appoint, in writing under their hands, any one or more suitable persons, from time to time, to execute all such warrants and other process as may be issued by them in the lawful performace of their respective duties; with authority to such commissioners, or the persons to be appointed by them, to execute process as aforesaid, to summon and call to their aid the bystander, or posse comitatus of the proper county, when necessary to ensure a faithful observance of the clause of the constitution referred to, in conformity with the provisions of this act; and all good citizens are hereby commanded to aid and assist in the prompt and efficient execution of this law, whenever their services may be required, as aforesaid, for that purpose; and said warrants shall run, and be executed by said officers, any where in the State within which they are issued.

Section 6

And be it further enacted, That when a person held to service or labor in any State or Territory of the United States, has heretofore or shall hereafter escape into another State or Territory of the United States, the person or persons to whom such service or labor may be due, or his, her, or their agent or attorney, duly authorized, by power of attorney, in writing, acknowledged and certified under the seal of some legal officer or court of the State of Territory in which the same may be executed, may pursue and reclaim such fugitive person, either by procuring a warrant from some one of the courts, judges, or commissioners aforesaid, of the proper circuit, district, or county, for the apprehension of such fugitive from service or labor, or by seizing and arresting such fugitive, where the same can be done without process, and by taking, or causing such person to be taken, forthwith before such court, judge, or commissioner, whose duty it shall be to hear and determine the case of such claimant in a summary manner; and upon satisfactory proof being made, by deposition or affidavit, in writing, to be taken and certified by such court, judge, or commissioner, or by other satisfactory testimony, duly taken and certified by some court, magistrate, justice of the peace, or other legal officer authorized to administer an oath and take depositions under the laws of the State or Territory from which such person owing service or labor may have escaped, with a certificate of such magistracy or other authority, as aforesaid, with the seal of the proper court or officer thereto attached, which seal shall be sufficient to establish the competency of the proof, and with proof, also by affidavit, of the identity of the person whose service or labor is claimed to be due as aforesaid, that the person so arrested does in fact owe service or labor to the person or persons claiming him or her, in the State or Territory from which such fugitive may have escaped as aforesaid, and that said person escaped, to make out and deliver to such claimant, his or her agent or attorney, a certificate setting forth the substantial facts as to the service or labor due from such fugitive to the claimant, and of his or her escape from the State or Territory in which he or she was arrested, with authority to such claimant, or his or her agent or attorney, to use such reasonable force and restraint as may be necessary, under the circumstances of the case, to take and remove such fugitive person back to the State or Territory whence he or she may have escaped as aforesaid. In no trial or hearing under this act shall the testimony of such alleged fugitive be admitted in evidence; and the certificates in this and the first [fourth] section mentioned, shall be conclusive of the right of the person or persons in whose favor granted, to remove such fugitive to the State or Territory from which he escaped, and shall prevent all molestation of such person or persons by any process issued by any court, judge, magistrate, or other person whomsoever.

Section 7

And be it further enacted, That any person who shall knowingly and willingly obstruct, hinder, or prevent such claimant, his agent or attorney, or any person or persons lawfully assisting him, her, or them, from arresting such a fugitive from service or labor, either with or without process as aforesaid, or shall rescue, or attempt to rescue, such fugitive from service or labor, from the custody of such claimant, his or her agent or attorney, or other person or persons lawfully assisting as aforesaid, when so arrested, pursuant to the authority herein given and declared; or shall aid, abet, or assist such person so owing service or labor as aforesaid, directly or indirectly, to escape from such claimant, his agent or attorney, or other person or persons legally authorized as aforesaid; or shall harbor or conceal such fugitive, so as to prevent the discovery and arrest of such person, after notice or knowledge of the fact that such person was a fugitive from service or labor as aforesaid, shall, for either of said offences, be subject to a fine not exceeding one thousand dollars, and imprisonment not exceeding six months, by indictment and conviction before the District Court of the United States for the district in which such offense may have been committed, or before the proper court of criminal jurisdiction, if committed within any one of the organized Territories of the United States; and shall moreover forfeit and pay, by way of civil damages to the party injured by such illegal conduct, the sum of one thousand dollars for each fugitive so lost as aforesaid, to be recovered by action of debt, in any of the District or Territorial Courts aforesaid, within whose jurisdiction the said offence may have been committed.

Section 8

And be it further enacted, That the marshals, their deputies, and the clerks of the said District and Territorial Courts, Shall be paid, for their services, the like fees as may be allowed for similar services in other cases; and where such services are rendered exclusively in the arrest, custody, and delivery of the fugitive to the claimant, his or her agent or attorney, or where such supposed fugitive may be discharged out of custody for the want of sufficient proof as aforesaid, then such fees are to be paid in whole by such claimant, his or her agent or attorney; and in all cases where the proceedings are before a commissioner, he shall be entitled to a fee of ten dollars in full for his services in each case, upon the delivery of the said certificate to the claimant, his agent or attorney; or a fee of five dollars in cases where the proof shall not, in the opinion of such commissioner, warrant such certificate and delivery, inclusive of all services incident to such arrest and examination, to be paid, in either case, by the claimant, his or her agent or attorney. The person or persons authorized to execute the process to be issued by such commissioner for the arrest and detention of fugitives from service or labor as afore-said, shall also be entitled to a fee of five dollars each for each person he or they may arrest, and take before any commissioner as aforesaid, at the instance and request of such claimant, with such other additional services as may be necessarily performed by him or them; such as attending at the examination, keeping the fugitive in custody, and providing him with food and lodging during his detention, and until the final determination of such commissioners; and, in general, for performing such other duties as may be required by such claimant, his or her attorney or agent, or commissioner in the premises, such fees to be made up in conformity with the fees usually charged by the officers of the courts of justice within the proper district or county, as near as may be practicable, and paid by such claimants, their agents or attorneys, whether such supposed fugitives from service or labor be ordered to be delivered to such claimant by the final determination of such commissioner or not.

Section 9

And be it further enacted, That, upon affidavit made by the claimant of such fugitive, his agent or attorney, after such certificate has been issued, that he has reason to apprehend that such fugitive will be rescued by force from his or their possession before he can be taken beyond the limits of the State in which the arrest is made, it shall be the duty of the officer making the arrest to retain such fugitive in his custody, and to remove him to the state whence he fled, and there to deliver him to said claimant, his agent, or attorney. And to this end, the officer aforesaid is hereby authorized and required to employ so many persons as he may deem necessary to overcome such force, and to retain them in his service so long as circumstances may require. The said officer and his assistants, while so employed, to receive the same compensation, and to be allowed the same expenses, as are now allowed by law for transportation of criminals, to be certified by the judge of the district within which the arrest is made, and paid out of the treasury of the United States.

Section 10

And be it further enacted, That when any person held to service or labor in any State or Territory, or in the District of Columbia, shall escape therefrom, the party to whom such service or labor shall be due, his, her, or their agent or attorney, may apply to any court of record therein, or judge thereof in vacation, and make satisfactory proof to such court, or judge in vacation, of the escape afore-said, and that the person escaping owed service or labor to such party. Where-upon the court shall cause a record to be made of the matters so proved, and also a general description of the person so escaping, with such convenient certainty as may be; and a transcript of such record, authenticated by the attestation of the clerk and of the seal of the said court, being produced in any other State, Terri-tory, or district in which the person so escaping may be found, and being exhib-ited to any judge, commissioner, or other office, authorized by the law of the United States to cause persons escaping from service or labor to be delivered up, shall be held and taken to be full and conclusive evidence of the fact of escape, and that the service or labor of the person escaping is due to the party in such record mentioned. And upon the production by the said party of other and further evidence if necessary, either oral or by affidavit, in addition to what is contained in the said record of the identity of the person escaping, he or she shall be delivered up to the claimant, And the said court, commissioner, judge, or other person authorized by this act to grant certificates to claimants or fugitives, shall, upon the production of the record and other evidences aforesaid, grant to such claimant a certificate of his right to take any such person identified and proved to be owing service or labor as aforesaid, which certificate shall authorize such claimant to seize or arrest and transport such person to the State or Territory from which he escaped: Provided, That nothing herein contained shall be construed as requiring the production of a transcript of such record as evidence as aforesaid. But in its absence the claim shall be heard and determined upon other satisfactory proofs, competent in law.

Approved, September 18, 1850.

IV. The Emancipation Proclamation.[4]

By the President of the United States of America

A Proclamation

Whereas, on the twenty-second day of September, in the year of our Lord one thousand eight hundred and sixty-two, a proclamation was issued by the President of the United States, containing among other things, the following, to wit:

"That on the first day of January, in the year of our Lord one thousand eight hundred and sixty-three, all persons held as slaves within any State or designated part of a State, the people whereof shall then be in rebellion against the United States, shall be then, thenceforward, and forever free; and the Executive Government of the United States, including the military and naval authority thereof, will recognize and maintain the freedom of such persons, and will do no act or acts to repress such persons, or any of them, in any efforts they may make for their actual freedom.

"That the Executive will, on the first day of January aforesaid, by proclamation, designate the States and parts of States, if any, in which the people thereof, respectively, shall on that day be, in good faith, represented in the congress of the United States by members chosen thereto at elections wherein a majority of the qualified voters of such State shall have participated, shall, in the absence of strong countervailing testimony, be deemed conclusive evidence that such State, and the people thereof, are not then in rebellion against the United States."

Now, therefore I, Abraham Lincoln, President of the United States, by virtue of the power in me vested as Commander-in-Chief, of the Army and Navy of the United States in time of actual armed rebellion against the authority and government of the United States, and as a fit and necessary war measure for suppressing said rebellion, do, on this first day of January, in the year of our Lord one thousand eight hundred and sixty-three, and in accordance with my purpose so to do publicly proclaimed for the full period of one hundred days, from the day first above mentioned, order and designate as the States and parts of States wherein the people thereof respectively, are this day in rebellion against the United States, the following, to wit:

Arkansas, Texas, Louisiana, (except the Parishes of St. Bernard, Plaquemines, Jefferson, St. John, St. Charles, St. James Ascension, Assumption, Terrebonne, Lafourche, St. Mary, St. Martin, and Orleans, including the City of New Orleans) Mississippi, Alabama, Florida, Georgia, South Carolina, North Carolina, and Virginia, (except the forty-eight counties designated as West Virginia, and also the counties of Berkley, Accomac, Northampton, Elizabeth City, York, Princess Ann, and Norfolk and Portsmouth), and which excepted parts, are for the present, left precisely as if this proclamation were not issued.

And by virtue of the power, and for the purpose aforesaid, I do order and declare that all persons held as slaves within said designated States, and parts of States, are, and henceforward shall be free; and that the Executive government of the United States, including the military and naval authorities thereof, will recognize and maintain the freedom of said persons.

And I hereby enjoy upon the people so declared to be free to abstain from all violence, unless in necessary self-defense; and I recommend to them that, in all cases when allowed, they labor faithfully for reasonable wages.

And I further declare and make known, that such persons of suitable condition, will be received into the armed service of the United States to garrison forts, positions, stations, and other places, and to man vessels of all sorts in said service.

And upon this act, sincerely believed to be an act of justice, warranted by the Constitution, upon military necessity, I invoke the considerable judgment of mankind, and the gracious favor of Almighty God.

In witness whereof, I have hereunto set my hand and caused the seal of the United States to be affixed.

Done at the City of Washington, this first day of January, in the year of our
Lord one thousand eight hundred and sixty three, and of the Independence of
the United States of America the eighty-seventh.
By the President: Abraham Lincoln
William H. Seward, Secretary of State.

V. The 13th Amendment to the U.S. Constitution.[5]

Amendment XIII

Section 1.

Neither slavery nor involuntary servitude, except as a punishment for crime
whereof the party shall have been duly convicted, shall exist within the United
States, or any place subject to their jurisdiction.

Section 2.

Congress shall have power to enforce this article by appropriate legislation.

Chapter Notes

Prologue

1. Ruth Abbott Rogers, "Reflections of Ruth Abbott Rogers" (clipping from the Salem County Historical Society).

Chapter 1

1. George Fox, *The Journal of George Fox* (London: Religious Society of Friends, 1975), pp. 1–2.
2. Will Durant and Ariel Durant, *The Story of Civilization Vol. 7: The Age of Reason Begins* (New York: Simon and Schuster, 1961), pp. 186, 212–216.
3. Benson Bobrick, *Wide as the Water: The Story of the English Bible and the Revolution It Inspired* (New York: Simon and Schuster, 2001), pp. 283–284.
4. Fox, pp. 3–8.
5. William C. Braithwaite, *The Beginnings of Quakerism* (Cambridge: Macmillan, 1912, 1961), pp. 46–47.
6. Fox, p. 36.
7. Braithwaite, pp. 48–49.
8. Thomas D. Hamm, *The Quakers in America* (New York: Columbia University Press, 2003), p. 17.
9. Braithwaite, pp. 126, 158, 187.
10. Hamm, pp. 17–18.
11. David M. Murray-Rust, *Quakers in Brief or Quakerism Made Easy: An Overview of the Quaker Movement from 1650 to 1990* (Merseyside, UK: Birkenhead Meeting, 1995), p. 16.
12. Elfrida Vipont, *George Fox and the Valiant Sixty* (London: Hamish Hamilton, 1975), pp. 73–75.
13. Braithwaite, p. 232.

14. Janetta Wright Schonover, ed., *A History of William Brinton Who Came from England to Chester County, Pennsylvania in 1684 and of His Descendants with Some Records of the English Brintons, Part I* (Trenton, NJ: 1924), p. 87.
15. Braithwaite, p. 232.
16. Hamm, pp. 18–22.
17. Fox, pp. 64–65.
18. Braithwaite, pp. 295–298.
19. Fox, pp. 398–399, 401–402, 404.
20. Hamm, p. 26.
21. Braithwaite, p. 143.

Chapter 2

1. Hamm, p. 22.
2. "Mary Barrett Dyer." http://www.rootsweb.ancestry.com/~nwa/dyer.html.
3. Hamm, pp. 23–24.
4. Braithwaite, p. 404.
5. Kenneth C. Davis, *America's Hidden History: Untold Tales of the First Pilgrims, Fighting Women, and Forgotten Founders Who Shaped a Nation* (New York: Smithsonian Books, 2008), p. 79.
6. Braithwaite, p. 404.
7. "Mary Barrett Dyer."
8. Braithwaite, p. 404.
9. Fox, pp. 411–414.
10. Hamm, pp. 22–24.
11. Vipont, pp. 68–69.
12. Hamm, p. 26.
13. Jeffrey M. Dorwart, *Camden County, NJ: The Making of a Metropolitan Community, 1626–2000* (New Brunswick, NJ: Rutgers University Press, 2001), pp. 12–14.
14. Robert W. Harper, *John Fenwick and Salem County in the Providence of West Jersey*

1609–1700, Including Burlington, Cape May, Cumberland, and Gloucester Counties (Salem, NJ: Salem County Cultural Heritage Commission, 1978), p. 35.

15. Charlotte M. Yonge, *Pictorial History of the World's Great Nations from the Earliest Dates to the Present Time, Vol. III* (New York: Selmar Hess, 1882), p. 988.

16. Barry Levy, *Quakers and the American Family: British Settlements in the Delaware Valley* (New York: Oxford University Press, 1988), pp. 110–114.

17. Harper, pp. 35–37.

18. Dorwart, pp. 15–26.

19. Salem County Tercentenary Committee, *Fenwick's Colony: Salem County Pictorial: 1675–1964* (Salem, NJ: Salem County Tercentenary Committee, 1964), p. 9.

20. Dorwart, p. 16.

21. John E. Pomfret, *Colonial New Jersey: A History* (New York: Charles Scribner's Sons, 1973), pp. 34–36.

22. Harper, p. 61.

23. Bessie Ayers Andrews, *Historical Sketches of Greenwich in Old Cohansey* (Vineland, NJ: Vineland Printing House, 1905), p. 16.

24. Harper, pp. 50, 62.

25. Pomfret, pp. 34–36.

26. Dorwart, pp. 16–18.

27. Ellis L. Derry, *Old and Historic Churches in New Jersey, Vol. 1* (Medford, NJ: Plexis Publishing, 2003), p. 21–23.

28. Hamm, p. 27.

29. William Penn, "Frame of Government of Pennsylvania," April 25, 1682. http://www.constitution.org/bcp/frampenn.htm.

30. Yonge, pp. 988–989.

31. Wallace N. Jamison, *Religion in New Jersey: A Brief History*. Vol. 13, The New Jersey Historical Series (Princeton, NJ: D. Van Nostrand Co., 1964), pp. 13–14.

Chapter 3

1. Betty Wood, *The Origins of American Slavery: Freedom and Bondage in the English Colonies* (New York: Hill and Wang, 1997), pp. 8, 14–16, 88.

2. William J. Switala, *The Underground Railroad in New York and New Jersey* (Mechanicsburg, PA: Stackpole, 2006), p. 28.

3. Gary B. Nash, *First City: Philadelphia and the Forging of Historical Memory* (Philadelphia: University of Pennsylvania Press, 2002), pp. 39, 41.

4. "New Jersey Slave Laws Summary and Records," www.slaveryinamerica.org/geography/slave_lawsNJ.html.

5. "Francis Daniel Pastorius," http://www.ushistory.org/germantown/people/pastorius.html.

6. "Pastorius, Francis Daniel (1651–1720)," http://www.germanheritage.com/biographies/mtoz/pastorius.html.

7. Thomas E. Drake, *Quakers and Slavery in America* (New Haven, CT: Yale University Press, 1965), p. 11.

8. "Resolutions of The Germantown Mennonites; February 18, 1688," http://avalon.law.yale.edu/17th_century/men01.asp.

9. Drake, pp. 12–13.

10. Phillip S. Foner, *History of Black Americans from the Compromise of 1850 to the End of the Civil War* (Santa Barbara, CA: Greenwood Press, 1983), p. 286.

11. George Keith, "An Exhortation and Caution to Friends Concerning Buying or Keeping of Negroes," http://www.qhpress.org/quakerpages/qwhp/gk-as1693.htm.

12. Pomfret, pp. 112–113.

13. Jamison, p. 49.

14. Drake, pp. 14–22.

15. Yonge, pp. 987, 989.

16. Julian P. Boyd, ed., *Fundamental Laws and Constitutions of New Jersey 1664–1964* (Princeton, NJ: D. Van Nostrand Co., 1964), pp. 148–151.

17. Thomas P. Farmer, *New Jersey in History: Fighting to be Heard* (Harvey Cedars, NJ: Down the Shore, 1996), pp. 8–10.

18. Hamm, pp. 29–30.

19. *History of the Gwynedd Friends*, www.gwyneddfriends.org/gwyneed_history_page1.html.

20. Drake, pp. 22–25.

21. Philadelphia Yearly Meeting (hereinafter PYM), 1714, p. 163.

22. PYM, 1715, pp. 165–166, 168.

23. PYM, 1716, pp. 174, 176.

24. Drake, pp. 28–35.

25. Ralph Sandiford, *A Brief Examination of the Practice of the Times* (Philadelphia: Franklin and Meredith, 1729), pp. 4–6, 9, 26–27, 62, 71.

26. Drake, pp. 27–32.

27. PYM, 1730, pp. 346–349.

28. Barbara J. Mitnick, *New Jersey in the American Revolution* (New Brunswick, NJ: Rivergate Books, 2005), p. 119.

29. PYM, 1737.

30. PYM, 1738.

31. John Greenleaf Whittier, Introduction to "The Journal of John Woolman." http://www.phillyburbs.com/undergroundrailroad/lay.shtml.

32. Drake, p. 46.

33. "John Woolman: An Appreciation by John Greenleaf Whittier, Part 1, Benjamin Lay." www.strecorsoc.org/jwoolman/apprel.html.

34. Whittier.

35. "John Woolman: An Appreciation by John Greenleaf Whittier, Part 1, Benjamin Lay."

36. Whittier.

37. "John Woolman: An Appreciation by John Greenleaf Whittier, Part 1, Benjamin Lay."

38. Benjamin Lay, *All Slave-Keepers That Keep the Innocent in Bondage* (Philadelphia: Benjamin Franklin, 1737), pp. 1–5, 7–9, 14.

39. PYM, 1738.

Chapter 4

1. John Woolman, *The Journal of John Woolman* (New York: Citadel Press, 1961), pp. 1–4, 15.

2. Drake, p. 52.

3. Woolman, pp. 19–22.

4. *The Pennsylvania Militia*, http://www.constitution.org/jw/acm_3-m.htm.

5. Edgar Jacob Fisher, *New Jersey as a Royal Province 1738–1776* (New York: AMS Press, 1967), pp. 322–325.

6. Daisy Newman, *A Procession of Friends: Quakers in America* (Garden City, NJ: Doubleday, 1972), p. 68.

7. Benjamin Franklin, *Benjamin Franklin: Autobiography, Poor Richard, and Later Writings* (New York: Library of America, 2005), p. 76.

8. Ronald W. Clark, *Benjamin Franklin: A Biography* (New York: Random House, 1983), p. 95.

9. Franklin, *Benjamin Franklin*, p. 76.

10. Esmond Wright, *Franklin of Philadelphia* (Cambridge, MA: Harvard University Press, 1986), pp. 77–79.

11. John Woolman, *The Works of John Woolman* (New York: Garrett Press, 1970), p. 29.

12. Drake, p. 54.

13. PYM, 1754.

14. Woolman, *Works*, p. 20.

15. PYM, 1754.

16. Drake, p. 59.

17. Woolman, *Works*, pp. 37, 258–261.

18. Whittier.

19. Hamm, pp. 31–32.

20. Woolman, *Journal*, pp. 51–67.

21. Woolman, *Journal*, pp. 78–79, 81–82, 84–91.

22. PYM, 1758, p. 42.

23. Drake, p. 46.

Chapter 5

1. Drake, pp. 73, 85.

2. "History of Camden," NJ, http://www.ci.camden.nj.us/history.

3. "New Jersey Slave Laws Summary and Records." http://www.slaveryinamerica.org/geography/slave_lawsNJ.html.

4. "History of Camden, NJ."

5. Dorwart, p. 29.

6. Elizabeth Donnan, *Documents Illustrative of the History of the Slave Trade in America, Vol. III, New England and the Middle Colonies* (New York: Octagon Books, 1969), pp. 453–456.

7. Woolman, *Journal*, pp. 127–128, 297.

8. C.E.N. Hartel, *Notes on Slaves in Haddonfield and Vincinity, Examination of Early Wills and Inventories of Estates* (Haddonfield, NJ: Haddonfield Historical Society, 1952), p. 2.

9. David Freeman Hawke, *Benjamin Rush: Revolutionary Gadfly* (New York: Bobbs-Merrill, 1971), p. 39.

10. Hartel, pp. 2–3.

11. Jacob-Fisher, p. 402.

12. *The Quakers Salem Quarterly Meeting Southern New Jersey 1675–1990* (Salem, NJ: Salem Quarterly Meeting, 1990), pp. 97–98.

13. Dubois, W.E.B., *The Philadelphia Negro*, "Chapter VIII, Education and Illiteracy." New York: Lippincott, 1899. www.2.pfeiffer.edu/2Iridener/DSS/DuBos/pnchviii.html.

14. Irv Brendlinger, "Anthony Benezet: True Champion of the Slave." *Wesleyan Theological Journal* 32, no. 1 (Spring 1997): http://wesley.nnu.edu/fileadmin/imported_site/wesleyjournal/1997-wtj-32-1.pdf.

15. Maurice Jackson, *Let This Voice Be Heard: Anthony Benezet, Father of Atlantic Abolitionism* (Philadelphia: University of Pennsylvania Press, 2009), pp. 61–63, 69–70, 109, 247–248.

16. Drake, pp. 71, 87.

17. Charles Rappleye, *Sons of Providence: The Brown Brothers, the Slave Trade and the*

American Revolution (New York: Simon and Schuster, 2006), p. 148.

18. Drake, p. 71.

19. Hamm, p. 35.

20. Willard Sterne Randall, *Benedict Arnold: Patriot and Traitor* (New York: William Morrow, 1990), p. 75.

21. Rappleye, *Sons of Providence*, p. 148.

22. "The Articles of Association," October 20, 1774, http://avalon.law.yale.edu/18th_century/contcong_10-20-74.asp.

23. Dumas Malone, *Jefferson the Virginian*. Vol. 1 of *Jefferson and His Times*. (Boston: Little, Brown, 1948), pp. 191–192.

24. Wilbur H. Siebert, "The Loyalists of Pennsylvania," *Ohio State Bulletin,* April 1, 1920.

25. *Pennsylvania Gazette*, September 10, 1777, pp. 1–2.

26. William H. Williams, *Slavery and Freedom in Delaware: 1639–1865* (Wilmington, DE: Scholarly Resources, 1996), p. 148.

27. Nash, p. 91.

28. Mitnick, pp. 121–122.

29. Siebert, "Loyalists," pp. 22–24.

30. Rappleye, *Sons of Providence*, p. 177.

31. Gary B. Nash, *The Unknown American Revolution: The Unruly Birth of Democracy and the Struggle to Create America* (New York: Penguin, 2005), p. 156.

32. David McCullough, *John Adams* (New York: Simon & Schuster, 2001), pp. 130–134.

33. *New Jersey State Loyalty Oath*, slic.njstatelib.org/slic_files/imported/NJ_Information/.../11.1.pdf.

34. Mitnick, pp. 42–43.

35. Elizabeth Drinker, *The Diary of Elizabeth Drinker: The Life Cycle of an Eighteenth Century Woman*. Edited by Elaine Forman Crane (Boston: Northeastern University Press, 1994), p. 58.

36. Mitnick, p. 88.

37. Drinker, pp. 58–60.

38. *Pennsylvania Gazette,* May 7, 1777, p. 3.

39. Drinker, p. 60.

40. Manumission papers, Stewart Collection, Rowan University, Glassboro, NJ.

41. Joan N. Burstyn, *Past and Promise: Lives of New Jersey Women* (Syracuse, NY: Syracuse University Press, 1997), p. 66.

42. *Pennsylvania Gazette*, September 10, 1777, p. 3; Drinker, p. 60.

43. Siebert, "Loyalists," pp. 35–37.

44. Drinker, pp. 60–64.

45. Siebert, "Loyalists," p. 46.

46. Robert Harper, *Old Gloucester County and the American Revolution 1763–1778, Including Atlantic, Burlington, Cape May, Cumberland, and Salem Counties* (Glassboro, NJ: Jefferson Printing Co., 1986), pp. 85–86.

47. Edith Hoelle, *Vignettes of Historic Woodbury* (Woodbury, NJ: Academy Business Forms), 1965.

48. Harper, *Old Gloucester County*, p. 86.

49. Ralph D. Paine, *The Battle of Red Bank* (Woodbury, NJ: Gloucester County Board of Chosen Freeholders).

50. *Gloucester County Times*, Sunday, March 1, 2009, p. D-2.

51. Harper, *Old Gloucester County*, pp. 86–88, 92–93.

52. Drinker, pp. 72–76.

53. Harper, *Old Gloucester County*, pp. 128–130.

54. *Gloucester County Times*, Sunday, March 1, 2009, p. D-2.

55. Charles Rappleye, *Robert Morris: Financier of the American Revolution* (New York: Simon and Schuster, 2010), p. 163.

56. William J. Jackson, *New Jerseyans in the Civil War: For Union and Liberty* (New Brunswick, NJ: Rutgers University Press, 2000), pp. 9–10.

57. Mrs. William Farr, *Slavery and the Underground Railroad in New Jersey* (Woodbury, NJ: Gloucester County Historical Society, 1964), p. 7.

58. Williams, *Slavery in Delaware*, pp. 148–149.

59. Nash, *Unknown American Revolution*, www.ancestry.com.uk, pp. 153–154.

60. "An Act for the Gradual Abolition of Slavery (PA)." www.yale.edu/lawweb/avalon/statec/statutes/penns07.htm.

61. *New Jersey Gazette*, September 20, 1780.

62. "John Cooper Advocates the Abolition of Slavery." http://slic.njstatelib.org/slic_files/imported/NJ_Information/Digital_Collections/NJInTheAmericanRevolution1763-1783/13.6.pdf.

63. Drinker, p. 91–92.

Chapter 6

1. Jackson, *Let This Voice Be Heard*, pp. 29–30.

2. James G. Basker, ed., *Early American Abolitionists: A Collection of Anti-Slavery Writings 1760–1820* (New York: The Gilder Lehrman Institute of American History, 2005), pp. 53, 56.

3. "To the U.S. Congress Assembled the Address from the Yearly Meeting of the People Called Quakers." http://www.rootsweb.ancestry.com/~quakers/petition.htm.

4. Rappleye, *Sons of Providence*, pp. 225–226.

5. "The Underground Railroad in Bucks, Burlington, and Montgomery County-Anthony Benezet." www.phillyburbs.com/undergroundrailroad/benzet.shtm.

6. Brendlinger, p. 2.

7. "The Underground Railroad in Bucks, Burlington, and Montgomery County-Anthony Benezet."

8. Williams, pp. 68–71, 146–148.

9. Ralph K. Andrist, ed., *George Washington: A Biography in His Own Words, Vol. 2* (New York: Newsweek, 1972), pp. 276–277.

10. Giles R. Wright, *Afro-Americans in New Jersey: A Short History* (Trenton, NJ: New Jersey Historical Commission, Department of State, 1988), p. 23.

11. Dorwart, p. 47.

12. Gaillard Hunt and James Brown Scott, eds., *The Debates in the Federal Convention of 1787 Which Formed the Constitution of the United States of America, Reported by James Madison, a Delegate from the State of Virginia* (Union, NJ: International Edition, The Lawbook Exchange, 1999), pp. 442–444.

13. Paul Finkelman, *Slavery and the Founders: Race and Liberty in the Age of Jefferson* (Armonk, NY: M.E. Sharpe, 1996), p. 26.

14. *Debates in the Federal Convention of 1787*, p. 445.

15. "Constitutional Convention 1787." http://avalon.law.yale.edu/18th_century/debates_825.asp.

16. Williams, pp. 148–149.

17. John M. Moore, ed., *Friends in the Delaware Valley: Philadelphia Yearly Meeting 1681–1981* (Haverford, PA: Friends Historical Association, 1981), p. 52.

18. William J. Switala, *The Underground Railroad in Delaware, Maryland, and West Virginia* (Mechanicsburg, PA: Stackpole Books, 2004), p. 32.

19. Samuel E. Morison, *The Oxford History of the United States 1783–1917, Vol. 1* (London: Oxford University Press, 1927), pp. 35–36.

20. Joseph J. Ellis, *Founding Brothers: The Revolutionary Generation* (New York: Vintage Books, 2000), p. 81.

21. Rappleye, *Sons of Providence*, p. 258.

22. Ellis, *Founding Brothers*, pp. 83–87.

23. *Journal of the House of Representatives.* February 12, 1790. http://memory.loc.gov/cgi-bin/query/r?ammem/hlaw:@field(DOCID+@lit(hj001204)), p. 157.

24. Winfred Bernhard, *Fisher Ames: Federalist and Statesman 1758–1808* (Chapel Hill: University of North Carolina Press, 1965), p. 141.

25. Ellis, *Founding Brothers*, p. 97.

26. John C. Fitzpatrick, ed., *The Diaries of George Washington, Vol. IV, 1789–1799* (New York: Houghton, Mifflin, 1925), pp. 103–104.

27. Bernhard, p. 141.

28. H.W. Brands, *The First American: The Life and Times of Benjamin Franklin* (New York: Anchor Books, 2000), p. 701.

29. Ellis, *Founding Brothers*, p. 110.

30. Brands, p. 702.

31. A. Leo Lemay, ed., *The Franklin Writings* (New York: Library of America, 1987), pp. 1154–1155.

32. Ellis, *Founding Brothers*, pp. 110–112, 116.

33. Jack N. Rakove, ed., *James Madison Writings* (New York: Library of America, 1999), p. 477–478.

34. "Maclay's Journal," http://memory.loc.gov/ammem/amlaw/lwmj.html, p. 222.

35. Lemay, *Writings*, pp. 1157–1160.

36. Bernhard, pp. 141–143.

37. Ellis, *Founding Brothers*, pp. 117–118.

38. Gary B. Nash, *The Unknown American Revolution: The Unruly Birth of Democracy and the Struggle to Create America* (New York: Viking Penguin, 2005), p. 412.

39. Manumission Papers, Historical Society of Pennsylvania.

40. Drake, p. 107.

41. *Eli Whitney's Patent for the Cotton Gin*, http://www.archives.gov/education/lessons/cotton-gin-patent/index.html, pp. 1–3; Brenda Stalcup, ed., *Turning Points in World History: The Industrial Revolution* (San Diego: Greenhaven Press, 2002), p. 85.

42. James M. McPherson, *Battle Cry of Freedom: The Civil War Era* (New York: Oxford University Press, 1988), pp. 78–81.

43. Finkelman, pp. 80–81, 86–87, 99.

44. Rappleye, *Sons of Providence*, pp. 296–297.

45. *Journal of the House of Representatives.* February 17, 1794, p. 64, www.lcweb2.loc.gov.

46. Rappleye, *Sons of Providence*, pp. 297–297.

47. Minutes of the Gloucester County Society for the Abolition of Slavery began in

Burlington on 5th month (May) 2, 1973, Stewart Collection, Rowan University, Glassboro, NJ.

48. Hartel, *Notes on Haddonfield*, p. 5.

49. Minutes of Gloucester County Society for Abolition.

50. Hartel, *Notes on Haddonfield*, p. 5.

51. *Journal of the House of Representatives*, November 30, 1797, http://memory.loc.gov.

52. "On the Evils of Slavery," http://www.loc.gov/cgi-bin/query/r?ammem/rbpe, pp. 1–2.

53. St. George Tucker, *A Dissertation on Slavery with a Proposal for the Gradual Abolition of It, in the State of Virginia* (Philadelphia: Mathew Carey, 1796), pp. 1–2.

54. Fergus M. Bordewich, *Bound for Canaan: The Underground Railroad and the War for the Soul of America* (New York: HarperCollins, 2005), pp. 44–45.

Chapter 7

1. Lydia Marie Child, *Isaac T. Hopper: A True Life* (Boston: John P. Jewett and Co., 1853), pp. 5, 14, 20–23.

2. "Minutes for the Gloucester County Society for the Abolition of Slavery," October 31, 1796, http://www.westjerseyhistory.org/docs/timhack/.

3. *List of Members of the Abolition Society in the County of Gloucester in the 9th month 1800–1802*, Historical Society of Haddonfield.

4. MaryAnn Ganges. "Neither Slave Nor Free: the Ganges Africans at the Lazaretto (1800)." http://www.sas.upenn.edu/~dbarnes/Ganges.html.

5. Wright, pp. 39–41.

6. Dennis Rizzo, *Parallel Communities: The Underground Railroad in South Jersey* (Charleston, SC: History Press, 2008), p. 135.

7. John Ferling, *Adams vs. Jefferson: The Tumultuous Election of 1800* (New York: Oxford University Press, 2004), pp. 15–16.

8. Child, pp. 30–32.

9. *Journal of the House of Representatives*, January 18, 1802, http://memory.loc.gov.

10. Child, pp. 36–39.

11. Wright, p. 26.

12. Frederick Tolles, *George Logan of Philadelphia* (New York: Oxford University Press, 1953), pp. 108, 243, 249–250.

13. *Journal of the Senate*, January 23, 1804, www.memory.loc.gov, p. 343.

14. Tolles, pp. 243–244.

15. *Journal of the Senate*, January 30, 1804, www.memory.loc.gov, p. 347.

16. Child, p. 43–45.

17. Margaret Hope Bacon, *Abby Hopper Gibbons: Prison Reformer and Social Activist*, (New York: State University of New York Press, 2000), p. 5.

18. Child, pp. 47–49.

19. Malone, *Jefferson the President, Second Term 1805–1809*. Vol. 5 of *Jefferson and His Times*, 1974, p. 543.

20. Child, pp. 54–55, 91.

21. John Parrish. "Notes on Abolition." 1805. http://trilogy.haverford.edu/speccoll/quakersandslavery/commentary/people/parrish_john.php.

22. Drake, p. 113.

23. *The Old Discipline: 19th century Friends' Disciplines in America* (Glenside, PA: Quaker Heritage Press, 1999), pp. 91–92.

24. Malone, *Jefferson the President*, p. 544.

25. *Journal of the House of Representatives*, December 31, 1806, January 8, 1807, March 3, 1807, www.memory.loc.gov, pp. 504, 517, 540.

26. Malone, *Jefferson the President*, pp. 546, 541–542.

Chapter 8

1. Drake, p. 116.

2. Elias Hicks, *Observations on the Slavery of the Africans and their Descendants and on the Use of the Produce of their Labour. Recommended to the serious perusal, and impartial considerations of the citizens of the United States of America, and others concerned* (New York: Samuel Wood, 1814), pp. 15–17.

3. Switala, *Underground Railroad in Delaware*, pp. 48–49.

4. *The African American Mosaic*, http://www.loc.gov/exhibits/african/intro.html.

5. *The Journal of Negro History* 2, no. 3 (July 1917), Henry Noble Sherwood, ed., www.gutenberg.org, p. 150.

6. T. Ellwood Chapman, "A Narrative of the Early Life, Travels and Gospel Labors of Jesse Kersey, Late of Chester County, PA," 1851, http://www.qhpress.org/quakerpages/qwhp/kntoc.htm.

7. Drake, p. 125.

8. *Journal of Negro History*, p. 153.

9. Drake, p. 125.

10. *Journal of Negro History*, pp. 151, 157–158.

11. Drake, p. 121.

12. Switala, *Underground Railroad in Delaware*, pp. 30–31.
13. Malone, *Jefferson and His Time (Vol. 6)*, pp. 328–331.
14. "The Missouri Compromise," http://www.citizensource.com/History/19thCen/MisCom.htm.
15. Ann Hagedorn, *Beyond the River: The Untold Story of the Heroes of the Underground Railroad*, (New York: Simon and Schuster, 2002), p. 14.
16. *Annals of Congress*, February 1820, www.memory.loc.gov, pp. 1559–1564.
17. Malone, *Jefferson and His Time*, vol. 6, p. 335.
18. William Still, *The Underground Railroad* (Philadelphia: Porter and Coates, 1872), pp. 642–643.
19. "Living the Experience." www.livingtheundergroundrailroad.com/historicalfigures.htm.
20. Still, pp. 643–647, 691–692.
21. Arna Bontemps, *Great Slave Narratives* (Boston: Beacon Press, 1969), pp. 214–219, 235–244; Still, p. 693.
22. Robert William Fagel, *Rise and Fall of American Slavery* (New York: W.W. Norton and Co., 1989), p. 253.
23. Hamm, pp. 39–43.
24. Larry Ceplair, ed., *The Public Years of Sarah and Angelina Grimké: Selected Writings 1835–1839* (New York: Columbia University Press, 1989), p. 3.

Chapter 9

1. Ceplair, *Public Years of Sarah and Angelina Grimké*, p. 4.
2. Richard J. Blackett, "'And There Shall Be No More Sea.' William Lloyd Garrison and the Transatlantic Abolitionist Movement." http://www.bu.edu/historicalconference08, pp. 1–7.
3. William Lloyd Garrison, *Selections from the Writings of William Lloyd Garrison* (Boston: R.F. Wallcut, 1852), pp. 235–236.
4. Julie Roy Jeffrey, *The Great Silent Army of Abolitionism: Ordinary Women in the Anti-Slavery Movement* (Chapel Hill: University of North Carolina Press, 1998), p. 15.
5. Drake, p. 118.
6. "Constitution of the Free Produce Society of Pennsylvania." http://triptych.brynmawr.edu/cdm/compoundobject/collection/HC_QuakSlav/id/4641/rec/1.
7. Drake, p. 118.
8. Peter P. Hinks, John R. McKivigan, R. Owen Williams, *Encyclopedia of Anti-Slavery and Abolition* (Westwood CT: Greenwood Press, 2007), p. 267.
9. George Taylor, *The Autobiography and Writings of George W. Taylor* (Philadelphia: Kessinger, 1891), pp. 40–43.
10. Hinks, pp. 267–268.
11. Mark E. Dixon, *The Hidden History of Chester County: Lost Tales from the Delaware and Brandywine Valleys* (Charleston, SC: The History Press), 2011, p. 2.
12. Margaret Hope Bacon, *But One Race: The Life of Robert Purvis* (Albany: State University of New York Press, 2007), p. 97.
13. Dixon, p. 2.
14. Hinks, p. 268.
15. Henry Mayer, *All on Fire: William Lloyd Garrison and the Abolition of Slavery* (New York: St. Martin's Press, 1998), pp. 120–121, 171–172.
16. Nash, *First City*, p. 150.
17. Mayer, *All on Fire*, p. 172.
18. Carlston Mabee, *Black Freedom: The Nonviolent Abolitionists from 1830 through the Civil War* (London: Macmillan, 1970), p. 20.
19. Mayer, *All on Fire*, p. 173.
20. Mabee, p. 20.
21. Mayer, *All on Fire*, p. 173.
22. Still, p. 650.
23. Margaret Hope Bacon, ed., "Lucretia Mott Speaking: Excerpts from the Sermons and Speeches of a Famous Nineteenth Century Quaker Minister and Reformer." Pendle Hill Pamphlet #234, 1980. http://www.pendlehill.org/images/pamphlets/php234b.pdf.
24. Mayer, *All on Fire*, pp. 174–176, 223.
25. William Lee Miller, *Arguing about Slavery: The Great Battles in the United States Congress* (New York: Alfred A. Knopf, 1996), p. 79.
26. *Public Years of Grimké*, p. 21.
27. Theodore Weld, ed., *American Slavery As It Is: Testimony of a Thousand Witnesses* (1839. Reprint, New York: Nabu Press, 2011), pp. 22–23.
28. Garrison, pp. 67–68.
29. "The Conflict with Slavery and Others, Complete, Volume VII." Letter to William Garrison from John Greenleaf Whittier, November 24, 1863. http://the-conflict-with-slavery-and-others-complete.t.ebooks2ebooks.com/71.html.
30. Mabee, p. 20.
31. Garrison, p. 69.

32. "The Conflict with Slavery and Others, Complete, Volume VII."
33. Garrison, pp. 69–71.
34. Miller, *Arguing about Slavery*, p. 314.
35. Jeffrey, pp. 141–142.

Chapter 10

1. Bessie Ayers Andrews, *Reminiscences of Greenwich* (Vineland, NJ: printed for the author, 1910), p. 31.
2. Charles Hall and Arlene T. Sayer, *The Monitor Register*, Woodstown, NJ, July 17, 1953 (clipping at the Salem County Historical Society).
3. Still, pp. 699–708.
4. William E. Schermerhorn, *The History of Burlington, New Jersey* (Burlington, NJ: Press of Enterprise Publishing Co., 1927), pp. 109–110.
5. P.H. Barnes, *The Underground Railroad and the Abolitionist Society*. June 12, 1939, p. 258—from folder in Gloucester County Historical Society Library.
6. Nash, *First City*, p. 149.
7. Kenneth Ives, ed., *Black Quakers* (Chicago: Progressive Press, 1991), pp. 48–52, 54–57.
8. Elizabeth Cady Stanton, Susan B. Anthony, Matilda Joslyn Gage, and Ida Husted Harper, eds., *The History of Woman Suffrage 1848–1861, Vol. 1* (New York: Fowler and Wells, 1881), pp. 334–335, 341–342.
9. "Turning the World Upside Down: The Anti-Slavery Convention of American Women, 1838." http://www.blackpast.org/bibliography/turning-world-upside-down-anti-slavery-convention-american-women-1838.
10. Prigg vs. Commonwealth of Pennsylvania, www.historicaldocuments.com, p. 6, 9–10.
11. Thomas D. Morris, *Free Men All: The Personal Liberty Laws of the North 1780–1861* (Baltimore: Johns Hopkins University Press, 1974), pp. 94–95.
12. Helen Tunnicliff Catterall with additions by James J. Hayden, *Judicial Cases Concerning American Slavery and the Negro, Vol. IV, Cases from the Courts of New England, the Middle States and the District of Columbia* (New York: Octagon Books, Inc., 1968), p. 292.
13. Morris, pp. 98–99.
14. Still, p. 693.

Chapter 11

1. William Henry Siebert, *The Underground Railroad from Slavery to Freedom* (New York: Macmillan, 1898), p. 45.
2. R.C. Smedley, *The History of the Underground Railroad* (New York: Arno Press and the New York Times, 1969), p. 35.
3. Switala, *The Underground Railroad in Delaware*, pp. 20–21.
4. Siebert, *The Underground Railroad*, p. 37.
5. David Brion Davis, *Inhuman Bondage: The Rise and Fall of Slavery in the New World* (New York: Oxford University Press, 2006), p. 269.
6. Switala, *The Underground Railroad in Delaware*, pp. 24–25.
7. Still, p. 647.
8. Switala, *The Underground Railroad in New York and New Jersey*, pp. 43–46.
9. Charles E. Smiley, *A True Story of Lawnside, NJ* (Camden, NJ: Robert J. Wythe, 1921), p. 31.
10. *Underground Railroad tour*, www.tourburlington.org, p. 4.
11. Switala, *The Underground Railroad in New York and New Jersey*, pp. 46–48.
12. Arthur D. Pierce, *Smugglers Woods: Jaunts and Journeys in Colonial and Revolutionary New Jersey* (New Brunswick, NJ: Rutgers University Press, 1960), p. 140.
13. Switala, *The Underground Railroad in New York and New Jersey* pp. 48–52.
14. *The Sunday Press*, Atlantic City, NJ, June 18, 1975, pp. 4–5.
15. Still, pp. 617–618.
16. *South Jersey Magazine*, January 1989 (Winter Issue), p. 12.
17. Still, pp. 619–620.
18. Switala, *The Underground Railroad in New York and New Jersey*, pp. 57–58.
19. *Sunday Press*, June 18, 1975, pp. 4–5.
20. Switala, *The Underground Railroad in New York and New Jersey*, p. 58.
21. "Underground Railroad, Thomas C. Oliver." http://www.phillyburbs.com/undergroundrailroad/Oliver.shtml.
22. Switala, *The Underground Railroad in New York and New Jersey*, pp. 58–59.
23. "Underground Railroad Tour." http://www.tourburlington.org/TourUGRR.html.
24. Switala, *The Underground Railroad in New York and New Jersey*, pp. 60–61.
25. Walter W. Evans, *The Story of Edgewater, the Historic Home at Evans Mill Pond,*

article at the Historical Society of Haddon-field, pp. 2–5.

26. Switala, *The Underground Railroad in New York and New Jersey* pp. 62–63.

27. *Courier Post*, February 7, 1988, p. 1.

28. "Underground Railroad Tour." http://www.tourburlington.org/TourUGRR.html.

29. *Courier Post,* February 7, 1988, p. 1.

30. Switala, *Underground Railroad in New York and New Jersey*, pp. 63–64.

31. Smedley, p. 29.

32. "Columbia, Pennsylvania." http://en.wikipedia.org/wiki/Columbia,_Pennsylvania.

33. Smedley, p. 29.

34. Still, pp. 695–696, 748–752.

35. Switala, *Underground Railroad in Delaware*, pp. 35–37.

36. "Woodburn." http://woodburn.dela ware.gov.

37. Switala, *Underground Railroad in Delaware*, pp. 38–39.

38. "Woodburn."

39. "John Alston." www.africanonline.com/slavery_delaware.htm.

40. Switala, *Underground Railroad in Delaware*, pp. 41–42.

41. Brian Temple, *The Union Prison at Fort Delaware: A Perfect Hell on Earth* (Jefferson, NC: McFarland, 2003), p. 18.

42. Switala, *Underground Railroad in Delaware*, p. 42

43. Still, p. 625.

44. "Johnson House Historic Site." http://www.johnsonhouse.org.

Chapter 12

1. James Miller and John Thompson, *Almanac of American History* (Washington DC: National Geographic, 2006), pp. 154–155.

2. Stanley W. Campbell, *The Slave Catchers: Enforcement of the Fugitive Slave Law 1850–1860* (Chapel Hill: University of North Carolina Press, 1968), pp. 5–7.

3. *Senate Journal*, January 29, 1850, www.memory.loc.gov, p. 118.

4. *Senate Journal*, March 4, 1850, www.memory.loc.gov. p. 192.

5. Campbell, p. 8.

6. "The Compromise of 1850 and the Fugitive Slave Act." http://www.pbs.org/wgbh/aia/part4/4p2951.html.

7. Campbell, p. 8.

8. Allen Douglas, *Stephen A. Douglas*

(1908. Reprint, New York: Chelsea House, 1983), pp. 180, 187.

9. "The Compromise of 1850 and the Fugitive Slave Act."

10. Campbell, pp. 11, 24.

11. "Fugitive Slave Act of 1793." http://www.ushistory.org/presidentshouse/history/slaveact1793.htm.

12. Siebert, *The Underground Railroad*, pp. 302–303.

13. Still, p. 613.

14. "The Compromise of 1850 and the Fugitive Slave Act."

Chapter 13

1. Siebert, *The Underground Railroad*, p. 274.

2. Barnes, *Underground Railroad and Abolitionist Society*, p. 258.

3. Siebert, *The Underground Railroad*, pp. 170–171.

4. Harper, *South Jersey's Angel*, pp. 4–5.

5. Siebert, *The Underground Railroad*, p. 50.

6. Smedley, pp. 57–58, 165–166.

7. Still, pp. 583–584, 624.

8. Burstyn, p. 66.

9. Still, p. 350.

10. Thomas P. Slaughter, *Bloody Dawn: The Christiana Riot and Racial Violence in the Antebellum North* (New York: Oxford University Press, 1991), p. 57.

11. Still, pp. 350–352.

12. Slaughter, *Bloody Dawn*, p. 70.

13. Smedley, pp. 92–93.

14. Still, p. 352.

15. *National Geographic*, July 1984, p. 35.

16. Campbell, *Slave Catchers*, p. 35.

17. Still, pp. 353–356.

18. *National Geographic,* July 1984, p. 35.

19. Still, p. 615.

20. Smedley, *Underground Railroad*, p. 124.

21. Siebert, *Underground Railroad*, pp. 280–281.

22. Still, p. 368.

23. Smedley, *Underground Railroad*, pp. 70, 86.

24. "Lindley Coates." http://www.muweb.millersville.edu.

25. Smedley, *Underground Railroad*, p. 86.

26. "Elizabeth Parker." http://www.afrolumens.org/ugrr/parker/html.

27. Still, pp. 551–555; Nagle, www.afrolumens.org, pp. 1–6.

28. William C. Kashatus, *Just over the Line* (West Chester, PA: Chester County Historical Society, 2002), p. 25.
29. Still, pp. 72–74.
30. Catherine Clinton, *Harriet Tubman: The Road to Freedom* (New York: Back Bay Books, 2004), pp. 114–115.
31. Jean M. Humez, *Harriet Tubman: The Life and the Life Stories* (Madison: University of Wisconsin Press, 2003), p. 231.
32. Smedley, *Underground Railroad*, pp. 254–255.
33. Still, p. 476.
34. "Thomas Garrett." http://www.hsd.org/DHE/DHE_who_garrett.htm.
35. Smedley, *Underground Railroad*, p. 241.
36. Harriet Beecher Stowe, *The Key to Uncle Tom's Cabin* (Cleveland, OH: Jewitt, Proctor, and Worthington, 1853), pp. 99–100.
37. Margaret Hope Bacon, *Quiet Rebels: The Story of the Quakers in America* (Philadelphia: New Society, 1985), p. 114.
38. Stowe, p. 100.
39. Bacon, *Quiet Rebels*, p. 114.
40. Siebert, *Underground Railroad*, pp. 322, 324.

Chapter 14

1. Bacon pp. 111–112.
2. Siebert, *Underground Railroad*, pp. 64, 67.
3. Smedley, *Underground Railroad*, p. 29.
4. Kashatus, p. 53.
5. Smedley, *Underground Railroad*, p. 46.
6. George and Willene Hendricks, *Fleeing for Freedom: Stories of the Underground Railroad, as Told by Levi Coffin and William Still* (Chicago: Ivan R. Dee, 2009), p. 15.
7. Still, pp. 749–750.
8. *Philadelphia Inquirer*, February 4, 1994, p. 1.
9. Smedley, p. 46.
10. Humez, p. 226.
11. *The Press of Atlantic City*, March 8, 1998, p. A-4.
12. Still, p. 647.
13. Smedley, *Underground Railroad*, pp. 82–83.
14. Still, pp. 502–503.
15. Loretta Rodgers, "The Trackless Train: Tracking Delco's Role in the Underground Railroad," http://www.delcohistory.org/articles/undergroundrr.htm.

16. *Cumberland Patriot,* The Cumberland County Historical Society, Greenwich, NJ, (clipping) Spring 1987, vol. 20, no. 1, p. 5.
17. Henry Box Brown, *Narrative of the Life of Henry Box Brown* (1850. Reprint, New York: Oxford University Press, 2002), pp. 47–62.
18. Still, pp. 82–84.
19. William L. Andrews and Henry Louis Gates, Jr. eds., *The Civitas Anthology of African American Slave Narratives (reprint of Running a Thousand Miles for Freedom or the Escape of William and Ellen Croft from Slavery by William and Ellen Croft)* (London: William Tweedee, 1860. Reprint, Washington, DC: Civitas Counterpoint, 1999), pp. 420–448.
20. Still, pp. 746.
21. Ziegenbein, www.africanaonline.com.
22. Still, pp. 746–747.

Chapter 15

1. Siebert, *Underground Railroad*, p. 10.
2. Still, p. 448.
3. Smedley, *Underground Railroad*, pp. 56–58, 72–73, 83–84.
4. *Philadelphia Inquirer*, Sunday, October 7, 2012, p. N-4.
5. *Burlington, NJ*, www.phillyburbs.com.
6. *The News*, February 24, 1997, p. B-5.
7. *Burlington, NJ*, www.phillyburbs.com.
8. Smedley, *Underground Railroad*, pp. 48–52.
9. "Mary Thomas." Interview. http://www.loc.gov/item/wpalh001409.
10. Smedley, *Underground Railroad*, pp. 77–78.
11. Still, pp. 694, 714–715.
12. Smedley, *Underground Railroad*, pp. 44–45.
13. Harper, *South Jersey Angel*, p. 5.
14. Still, pp. 88–91.
15. Campbell, *The Slave Catchers*, p. 142.
16. Still, p. 90.
17. Campbell, pp. 142–143.
18. Still, pp. 93–94.
19. Campbell, pp. 143–144.
20. Dennis C. Rizzo, *Mount Holly, New Jersey: A Hometown Reinvented* (Charleston, SC: History Press, 2007), p. 106.
21. Still, pp. 129–131.
22. Harper, *South Jersey Angel*, p. 5.
23. Humez, pp. 292–293.
24. Still, pp. 394–395, 422–425, 445–448.

25. Harper, *South Jersey Angel*, p. 5.
26. Burstyn, p. 66.
27. Still, pp. 530–531, 618.

Chapter 16

1. Still, p. 627.
2. Harper, *South Jersey's Angel*, p. 5.
3. Still, p. 622.
4. McPherson, *Battle Cry*, pp. 495–496, 502, 505.
5. "The Emancipation Proclamation." http://www.archives.gov/exhibits/featured_documents/emancipation_proclamation.
6. Still, p. 641.
7. "13th Amendment to the Constitution." http://www.loc.gov/rr/program/bib/ourdocs/13thamendment.html.
8. *The Congressional Globe*, House of Representatives, 38th Congress, 2nd session, #34, February 2, 1865, http://www.memory.loc.gov/cgi-bin/ampage?collId=llcg&fileName=068/llcg068.db&recNum, p. 531.
9. McPherson, *Battle Cry*, pp. 840–841.

10. Harper, *South Jersey's Angel*, p. 5.
11. Smedley, *Underground Railroad*, pp. 256–257.
12. Still, pp. 627–629, 697.

Appendix

1. "Resolutions of The Germantown Mennonites; February 18, 1688," http://avalon.law.yale.edu/17th_century/men01.asp.
2. "Fugitive Slave Act of 1793," http://www.ushistory.org/presidentshouse/history/slaveact1793.htm.
3. "Fugitive Slave Act of 1850," www.yale.edu/lawweb/avalon/fugitive.htm.
4. "The Emancipation Proclamation." http://www.archives.gov/exhibits/featured_documents/emancipation_proclamation.
5. "The 13th Amendment to the Unites States Constitution." http://www.ourdocuments.gov/print_friendly.php?flash=true&page=transcript&doc=40&title=Transc.

Bibliography

Books

Andrews, Bessie Ayers. *Historical Sketches of Greenwich in Old Cohansey*. Vineland, NJ: Vineland Printing House, 1905.

_____. *Reminiscences of Greenwich*. Vineland, NJ: Vineland Printing House, 1910.

Andrews, William L., and Henry Louis Gates, Jr., eds. *The Civitas Anthology of African American Slave Narratives*. Washington, DC: Civitas Counterpoint, 1999 (reprint of *Running a Thousand Miles for Freedom or The Escape from Slavery*, 1860).

Andrist, Ralph K., ed. *George Washington: A Biography in His Own Words, Vol. 2*. New York: Newsweek, 1972.

Anthony, Susan B., Elizabeth Cady Stanton, Matilda Joslyn Gage, and Ida Husted Harper, eds. *The History of Woman Suffrage 1848–1861, Vol. 1*. New York: Fowler and Wells, 1881.

Bacon, Margaret Hope. *Abby Hopper Gibbons: Prison Reformer and Social Activist*. Albany: State University of New York Press, 2000.

_____. *But One Race: The Life of Robert Purvis*. Albany: State University of New York Press, 2007.

_____. *Quiet Rebels: The Story of the Quakers in America*. Philadelphia: New Society, 1985.

Barnes, P.H. *Underground Railroad and the Abolitionist Society*, June 12, 1939, from folder of Gloucester County Historical Society.

Basker, James G., ed. *Early American Abolitionists: A Collection of Anti-Slavery Writings 1760–1820*. New York: The Gilder Lehrman Institute of American History, 2005.

Benezet, Anthony. *Views of American Slavery*. Philadelphia: Association of Friends for the Diffusion of Religious and Useful Knowledge, 1855.

Bernhard, Winfred. *Fisher Ames: Federalist and Statesman, 1758–1808*. Chapel Hill: University of North Carolina Press, 1965.

Bobrick, Benson. *Wide as the Water: The Story of the English Bible and the Revolution It Inspired*. New York: Simon & Schuster, 2001.

Bontemps, Anna, ed. *Great Slave Narratives (The Fugitive Blacksmith or Events in the History of James W.C. Pennington: Pastor of a Presbyterian Church, New York, Formerly a Slave in the State of Maryland)*. Boston: Beacon Press, 1969.

Bordewich, Fergus M. *Bound for Canaan: The Underground Railroad and the War for the Soul of America*. New York: HarperCollins, 2005.

Boyd, Julian P., ed. *Fundamental Laws and Constitutions of New Jersey 1664–1964*. Princeton, NJ: D. Van Nostrand Co., 1964.

Braithwaite, William C. *The Beginnings of Quakerism*. Macmillan, 1912. Reprint, Cambridge: Cambridge University Press, 1961.

Brands, H. *The First American: The Life and Times of Benjamin Franklin*. New York: Anchor, 2000.

Brown, Henry Box. *Narrative of the Life of*

Henry Box Brown. 1850. Reprint, New York: Oxford University Press, 2002.

Burstyn, Joan N. *Past and Promise: Lives of New Jersey Women*. Syracuse, NY: Syracuse University Press, 1997.

Campbell, Stanley W. *The Slave Catchers: Enforcement of the Fugitive Slave Law 1850–1860*. Chapel Hill: University of North Carolina Press, 1968.

Catterall, Helen Tunnicliff, and James J. Hayden, eds. *Judicial Cases Concerning American Slavery and the Negro, Vol. IV: Cases from the Courts of New England, the Middle States and the District of Columbia*. New York: Octagon, 1968.

Ceplair, Larry, ed. *The Public Years of Sarah and Angelina Grimké: Selected Writings, 1835–1839*. New York: Columbia University Press, 1989.

Child, Lydia Maria. *Isaac T. Hopper: A True Life*. Boston: John P. Jewett, 1853.

Clark, Ronald W. *Benjamin Franklin: A Biography*. New York: Random House, 1983.

Clinton, Catherine. *Harriet Tubman: The Road to Freedom*. New York: Back Bay, 2004.

Davis, David Brion. *Inhuman Bondage: The Rise and Fall of Slavery in the New World*. New York: Oxford University Press, 2006.

Davis, Kenneth C. *America's Hidden History: Untold Tales of the First Pilgrims, Fighting Women, and Forgotten Founders Who Shaped a Nation*. New York: Smithsonian, 2008.

Derry, Ellis L. *Old and Historic Churches in New Jersey, Vol. 1*. Medford, NJ: Plexus Publishing, 2003.

Dixon, Mark E. *The Hidden History of Chester County: Lost Tales from the Delaware and Brandywine Valleys*. Charleston, SC: The History Press, 2011.

Donnan, Elizabeth. *Documents Illustrative of the History of the Slave Trade in America, Vol. III, New England and the Middle Colonies*. New York: Octagon, 1969.

Dorwart, Jeffrey M. *Camden County, NJ: The Making of a Metropolitan Community, 1626–2000*. New Brunswick, NJ: Rutgers University Press, 2001.

Douglas, Allen. *Stephen A. Douglas*. 1908. Reprint, New York: Chelsea House, 1983.

Drake, Thomas E. *Quakers and Slavery in America*. New Haven, CT: Yale University Press, 1950, 1965.

Drinker, Elizabeth. *The Diary of Elizabeth Drinker: The Life Cycle of an Eighteenth Century Woman*. Edited by Elaine Forman Crane. Boston: Northeastern University Press, 1994.

Durant, Will, and Ariel Durant. *The Story of Civilization Vol. 7: The Age of Reason Begins*. New York: Simon & Schuster, 1961.

Ellis, Joseph J. *Founding Brothers: The Revolutionary Generation*. New York: Vintage, 2000.

Evans, Walter W. *The Story of Edgewater: The Historic Home at Evans Mill Pond*, 1918. Manuscript at the Historical Society of Haddonfield, NJ

Fagel, Robert William. *The Rise and Fall of American Slavery*. New York: W.W. Norton, 1989.

Farmer, Thomas P. *New Jersey in History: Fighting to be Heard*. Harvey Cedars, NJ: Down the Shore, 1996.

Farr, Mrs. William. *Slavery and the Underground Railroad*. Woodbury, NJ: Gloucester County Historical Society.

Ferling, John. *Adams vs. Jefferson: The Tumultuous Election of 1800*. New York: Oxford University Press, 2004.

Finkelman, Paul. *Slavery and the Founders: Race and Liberty in the Age of Jefferson*. Armonk, NY: M.E. Sharpe, 1996.

Fisher, Edgar Jacob. *New Jersey as a Royal Province 1738–1776*. Studies in History, Economics and Public Law. New York: AMS Press, 1967.

Fitzpatrick, John C., ed. *The Diaries of George Washington, Vol. IV, 1789–1799*. New York: Houghton Mifflin, 1925.

Foner, Phillip S. *History of Black Americans from the Compromise of 1850 to the End of the Civil War*. Westport, CT: Greenwood Press, 1983.

Fox, George. *The Journal of George Fox*. London: Religious Society of Friends, 1975.

Franklin, Benjamin. *Benjamin Franklin: Autobiography, Poor Richard and Later Writings*. New York: Library of America, 2005.

_____. *Writings*. New York: Library of America, 1987.

Garrison, William Lloyd. *Selections from the Writings of W.L. Garrison*. Boston: R.F. Wallcut, 1852.

Hagedorn, Ann. *Beyond the River: The Untold Stories of the Heroes of the Underground Railroad*. New York: Simon & Schuster, 2002.

Hamm, Thomas D. *The Quakers in America*. New York: Columbia University Press, 2003.

Harper, Robert W. *John Fenwick and Salem County in the Province of West Jersey 1609–1700, Including Burlington, Cape May, Cumberland and Gloucester Counties*. Salem, NJ: Salem County Cultural Heritage Commission, 1978.

_____. *Old Gloucester County and the American Revolution 1763–1778, Including Atlantic, Burlington, Cape May, Cumberland and Salem Counties*. Glassboro, NJ: The Jefferson Printing Co., 1986.

Hartel, C.E.N. *Notes on Slaves in Haddonfield and Vicinity: Examination of Early Wills and Inventories of Estates*. Haddonfield, NJ: Haddonfield Historical Society, February and August 1952.

Hawke, David Freeman. *Benjamin Rush: Revolutionary Gadfly*. New York: Bobbs-Merrill, 1971.

Hendricks, George, and Willine Hendricks. *Fleeing for Freedom: Stories of the Underground Railroad as Told by Levi Coffin and William Still*. Chicago: Ivan R. Dee, 2009.

Hicks, Elias. *Observations on the Slavery of the Africans and their Descendants and on the Use of the produce of their labour. Recommended to the serious perusal, and impartial considerations of the citizens of the USA, and other concerned*. New York: Samuel Wood, 1814.

Hinks, Peter P., John R. McKivigan, and R. Owen Williams, eds. *Encyclopedia of Anti-Slavery and Abolition*. Westport, CT: Greenwood Press, 2007.

Hoelle, Edith. *Vignettes of Historic Woodbury*. Woodbury, NJ: Academy Business Forms, 1965.

Humez, Jean M. *Harriet Tubman: The Life and the Life Stories*. Madison: University of Wisconsin Press, 2003.

Hunt, Gaillord, and James Brown Scott, eds. *The Debates in the Federal Convention of 1787 Which Framed the Constitution of the United States of America, Reported by James Madison, a Delegate from the State of Virginia*. Union, NJ: The Lawbook Exchange, 1999.

Ives, Kenneth, ed. *Black Quakers*. Chicago: Progressive Press, 1991.

Jackson, Maurice. *Let This Voice Be Heard: Anthony Benezet, Father of Atlantic Abolitionism*. Philadelphia: University of Pennsylvania Press, 2009.

Jackson, William J. *New Jerseyans in the Civil War: For Union and Liberty*. New Brunswick, NJ: Rutgers University Press, 2000.

Jamison, Wallace N. *Religion in New Jersey: A Brief History*. Vol. 13, The New Jersey Historical Series. Princeton, NJ: D. Van Nostrand & Co., 1964.

Jeffrey, Julie Roy. *The Great Silent Army of Abolitionism: Ordinary Women in the Antislavery Movement*. Chapel Hill: University of North Carolina Press, 1998.

Kashatus, William C. *Just over the Line*. West Chester, PA: Chester County Historical Society, 2002.

Lay, Benjamin. *All Slave-Keepers That Keep the Innocent in Bondage*. Philadelphia: Benjamin Franklin, 1737.

Levy, Barry. *Quakers and the American Family: British Settlement in the Delaware Valley*. New York: Oxford University Press, 1968.

Mabee, Carlston. *Black Freedom: The Nonviolent Abolitionists from 1830 through the Civil War*. London: Macmillan, 1970.

Madison, James. *Writings*. New York: Library of America, 1999.

Malone, Dumas. *Jefferson the President: Second Term,1805–1809, Vol. 5*. Boston: Little, Brown, 1974.

_____. *Jefferson the Virginian*. (*Jefferson and His Times*. Vol. 1) Boston: Little, Brown, 1948.

Mayer, Henry. *All on Fire: William Lloyd Garrison and the Abolition of Slavery*. New York: St. Martin's Press, 1998.

McCullough, David. *John Adams*. New York: Simon & Schuster, 2001.

McPherson, James M. *Battle Cry of Freedom: The Civil War Era*. New York: Oxford University Press, 1988.

Miller, William Lee. *Arguing about Slavery: The Great Battles in the United States Congress*. New York: Alfred A. Knopf, 1996.

Miller, William Lee, and John Thompson. *Almanac of American History*. Washington, DC: National Geographic, 2006.

Mitnick, Barbara J. *New Jersey in the American Revolution*. New Brunswick, NJ: Rivergate, 2005.

Moore, John M., ed. *Friends in the Delaware Valley: Philadelphia Yearly Meeting 1681–1981*. Haverford, PA: Friends Historical Association, 1981.

Morison, Samuel E. *The Oxford History of the United States, 1783–1917, Vol. 1*. London: Oxford University Press, 1927.

Morris, Thomas D. *Free Men All: The Personal Liberty Laws of the North, 1780–1861*. Baltimore: Johns Hopkins University Press, 1974.

Murray-Rust, David M. *Quakers in Brief or Quakerism Made Easy: An Overview of the Quaker Movement from 1650 to 1990*. Merseyside, UK: Birkenhead Meeting, 1995.

Nash, Gary B. *First City: Philadelphia and the Forging of Historical Memory*. Philadelphia: University of Pennsylvania Press, 2002.

_____. *The Unknown American Revolution: The Unruly Birth of Democracy and the Struggle to Create America*. New York: Penguin, 2005.

Newman, Daisy. *A Procession of Friends: Quakers in America*. Garden City, NJ: Doubleday, 1972.

The Old Discipline: 19th Century Friends' Disciplines in America. Glenside, PA: Quaker Heritage Press, 1999.

Paine, Ralph D. *The Battle of Red Bank*. Woodbury, NJ: Gloucester County Board of Chosen Freeholders, 1967.

Pierce, Arthur D. *Smugglers Woods: Jaunts and Journeys in Colonial and Revolutionary New Jersey*. New Brunswick, NJ: Rutgers University Press, 1960.

Pomfret, John E. *Colonial New Jersey: A History*. New York: Charles Scribner's Sons, 1973.

The Quakers Salem Quarterly Meeting Southern New Jersey 1675–1990. Salem, NJ: Salem Quarterly Meeting, 1990.

Randall, Willard Sterne. *Benedict Arnold: Patriot and Traitor*. New York: William Morrow, 1990.

Rappleye, Charles. *Robert Morris: Financier of the American Revolution*. New York: Simon & Schuster, 2010.

_____. *Sons of Providence: The Brown Brothers, the Slave Trade and the American Revolution*. New York: Simon & Schuster, 2006.

Rizzo, Dennis. *Mount Holly, New Jersey: A Hometown Reinvented*. Charleston, SC: The History Press, 2007.

_____. *Parallel Communities: The Underground Railroad in South Jersey*. Charleston, SC: The History Press, 2008.

Salem County Tercentenary Committee. *Fenwick's Colony: Salem County Pictorial: 1675–1964*. Salem, NJ: Salem County Tercentenary Committee, 1964.

Sandiford, Ralph. *A Brief Examination of the Practice of the Times*. Philadelphia: Franklin and Meredith, 1729.

Schermerhorn, William E. *The History of Burlington, New Jersey*. Burlington, NJ: Press of Enterprise, 1927.

Schonover, Janetta Wright, ed. *A History of William Brinton Who Came from England to Chester County, Pennsylvania in 1684 and of His Descendants with Some Records of the English Brintons, Part I*. Trenton, NJ, 1924.

Siebert, Wilbur Henry. *The Underground Railroad from Slavery to Freedom*. New York: Macmillan, 1898.

Slaughter, Thomas P. *Bloody Dawn: The Christiana Riot and Racial Violence in the Antebellum North*. New York: Oxford University Press, 1991.

Smedley, R.C. *The History of the Underground Railroad*. 1883. Reprint, New York: Arno Press and New York Times, 1969.

Smiley, Charles C., ed. *A True Story of Lawnside, NJ*. Camden, NJ: Robert J. Wythe, Jr., 1921.

Stalcup, Brenda, ed. *Turning Points in World History: The Industrial Revolution*. San Diego, CA: Greenhaven Press, 2002.

Still, William. *The Underground Railroad*. Philadelphia: Porter and Coates, 1872.

Stowe, Harriet Beecher. *The Key to Uncle Tom's Cabin*. Cleveland, OH: Jewitt, Proctor and Worthington, 1853.

Switala, William J. *The Underground Railroad in Delaware, Maryland, and West Virginia*. Mechanicsburg, PA: Stackpole, 2004.

_____. *The Underground Railroad in New York and New Jersey*. Mechanicsburg, PA: Stackpole, 2006.

Taylor, George W. *The Autobiography and Writings of George W. Taylor*. 1891. Reprint, Philadelphia: Kessinger, 2009.

Temple, Brian. *The Union Prison at Fort Delaware: A Perfect Hell on Earth*. Jefferson, NC: McFarland, 2003.

Tolles, Frederick. *George Logan of Philadelphia*. New York: Oxford University Press, 1953.

Tucker, St. George. *A Dissertation on Slavery with a Proposal for the Gradual Abolition of It, in the State of Virginia*. Philadelphia: Mathew Carey, 1796.

Vipont, Elfrida. *George Fox and the Valiant Sixty*. London: Hamish Hamilton, 1975.

Weld, Theodore, ed. *American Slavery as It Is: Testimony of a Thousand Witnesses*. 1839. Reprint, New York: Nabu Press, 2011.

Williams, William H. *Slavery and Freedom in Delaware: 1639–1865*. Wilmington, DE: Scholarly Resources, 1996.

Wood, Betty. *The Origins of American Slavery: Freedom and Bondage in the English Colonies*. New York: Hill and Wang, 1997.

Woolman, John. *The Journal of John Woolman*. New York: Citadel Press, 1961.

_____. *The Works of John Woolman*. New York: J.W. Garrett Press, 1970.

Wright, Esmond. *Franklin of Philadelphia*. Cambridge, MA: Belknap Press of Harvard University Press, 1986.

Wright, Giles R. *Afro-Americans in New Jersey: A Short History*. Trenton, NJ: New Jersey Historical Commission, 1988.

Yonge, Charlotte M. *A Pictorial History of the World's Great Nations from the Earliest Dates to the Present Time*. New York: Selmar Hess, 1882.

Documents

Manumission Papers, Stewart Collection, Rowan University, Glassboro, NJ.

Online

"An Act for the Gradual Abolition of Slavery (PA)." www.yale.edu/lawweb/avalon/statec/statutes/penns07.htm.

"The African American Mosaic." http://www.loc.gov/exhibits/african/intro.html.

"The Articles of Association." October 20, 1774. http://avalon.law.yale.edu/18th_century/contcong_10-20-74.asp.

Bacon, Margaret Hope, ed. "Lucretia Mott Speaking: Excerpts from the Sermons and Speeches of a Famous Nineteenth Century Quaker Minister and Reformer." Pendle Hill Pamphlet #234, 1980. http://www.pendlehill.org/images/pamphlets/php234b.pdf.

Blackett, Richard J. "'And There Shall Be No More Sea.' William Lloyd Garrison and the Transatlantic Abolitionist Movement." http://www.bu.edu/historicalconference08.

Brendlinger, Irv. "Anthony Benezet: True Champion of the Slave." *Wesleyan Theological Journal* 32, no. 1 (Spring 1997): http://wesley.nnu.edu/fileadmin/imported_site/wesleyjournal/1997-wtj-32-1.pdf.

Chapman, T. Ellwood. "A Narrative of the Early Life, Travels and Gospel Labors of Jesse Kersey, Late of Chester County, PA." 1851. http://www.qhpress.org/quakerpages/qwhp/kntoc.htm.

"Columbia, Pennsylvania." http://en.wikipedia.org/wiki/Columbia,_Pennsylvania.

"The Compromise of 1850 and the Fugitive Slave Act." http://www.pbs.org/wgbh/aia/part4/4p2951.html.

"The Conflict with Slavery and Others, Complete, Volume VII." Letter to William Garrison from John Greenleaf Whittier, November 24, 1863. http://the-conflict-with-slavery-and-others-complete.t.ebooks2ebooks.com/71.html.

The Congressional Globe. House of Representatives, 38th Congress, 2nd session, #34. Thursday, February 2, 1865. http://www.memory.loc.gov/cgi-bin/ampage?collId=llcg&fileName=068/llcg068.db&recNum.

"Constitution of the Free Produce Society

of Pennsylvania." http://triptych.bryn
mawr.edu/cdm/compoundobject/col
lection/HC_QuakSlav/id/4641/rec/1.
"Constitutional Convention 1787." http://
avalon.law.yale.edu/18th_century/
debates_825.asp.
Dubois, W.E.B., *The Philadelphia Negro.*
"Chapter VIII, Education and Illiteracy."
New York: Lippincott, 1899. www.2.
pfeiffer.edu/2Iridener/DSS/DuBos/
pnchviii.html.
"Eli Whitney's Patent for the Cotton Gin."
http://www.archives.gov/education/
lessons/cotton-gin-patent/index.html.
"Elizabeth Parker." http://www.afrolumens.
org/ugrr/parker/html.
"The Emancipation Proclamation." http://
www.archives.gov/exhibits/featured_
documents/emancipation_proclamation.
"Formation of the American Anti-Slavery
Society." Letter to American Anti-Slavery
Society from John Greenleaf Whittier,
November 30, 1863. http://www.apstu
dent.com/ushistory/docs1851/antislv2.
htm.
"Fugitive Slave Act of 1850." www.yale.edu/
lawweb/avalon/fugitive.htm.
"Fugitive Slave Act of 1793." http://www.
ushistory.org/presidentshouse/history/
slaveact1793.htm.
Ganges, MaryAnn. "Neither Slave Nor Free:
the Ganges Africans at the Lazaretto
(1800)." http://www.sas.upenn.edu/~d
barnes/Ganges.html.
"Historic Germantown, Philadelphia, PA,
Francis Daniel Pastorius." http://www.
ushistory.org/Germantown/people/
pastorius.html.
Historical Society of Pennsylvania. http://
www.hsp.org.
"History of Camden, NJ." http://www.ci.
camden.nj.us/history.
"History of Congress, House of Representatives." February 29, 1820. www.memory.
loc.gov/cgi-bin/ampage?collID=
llac&fileName=036.db&recNum=141.
"History of the Gwynedd Friends." http://
www.gwyneddfriends.org/gwyneed_
history_page1.html.
"John Alston." http://www.africanonline.
com/slavery_delaware.htm.
"John C. Calhoun's Speech." March 4, 1850.

http://memory.loc.gov/cgi-bin/query/r
?ammem/mcc:@field%28DOCID
+@lit%28mcc/009%29%29.
"John Cooper Advocates the Abolition of
Slavery." http://slic.njstatelib.org/slic_
files/imported/NJ_Information/
Digital_Collections/NJInTheAmerican-
Revolution1763-1783/13.6.pdf.
"John Woolman: An Appreciation by John
Greenleaf Whittier, Part 1, Benjamin
Lay." http://www.strecorsoc.org/jwool
man/apprel.html.
"Johnson House Historic Site." http://www.
johnsonhouse.org.
Journal of the House of Representatives. February 12, 1790; February 17, 1794; November 30, 1797; January 18, 1802; December 31, 1806; January 8, 1807; March
3, 1807. http://memory.loc.gov.
Journal of the Senate. January 23, 1804; January 30, 1804; January 29, 1850. http://
memory.loc.gov.
"Maclay's Journal." http://memory.loc.gov/
ammem/amlaw/lwmj.html.
Keith, George. "An Exhortation and Caution
to Friends Concerning Buying or Keeping
of Negroes." http://www.qhpress.org/qua
kerpages/qwhp/gk-as1693.htm.
"Lindley Coates." http://www.muweb.mil
lersville.edu.
"Living the Experience." http://www.living
theundergroundrailroad.com/histor
icalfigures.htm.
"Mary Barrett Dyer." http://www.rootsweb.
ancestry.com/~nwa/dyer.html.
"Mary Thomas." Interview. http://www.loc.
gov/item/wpalh001409.
"Minutes for the Gloucester County Society
for the Abolition of Slavery." October 31,
1796. http://www.westjerseyhistory.org/
docs/timhack/.
"The Missouri Compromise." http://www.
citizensource.com/History/19thCen/
MisCom.htm.
"New Jersey Slave Laws Summary and
Records." http://www.slaveryinamerica.
org/geography/slave_lawsNJ.html.
"New Jersey State Loyalty Oath." slic.njs-
tatelib.org/slic_files/imported/NJ_In-
formation/.../11.1.pdf.
"On the Evils of Slavery." http://www.loc.
gov/cgi-bin/query/r?ammem/rbpe.

Parrish, John. "Notes on Abolition." 1805. http://trilogy.haverford.edu/speccoll/quakersandslavery/commentary/people/parrish_john.php.

"Pastorius, Francis Daniel (1651–1720)." http://www.germanheritage.com/biographies/mtoz/pastorius.html.

Penn, William. "Frame of Government of Pennsylvania." April 25, 1682. http://www.constitution.org/bcp/frampenn.htm.

"Pennsylvania Hall Fire (1838)." http://www.blackpast.org/aah/pennsylvania-hall-fire-1838.

"The Pennsylvania Militia." http://www.constitution.org/jw/acm_3-m.htm.

"Petition from the Pennsylvania Society for the Abolition of Slavery." February 3, 1796. http://www.ushistory.org/documents/antislavery.htm.

"Prigg vs. Commonwealth of Pennsylvania." http://supreme.justia.com/cases/federal/us/41/539/case.html.

"Resolutions of The Germantown Mennonites; February 18, 1688." http://avalon.law.yale.edu/17th_century/men01.asp.

Rodgers, Loretta. "The Trackless Train: Tracking Delco's Role in the Underground Railroad." http://www.delcohistory.org/articles/undergroundrr.htm.

"13th Amendment to the Constitution." http://www.loc.gov/rr/program/bib/ourdocs/13thamendment.html.

"The 13th Amendment to the Unites States Constitution." http://www.ourdocuments.gov/print_friendly.php?flash=true&page=transcript&doc=40&title=Transc.

"Thomas Garrett." http://www.hsd.org/DHE/DHE_who_garrett.htm.

"To the U.S. Congress Assembled the Address from the Yearly Meeting of the People Called Quakers." http://www.rootsweb.ancestry.com/~quakers/petition.htm.

"Turning the World Upside Down: The Anti-Slavery Convention of American Women, 1838." http://www.blackpast.org/bibliography/turning-world-upside-down-anti-slavery-convention-american-women-1838.

"The Underground Railroad in Bucks, Burlington, and Montgomery County—

Anthony Benezet." www.phillyburbs.com/undergroundrailroad/benzet.shtm.

"Underground Railroad, Thomas C. Oliver." http://www.phillyburbs.com/undergroundrailroad/Oliver.shtml.

"Underground Railroad Tour." http://www.tourburlington.org/TourUGRR.html.

Whittier, John Greenleaf. Introduction to "The Journal of John Woolman." http://www.phillyburbs.com/undergroundrailroad/lay.shtml.

"Woodburn." http://woodburn.delaware.gov/.

Minutes

Gloucester County Society for the Abolition of Slavery began in Burlington on 5th month (May) 2, 1793. Stewart Collection, Rowan University, Glassboro, NJ.

List of Members of the Abolition Society in the County of Gloucester in the 9th month 1800–1802. Historical Society of Haddonfield, Haddonfield, NJ.

Periodicals

Blockson, Charles. "Escape From Slavery: The Underground Railroad." *National Geographic*, July 1984 (clipping from the Cumberland County Historical Society, Greenwich, NJ).

Courier-Post (Cherry Hill, NJ), February 7, 1988.

Cumberland Patriot (Bridgeton, NJ) 20 no. 1, Spring 1987 (clipping from the Cumberland County Historical Society, Greenwich, NJ).

Garcia-Barrio, Constance. "Underground Railroad Stations: Reminders of Perilous Journeys A Few Remain, Keeping the History Alive ." *Philadelphia Inquirer*, February 4, 1994,

Goldy, Jim, Sr. "A Friend of Slaves: The Story of Abigail Goodwin." *South Jersey Magazine*, January 1989.

Hall, Charles, and Arlene T. Sayer. *The Monitor Register* (Woodstown, NJ), July 17, 1953 (clipping from the Salem County Historical Society, Salem, NJ).

Harper, Robert W. "South Jersey's Angel to

Runaway Slaves." *The Sunday Press*, June 18, 1975.

Kephart, Bill, and Mary Kephart. "The Revolutionary War in Gloucester County." *Gloucester County Times*, March 1, 2009.

Lee, James F. "A Little Enclave of History in Delaware." *Philadelphia Inquirer*, October 7, 2012.

The News, Monday, February 24, 1997 (clipping from the Cumberland County Historical Society, Greenwich, NJ).

Pennsylvania Gazette, #2515, May 7, 1777.

Press of Atlantic City, March 8, 1998 (clipping from the Cumberland County Historical Society, Greenwich, NJ).

Sherwood, Henry Noble. "The Formation of the American Colonization Society." *The Journal of Negro History* 2, no. 3 (July 1917).

Siebert, Wilbur H. "The Loyalists of Pennsylvania." *Ohio State University Bulletin*, April 1, 1920.

"The Testimony of the People called Quakers Given Forth by a Meeting of the Representatives of Said People in Pennsylvania and New Jersey, Held at Philadelphia the 24th day of the 9th month 1775." *Pennsylvania Gazette*, September 10, 1777.

Quaker Records

Philadelphia Yearly Meeting, 1714, 1715, 1716, 1730, 1737, 1738, 1754, 1758. Friends Historical Library, Swarthmore College, Swarthmore, PA

Index